The Surge

The Surge

2014's Big GOP Win and What It Means for the Next Presidential Election

Edited by
Larry J. Sabato,

with Kyle Kondik
and Geoffrey Skelley

ROWMAN & LITTLEFIELD
Lanham • Boulder • New York • London

Published by Rowman & Littlefield
A wholly owned subsidiary of The Rowman & Littlefield Publishing Group, Inc.
4501 Forbes Boulevard, Suite 200, Lanham, Maryland 20706
www.rowman.com

Unit A, Whitacre Mews, 26–34 Stannary Street, London SE11 4AB

British Library Cataloguing in Publication Information Available

Library of Congress Cataloging-in-Publication Data

The surge : 2014's big GOP win and what it means for the next presidential
election / edited by Larry J. Sabato, with Kyle Kondik and Geoffrey Skelley.
    pages cm
    Includes index.
    ISBN 978-1-4422-4632-4 (cloth : alk. paper) — ISBN 978-1-4422-4634-8
(pbk. : alk. paper) — ISBN 978-1-4422-4633-1 (electronic)   1. United States.
Congress—Elections, 2014.   2. Elections—United States.   I. Sabato, Larry J.
JK19682014 .A18   2015
324.973'0932—dc23   2015000497

♾ ™The paper used in this publication meets the minimum requirements of
American National Standard for Information Sciences—Permanence of Paper for
Printed Library Materials, ANSI/NISO Z39.48-1992.

Printed in the United States of America

Contents

1

A Midterm Course Correction

Larry J. Sabato

In the University of Virginia Center for Politics' recent books analyzing national elections, stretching back to 1996, the titles usually sum up the results. President Obama has featured prominently in the most recent four: *The Year of Obama* (2008), *Pendulum Swing* (2010), *Barack Obama and the New America* (2012), and now *The Surge* (2015).

This quartet of headings immediately suggests two themes we will explore. First, there is a "surge and decline" quality to American elections (and for that matter, the elections in most democratic countries) that has been visible throughout history. Voters regularly seek to elevate one party in order to limit or replace the other.

Second, the recent U.S. pattern has emphasized the very different electorates of presidential and midterm years. The turnout of eligible adults hovered around 60 percent in 2008 and 2012, while voter participation in 2010 was 40 percent and in 2014, just 36 percent—the lowest midterm turnout since 1942, when the United States was almost a year into World War II and experiencing severe disruption in the patterns of normal life. It matters greatly, because the presidential electorate is made up of larger numbers of Democratically inclined minority and young voters, while midterm voters skew toward Republican-tilting seniors and whites.

The headline for 2014 is obvious: Republicans captured the U.S. Senate while keeping the House of Representatives (with an enlarged majority) as well as adding a couple of net governorships and loads of state legislative seats. It's not as though this was an enormous surprise. The sixth-year election in a two-term presidency is usually an unhappy one for the party that holds the White House, and it heralds the start of diminished influence for the president in his final two years.

Throughout 2014, election analysts debated not whether the GOP would gain seats in both houses of Congress, but how many. The House was nearly guaranteed to stay Republican, and most conceded the GOP would add to their majority (in the end, the party grabbed an additional thirteen seats, taking it to 247—the largest Republican total since 1929).

The big question was whether the GOP could net at least six seats to take control of the Senate. This was not a sure thing because Republicans had fumbled away real opportunities to obtain a majority in both 2010 and 2012. However, the math and the map certainly favored Republicans this time. In 2014, Democrats were defending twenty-one seats, including seven in states Mitt Romney carried in 2012. Republicans had to worry about far fewer seats (fifteen were held by the GOP), and all but one of them (Maine) had been won by Romney, mostly by wide margins. Sure enough, Republicans won all seven Democratic seats in Romney states while losing none of their own. Two marginal 2012 Obama states that were considered competitive, Iowa and Colorado, also fell to the GOP.

In retrospect, President George W. Bush's sixth-year election was a solid predictor of what was to happen in his successor's sixth-year Waterloo. The Democrats took control of both the House and Senate in 2006, which was in essence a repudiation of much of the Bush agenda—from the Iraq War to disaster relief operations after Hurricane Katrina. An earlier midterm book, *The Sixth Year Itch*, covered the events of that November.[1] President Obama felt a similar sting in 2014. While his national job approval (42 percent) in the early November *RealClearPolitics* polling average was higher than Bush's just before the 2006 midterm (38 percent), Obama's economic, health care, and immigration policies generated strong opposition and spurred turnout among the GOP base.

In *The Surge*, my coauthors and I will try to bring the 2014 midterm into focus for you, followed by a sustained look ahead to the forthcoming 2016 battle for the White House. First, we will analyze the demographics of 2014, and then Rhodes Cook will focus on the primary season that produced the candidates. That's followed by a chapter-by-chapter focus on the Senate (James Hohmann), the House (Kyle Kondik), and the governorships (Geoffrey Skelley). Michael Toner and Karen Trainer give us the big picture on campaign financing and the expanding, less disclosed ways that help candidates win elections. The polling industry continued to have problems in 2014, and Mark Blumenthal and Ariel Edwards-Levy tell us why and what can be done about it.

Jill Lawrence then reminds us that for all our early obsession about the next election, President Obama's final quarter in office comes first—and will certainly affect the contours of the contest to succeed him. Next is the post-2014 state of both parties: Jamelle Bouie looks at the Democrats and Robert Costa explores the Republicans.

Then it's on to 2016. Josh Putnam reviews the likely shape of the presidential nominating process, Sean Trende gives an early sense of how the Electoral College may align, and Alan Abramowitz sketches the fundamentals of the race for the White House.

THE MIDTERM ELECTION'S EFFECT: COURSE CORRECTION

The midterm election is a remarkable phenomenon that has become a critical part of democracy's superstructure in the United States. Coming at the midpoint of each presidential term, the elections for about a third of the U.S. Senate, the entire U.S. House of Representatives, and nearly three-quarters of the state governorships give voters an opportunity to pass preliminary judgment on the person in the White House.

In the strictest sense, a midterm is not a referendum on the president. The president's name is not on the ballot. But increasingly, political scientists have come to realize that campaign outcomes for Congress, governors, and even thousands of state legislative posts around the country have a strong relationship to the voters' level of approval for the White House administration.

Of course, it is not a perfect measure since, as noted above, a much lower proportion of Americans turns out to vote in a midterm year than in a presidential year, and the circumstances vary depending on the political climate. One party's activists may be more enthused and thus turn out at a higher rate than the other party's, giving them a leg up in producing victories—as was true for Republicans in both 2010 and 2014.

Another reason why a midterm is not a perfect measure of popular opinion is that some states and districts do not have competitive contests in any given year. For example, in 2014, fourteen states had no election for governor, sixteen lacked a Senate contest, and hundreds of the 435 U.S. House races were either unopposed or lightly opposed. Naturally, voter turnout was generally lower in the locales that lacked any high-profile statewide contested race.

Yet another basis on which to question midterm elections can be found by examining the contests individually. While the balance of the voters' identification with one major party versus the other is the overarching factor in most states and districts (plus turnout of the two party bases), the skills of the candidates, as well as the campaigns they run, influence the results. Especially in competitive places where the two parties are closely balanced, election outcomes can depend heavily on the abilities and characteristics of the people running for office—their strengths, weaknesses, financial war chests, policies, and so on. Some politicians are a better fit for their states or districts than their opponents, and they may raise more money and run smarter campaigns. Also, incumbents running for reelection can skew the results because they usually have higher name recognition and better contacts with donors. A combination of these factors can occasionally produce victory for a candidate even though the national tide is running in the other party's direction.

Most analysts start from the national perspective because the conditions existing in the nation set the tone for virtually every campaign across the United States. From the second midterm of Franklin Roosevelt's presidency in 1938 through the first midterm of Bill Clinton's presidency in 1994, the party in charge of the White House lost House seats in the congressional elections without exception.

Political scientists have laid out logical reasons for why this is the case. Some have theorized that midterms serve as natural electoral "reflexes" to counterbalance strong party showings in presidential cycles. The notion of "checks and balances" is deeply rooted in our Constitution and our national psyche. Generally, we recoil from giving one political party too much power for too long.

In the nearly seventy years since the end of World War II, Americans have switched control of the presidency from one party to another eight times, control of the Senate ten times, and control of the House seven times. Unified party control of both the executive and legislative branches is becoming rare. More than half the time (forty of the seventy post-war years), the parties have shared power in one combination or another, and the 2014 election has guaranteed that two more years will be added to the split-control total. This is quite remarkable: Since President Richard Nixon came to power in 1969, there have been just a dozen years when one party simultaneously had the White House and majorities of both houses of Congress.

This has considerable implications for governance. It is much easier for a party to enact its platform if its officials are in charge across the board. It was only because of large Democratic majorities in both houses of Congress that President Obama was able to (narrowly) secure passage of a roughly $800 billion stimulus bill, health care reform ("Obamacare"), and financial services reform from 2009 to 2010. Divided control usually produces gridlock, and not much is accomplished legislatively. On the other hand, conservatives would argue, invoking Henry David Thoreau and Thomas Jefferson, "That government is best which governs least." To those who favor smaller and less government, gridlock may be a good thing.

Almost always, voters view the midterm as the designated time for a course correction in the White House, and they send messages by means of their ballots. Even in good times, voters are inclined to trim at least a few seats from the governing White House party, perhaps to remind those in power that the people are the boss. In rocky stretches, when the economy seems to be underperforming or a president has embraced controversial stands, Americans eagerly express their frustrations at the polls. In 2010 and 2014 the electorate applied the brakes to President Obama's agenda.

Usually, but not always, the president's party loses fewer seats in the first midterm than in the second, which occurs in the sixth year of a two-term presidency. There have been eight of these sixth-year elections in the post–World War II era: 1950, 1958, 1966, 1974, 1986, 1998, 2006, and 2014. This tendency is called the "sixth-year itch." But history can play tricks. There are no iron laws in politics, and the previous two midterms proved this yet again. Republicans gained 63 House seats in 2010, but only 13 in 2014—in part because the GOP already controlled the vast majority of territory friendly to Republican candidates before the 2014 voting commenced. In the Senate, the pattern was reversed. Back in 2010 the GOP gained just six seats in the Senate, but in 2014 it won nine net seats.

Lately, we have had a couple of other midterm elections that didn't precisely follow the usual pattern. The durability of the sixth-year itch prior to 1998 led most analysts to speculate about how many seats President Clinton's Democrats would lose, especially in the midst of an impeachment effort following the Monica Lewinsky sex scandal. Yet the Democrats actually gained a few House seats and held their own in the Senate, as voters appeared to resent Republican efforts to oust Clinton. The next midterm election in 2002, the first of the George W. Bush presidency, also broke the pattern. In the wake of the terrorist attacks on September 11, 2001, the narrowly elected Bush soared to near-unanimous approval in the opinion polls, and a year later he retained enough of that popularity to add GOP seats in both the House and Senate. This was something that had not occurred in the first midterm election of a presidency since 1934 when Franklin Roosevelt's New Deal program to combat the Great Depression was exceptionally popular.

In truth, every midterm differs from its predecessors in one respect or another. As an introduction to the 2014 analysis, a short history lesson may be in order, so that you can see for yourself the ebb and flow of public opinion in modern midterm years.

CHRONOLOGICAL COUNTDOWN TO 2014

Just for starters, let's glance at the midterm results from 1946 to 2010 (also see Tables 1.1 and 1.2, as well as Figures 1.1, 1.2, and 1.3 for reference). It is easy to analyze in retrospect, and every bit of it falls neatly into a sentence or two:

- 1946: After fourteen years of solid Democratic control under Franklin D. Roosevelt (FDR) and Truman, voters wanted change. The end of

Table 1.1. Gain or Loss for President's Party: Presidential Election Years

Year	President	House	Senate	Governor
1948	Truman (D)	+75	+9	+5
1952	Eisenhower (R)	+22	+2	+5
1956	Eisenhower (R)	−2	0	−2
1960	Kennedy (D)	−20	−1	+1
1964	Johnson (D)	+37	+2	−1
1968	Nixon (R)	+5	+5	+5
1972	Nixon (R)	+12	−2	−1
1976	Carter (D)	+1	0	+1
1980	Reagan (R)	+34	+12	+4
1984	Reagan (R)	+16	−2	+1
1988	G.H.W. Bush (R)	−3	−1	−1
1992	Clinton (D)	−9	0	+2
1996	Clinton (D)	+3	−2	0
2000	G.W. Bush (R)	−2	−4	−1
2004	G.W. Bush (R)	+3	+4	0
2008	Obama (D)	+23	+8	+1
2012	Obama (D)	+8	+2	−1

Notes: Because of independent or third-party members, vacancies, and other factors, gains or losses for the president's party do not imply the exact opposite result for the other major party.
Sources: Crystal Ball research, *Vital Statistics on American Politics 2011–2012.*

World War II and postwar economic dislocation encouraged the "time for a change" theme. Truman did not seem up to the job—who would, after Franklin Roosevelt?—and the mantra became "To err is Truman." So Republicans captured both houses of Congress, grabbing fifty-five House seats and eleven Senate seats, plus two more governorships (for a total of twenty-five out of forty-eight).

- 1950: Truman's come-from-behind presidential victory in 1948 had restored Democratic rule by adding seventy-five House and nine Senate seats. But eighteen straight years of Democratic presidencies and an unpopular war in Korea took their toll again in the midterm, and Democrats gave back twenty-nine House and five Senate seats. Democratic losses in 1950 were nearly identical to the Republican losses in 2006, when another unpopular foreign war, this time in Iraq, dealt the governing party a severe setback.
- 1954: Eisenhower's triumph two years earlier gave the GOP narrow majorities in Congress, even though his coattails were not particularly long. By the time of the midterm, a slight swing away from the Republicans cost eighteen of the party's twenty-two newly gained House seats and two Senate seats.

- 1958: This is the first dramatic modern example of the so-called "sixth-year itch," when voters decide to give the other party sizeable congressional majorities after the first six years of a two-term presidency. While Democrats had already won back control of Congress in 1956, despite Eisenhower's landslide reelection, the additional forty-seven House and thirteen Senate berths for Democrats ensured that Ike's legislative influence would be minimal in his final two years in office.
- 1962: John F. Kennedy had almost no coattails in his 1960 presidential squeaker; Democrats actually lost twenty House seats and one Senate seat. JFK feared more losses in his 1962 midterm, but the Cuban Missile Crisis—the "Missiles of October"—boosted support for his administration just before the balloting. The result was a wash, with Democrats losing five House seats but picking up four Senate seats. "October Surprises" can affect congressional elections every bit as much as presidential contests do.

Table 1.2. Gain or Loss for President's Party: Midterm Election Years

Year	President	House	Senate	Governor
1946	Truman (D)	−55	−11	−2
1950	Truman (D)	−29	−5	−6
1954	Eisenhower (R)	−18	−2	−8
1958	Eisenhower (R)	−47	−13	−5
1962	Kennedy (D)	−5	+4	0
1966	Johnson (D)	−47	−3	−8
1970	Nixon (R)	−12	+1	−11
1974	Ford (R)	−48	−4	−5
1978	Carter (D)	−15	−3	−5
1982	Reagan (R)	−26	0	−7
1986	Reagan (R)	−5	−8	+8
1990	G.H.W. Bush (R)	−7	−1	−1
1994	Clinton (D)	−54	−8	−10
1998	Clinton (D)	+4	0	0
2002	G.W. Bush (R)	+8	+2	−1
2006	G.W. Bush (R)	−30	−6	−6
2010	Obama (D)	−63	−6	−7*
2014	Obama (D)	−13	−9	−3

Notes: Because of independent or third-party members, vacancies, and other factors, gains or losses for the president's party do not imply the exact opposite result for the other major party.

*This total of seven includes Florida, which switched on Election Day from an independent governor, Charlie Crist, to a Republican governor, Rick Scott. Crist was elected as a Republican in 2006 but left the party in spring 2010 to run unsuccessfully for the U.S. Senate (and later became a Democrat to run unsuccessfully for governor again in 2014). We traditionally count party switches in this fashion, though one could argue that there was no change between the elections of 2006 and 2010, and thus the national gain for the GOP in 2010 was six governorships. Take your pick.

Sources: Crystal Ball research, Vital Statistics on American Politics 2011–2012.

- 1966: Lyndon Johnson's historic 61 percent landslide in 1964 appeared to presage a new era of Democratic rule, as he carried in thirty-seven House freshmen and two additional senators to an already heavily Democratic Congress. But that was before the Vietnam War began to devour LBJ. Already by 1966, voters were turning against the president's conduct of the war, and it cost the Democrats forty-seven House seats and three Senate seats—though not overall control of Congress.
- 1970: Richard Nixon's close 43 percent victory in 1968 did not stop him from dreaming of a "silent majority" of Republicans and conservative Southern Democrats, and he made a major effort to improve the GOP's weak position in Congress. (Nixon had added but five House members and five senators to the Republican minority in 1968.) His efforts paid off to a certain degree, as the GOP added one Senate seat in 1970, while holding House losses to a relatively small twelve seats. Democrats still ruled the Capitol Hill roost, though.
- 1974: Oddly, Nixon's 61 percent reelection landslide in 1972 almost precisely returned his party to its paltry 1968 levels in both chambers. The Republicans could ill afford a coattail-less election, given what was soon to happen: Nixon's resignation in disgrace, a recession, and an unelected successor GOP president (Gerald Ford) who squandered his initial popularity by pardoning Nixon—all just in time for November 1974. Democrats picked up forty-eight House seats and four Senate seats; Ford was left mainly with his veto power for his remaining two years in office.
- 1978: Jimmy Carter's narrow 1976 election left Congress virtually unchanged, though still heavily Democratic. And Carter's fall from grace had barely started in 1978. A quiet midterm before the storm of 1980 nonetheless subtracted fifteen House and three Senate seats from the Democratic totals.
- 1982: Ronald Reagan's ten-point slaughter of Carter in 1980 was a now-rare coattail election, as the GOP also won thirty-four House seats and twelve Senate seats, defeating many long-time Democratic incumbents. That was enough to take over the Senate outright and obtain a working majority on some issues with conservative House Democrats. But this tumultuous period in American politics continued through 1982, when a serious recession deprived the GOP of twenty-six House seats. The Senate stayed Republican, however, with no net change.
- 1986: After yet another coattail-less reelection of a president—Reagan's massive 59 percent win in 1984—the sixth-year itch returned in 1986, at least in federal elections. Voters handed eight Senate seats to the Democrats, and thus control of that body. The GOP lost only five House seats, but the Democrats were solidly in charge of the House in

any event. Remarkably, the Republicans did gain eight governorships, in part because of a large number of Democratic incumbents were either term limited or didn't seek reelection.

- 1990: Vice President Bush had won Reagan's "third term" in 1988 with 53 percent of the popular vote, but the Republicans suffered from having no coattails again, losing three House seats and one Senate seat. With partisan politics somewhat at abeyance due to the pre-Persian Gulf War military buildup, a quiet midterm saw Republicans lose seven House seats and one Senate berth. Much like Carter in 1978, Bush did not see the gathering storm clouds due to this eerie calm.
- 1994: A recession and a disengaged administration took George H.W. Bush from the all-time height of 90 percent popularity to a humiliating

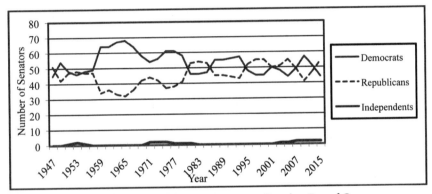

Figure 1.1   Political Divisions of the U.S. Senate on Opening Day of Congress

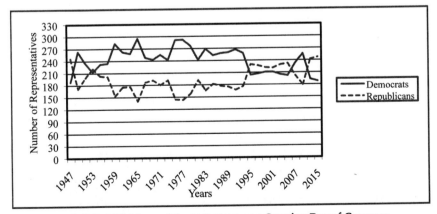

Figure 1.2   Political Divisions of the U.S. House on Opening Day of Congress

37 percent finish in the 1992 election. With Ross Perot securing 19 percent, Bill Clinton's 43 percent victory was not impressive, and Democrats lost nine House seats and stayed even in the Senate. A disastrous overreaching by new President Clinton on health care reform, gays in the military, and other issues, coupled with a slow economy, produced a sixth-year itch in the second year. In 1994 Republicans gained an eye-popping fifty-four House seats and eight Senate seats (nine when Democratic Alabama Senator Richard Shelby switched parties the day after the election) to win control of both houses.

- 1998: Proving that every defeat can yield the seeds of victory, Clinton let Republicans overreach just as he had in the runup to the 1996 election. Running against both ex-Senate Majority Leader Bob Dole (the GOP nominee) and Speaker Newt Gingrich (the unpopular foil), Clinton won a 49 percent reelection. But Democrats captured only three House seats and actually lost two more Senate seats, leaving Republicans in charge of Congress. Would Clinton have another catastrophic midterm election in 1998? It certainly looked that way as the Monica Lewinsky scandal unfolded. But Republicans again overplayed their hand, beginning unpopular impeachment proceedings that yielded a Democratic gain of four House seats (with the Senate unchanged).

- 2002: "The George W. Bush Midterm," plain and simple. In an election dominated by terrorism, Iraq, and the president himself, the Republicans defied conventional wisdom by gaining seats in both houses of Congress, making Bush the first president since FDR in 1934 to net seats in both chambers in a midterm election. The Democrats were unable to link the poor economy to Bush, and the media's extensive coverage of the impending confrontation with Iraq and the Washington, D.C.-area sniper incidents overshadowed the somewhat fuzzy Democratic election agenda. In the final two weeks of the general election, key White House adviser Karl Rove sent Bush on a whirlwind campaign tour of the battleground states, which ended up reaping rich rewards for the GOP. The Republicans gained two seats in the Senate and eight House seats. The only positive note for the Democrats was a net gain of one governorship, but the GOP maintained a narrow overall statehouse majority (26 to 24).

- 2006: The unpopularity of the Iraq War, the failure of much of President Bush's second-term legislative agenda, and a series of financial and sex scandals that rocked the Republican congressional caucus combined to produce a major sixth-year itch. On Election Day, Democrats won thirty net House seats, six Senate seats, and six governorships. With the help of two independents, Democrats took control of

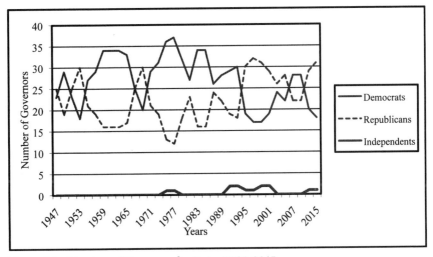

Figure 1.3   Number of Governors by Party, 1947–2015

the Senate by a narrow 51–49 margin, while the party also won a comfortable majority of 233 in the House. The 2006 election marked the effective end of George W. Bush's domestic presidency. He was unable to influence Congress, at least until the bank and Wall Street crisis of September 2008, when both parties joined together to prevent what they feared would be a descent into another Great Depression.

- 2010: When Barack Obama won the White House, he added twenty-three House seats and eight Senate seats for Democrats, swelling their congressional majorities. But only two years later, the electorate applied the brakes to President Obama's agenda in dramatic fashion. After just four years of control in the House, Democrats gave way to Republicans as the GOP scored a massive landslide, gaining sixty-three seats and posting a majority of two hundred and forty-two seats. Democrats also lost six net seats in the Senate, but still managed to hold on to a fifty-three-seat majority (again with the help of two independents). In the statehouse ranks, Democrats lost a net seven governorships. The congressional results at the second year of Obama's presidency were reminiscent of 1994. Voters reacted strongly and negatively to reforms introduced by the new president. In both Clinton's and Obama's cases, health care programs and other liberal initiatives appeared to be the motivators for a large GOP base turnout. Also, for both new Democratic presidents, a balky economy that was only slowly recovering from a recession contributed significantly to low job approval and thus produced large congressional turnover. History does not repeat itself, but it does rhyme.

- 2014: The same slow economy continued right through President Obama's reelection campaign in 2012, yet Obama won by four percentage points and carried in a modest number of additional Democrats (eight in the House and two in the Senate). Following the first-term path, conditions changed rapidly. With Obama once again registering job approval in the low forties—and much lower approval in many states with key contests—voters completed the transition of Congress from Democratic to Republican control in 2014 by giving the Senate to the GOP. On Election Day, Republicans added eight Senate seats, which was expanded to nine once the Louisiana runoff was held in early December. The new GOP Senate majority of fifty-four seats guaranteed trouble for President Obama's final two years in the White House. Republicans also added thirteen seats to their House total, bringing their majority to two hundred and forty-seven, one seat greater than the GOP delegation at the start of 1947 and the highest number for the party since 1929. Two additional net governorships went to Republicans, leaving the GOP occupying the top executive office in thirty-one states.

MAKING SENSE OF THE
2014 MIDTERM ELECTION

Elections can be sliced and diced in numerous ways and from many perspectives in order to augment our understanding. For 2014, some aspects (such as the Republican takeover of the Senate) were dramatic, but others, less so. Compared to the upheaval in 2010, for instance, Obama's second midterm seems tame in terms of the number of incumbents defeated. In 2010, fifty-four House members (fifty-two Democrats) lost their seats in November; in 2014, the overall number for the general election was a mere fourteen (twelve of them Democrats). Partisan redistricting of the House has made most congressional districts uncompetitive (except potentially in primaries), so even in years when one party has a big edge, relatively few House seats register a party turnover. Meanwhile, in the Senate's thirty-six races, a total of five incumbents, all Democrats, lost. This was the first time since 1980 that Republicans had managed to defeat more than two incumbent Democratic senators. Of the twenty-two senators in the eleven Southern states, the GOP now has nineteen (all but two in Virginia and one in Florida).

In the thirty-six gubernatorial contests of 2014, just six states switched parties. The GOP captured the heavily Democratic states of Illinois, Maryland, and Massachusetts, plus strongly Republican Arkansas. The Democrats gained only Pennsylvania, while an independent on a fusion ticket representing both parties defeated the incumbent GOP governor of Alaska. (More detailed analysis of these contests is contained in later chapters.)

Republicans may have achieved their most vital gains in state legislatures, since these lower-level posts fill the benches from which parties draw many of their nominees for top offices. Overall, the GOP added 310 seats in the ninety-eight partisan legislative houses (Nebraska is unicameral and technically nonpartisan). Republicans gained control of eleven more legislative chambers, and now control sixty-eight to the Democrats' thirty. Republicans have complete control of thirty legislatures to the Democrats' eleven (with eight under split control); and the GOP has total dominance in 23 states (governor plus both houses) while Democrats have been left with a mere seven in their grasp (with 19 under split control). Just as in the national House of Representatives, the GOP has secured its largest majority of state legislative seats since 1929 (56.3 percent of the 7,334 seats in 49 states besides Nebraska). Since the start of his presidency, Obama has presided over the loss of 910 Democratic net seats in state legislatures—almost three times as many as in the presidency of George W. Bush.[2]

WHO TURNED OUT TO VOTE?

Every election is determined by the subsample of Americans who show up—and it differs widely from year to year. This truism is amply demonstrated in the 2014 election. Often political observers make the fundamental error of equating all electorates, but in fact, the smaller midterm

Table 1.3. Defeated House Incumbents, 1980–2014

Year	Primary	General
1980	6	30
1982	10	28
1984	3	15
1986	3	6
1988	1	6
1990	1	15
1992	19	24
1994	4	34
1996	2	21
1998	1	6
2000	3	6
2002	8	8
2004	2	7
2006	2	22
2008	3	19
2010	4	54
2012	13	27
2014	4	14

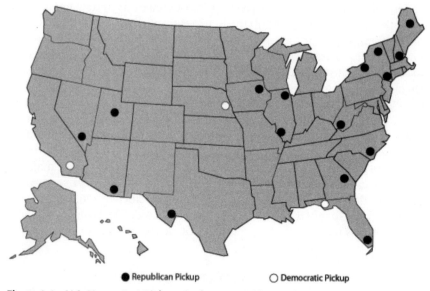

Figure 1.4   U.S. House Seat Pickups in the 2014 Midterm Election. *Map credit:* **Tim Robinson, U.Va. Center for Politics**

electorate is *not* a random sampling of the big-turnout presidential group of voters. As I mentioned at the outset, the turnout in 2014 of the voting eligible population (VEP—see definition in Table 1.7) was a paltry 36 percent—the lowest since 1942, when the world was at war and many Americans were distracted or abroad.[3] This is well below the average turnout of about 40 percent in the nation's midterm elections in the previous four decades, beginning in 1974 (the first midterm that included the newly enfranchised eighteen to twenty-year-olds). The previous GOP landslide year of 2010 had produced almost exactly a 40 percent voter participation rate.

In looking at the total votes by party (Table 1.9), notice how uniform the proportions are, even though there are different combinations of states and districts electing the Senate, House, and governors in 2014. Republican candidates garnered a majority of the vote in all three categories (between 50.4 percent and 51 percent), and Democratic candidates secured between 44.4 percent and 46.1 percent. These proportions constitute a decisive Republican victory by any reasonable measure. In the House alone—the only category where an election was held everywhere in the United States—Republicans outpolled Democrats by 5.7 percent. While a solid margin, this percentage was less than the 7.5 percent of 2010, which was the largest GOP advantage since the 9 percent gap that occurred in 1946.

Table 1.4.   Defeated Senate Incumbents, 1980–2014

Year	Primary	General
1980	4	9
1982	0	2
1984	0	3
1986	0	7
1988	0	4
1990	0	1
1992	1	4
1994	0	2
1996	1	1
1998	0	3
2000	0	6
2002	1	3
2004	0	1
2006	0*	6
2008	0	4
2010	2†	2
2012	1	1
2014	0	5

Notes: * In 2006, Sen. Joseph Lieberman (D) of Connecticut was defeated for renomination in an August 8 primary but won the general election as a petitioning independent, so he is not included.

† In 2010, Sen. Robert Bennett (R) of Utah lost renomination at a convention and is included in the total. Also that year, Sen. Lisa Murkowski (R) was defeated in the Republican primary, but won the general election as a write-in, so she is not counted in the total.

On the other hand, the 2014 voter turnout is 22 full percentage points below that of the 2012 presidential election, greater than the 20.7 point gap between the 2008 election for president and the 2010 midterm. And just as in 2010, the citizens who chose to cast a ballot in 2014 were dramatically more Republican, more conservative, and older than in 2008 or 2012. They were also disproportionately white—a GOP-tilting demographic.

Take a glance at Table 1.8. While the 2014 electorate was split almost evenly between Democrats and Republicans (35 percent Democratic, 36 percent Republican), this profile is far less Democratic than in 2008 and 2012 (which featured a six-to-seven-point gap in favor of the Democrats). Furthermore, as we shall see, the independents who cast a ballot (28–29 percent of the total in the last four national elections) were more heavily drawn from the conservative end of the ideological spectrum in 2014 than in either of the last couple of White House election years. By the way, a large majority of these so-called independents are in fact "hidden partisans"—people who vote for their undisclosed party by about the same margins as those who openly call themselves Republicans or Democrats.

Table 1.5.   Senate Races, 2014

State	Candidate	Percentage	Total
Alabama	Jeff Sessions (R)*	97	795,606
	Write-Ins	3	22,484
Alaska	Dan Sullivan (R)	48	135,445
	Mark Begich (D)*	46	129,431
Arkansas	Tom Cotton (R)	56	478,819
	Mark Pryor (D)*	39	334,174
Colorado	Cory Gardner (R)	48	983,891
	Mark Udall (D)*	46	944,203
Delaware	Chris Coons (D)*	56	130,655
	Kevin Wade (R)	42	98,823
Georgia	David Perdue (R)	53	1,358,088
	Michelle Nunn (D)	45	1,160,811
Hawaii (S)	Brian Schatz (D)*	70	246,827
	Cam Cavasso (R)	28	98,006
Idaho	Jim Risch (R)*	65	285,596
	Nels Mitchell (D)	35	151,574
Illinois	Richard Durbin (D)*	54	1,929,637
	Jim Oberweis (R)	43	1,538,522
Iowa	Joni Ernst (R)	52	588,575
	Bruce Braley (D)	44	494,370
Kansas	Pat Roberts (R)*	53	460,350
	Greg Orman (I)	43	368,372
Kentucky	Mitch McConnell (R)*	56	806,787
	Alison L. Grimes (D)	41	584,698
Louisiana†	Mary Landrieu (D)*	42	619,402
	Bill Cassidy (R)	41	603,048
	Rob Maness (R)	14	202,556
Louisiana[a]	Bill Cassidy (R)	56	712,379
	Mary Landrieu (D)*	44	561,210
Maine	Susan Collins (R)*	68	413,505
	Shenna Bellows (D)	31	190,254

Table 1.5.   (Continued)

State	Candidate	Percentage	Total
Massachusetts	Ed Markey (D)*	62	1,289,944
	Brian Herr (R)	38	791,950
Michigan	Gary Peters (D)	55	1,704,936
	Terri Lynn Land (R)	41	1,290,199
Minnesota	Al Franken (D)*	53	1,053,205
	Mike McFadden (R)	43	850,227
Mississippi	Thad Cochran (R)*	60	378,481
	Travis Childers (D)	38	239,439
Montana	Steve Daines (R)	58	213,709
	Amanda Curtis (D)	40	148,184
Nebraska	Ben Sasse (R)	64	347,636
	Dan Domina (D)	31	170,127
New Hampshire	Jeanne Shaheen (D)*	51	251,184
	Scott Brown (R)	48	235,347
New Jersey	Cory Booker (D)*	56	1,043,866
	Jeff Bell (R)	42	791,297
New Mexico	Tom Udall (D)*	56	286,409
	Allen Weh (R)	44	229,097
North Carolina	Thom Tillis (R)	49	1,423,259
	Kay Hagan (D)*	47	1,377,651
Oklahoma	Jim Inhofe (R)*	68	558,166
	Matt Silverstein (D)	29	234,307
Oklahoma (S)	James Lankford (R)	68	557,002
	Connie Johnson (D)	29	237,923
Oregon	Jeff Merkley (D)*	56	814,537
	Monica Wehby (R)	37	538,847
Rhode Island	Jack Reed (D)*	71	223,675
	Mark Zaccaria (R)	29	92,684
South Carolina	Lindsey Graham (R)*	54	672,941
	Brad Hutto (D)	39	480,933

Table 1.5. (Continued)

State	Candidate	Percentage	Total
South Carolina (S)	Tim Scott (R)*	61	757,215
	Joyce Dickerson (D)	37	459,583
South Dakota	Mike Rounds (R)	50	140,741
	Rick Weiland (D)	30	82,456
	Larry Pressler (I)	17	47,741
Tennessee	Lamar Alexander (R)*	62	850,087
	Gordon Ball (D)	32	437,848
Texas	John Cornyn (R)*	62	2,861,531
	David Alameel (D)	34	1,597,387
Virginia	Mark Warner (D)*	49	1,073,667
	Ed Gillespie (R)	48	1,055,940
West Virginia	Shelley Moore Capito (R)	62	281,820
	Natalie Tennant (D)	34	156,360
Wyoming	Mike Enzi (R)*	72	121,554
	Charlie Hardy (D)	17	29,377

Source: Official Sources
* Indicates incumbent.
† Indicates November 4 result.
ᵃ Indicates December 6 runoff result.
(S) Indicates a special election.
Note: Percentages may not total 100 because of rounding

The Republican coloration of the 2014 voters—and the sharp distinctions with the 2012 voters who elected President Obama—can best be seen in the exit poll data. The exit poll was conducted by a professional, nonpartisan polling organization and financed by a consortium of news organizations. In total, 19,441 voters were interviewed by telephone or at polling places.[4] Early and mail-in voters (especially in Colorado, Oregon, and Washington state, where most voters vote by mail) were included in the sample.

The comparisons between 2012 and 2014 are stunning. One of the most Democratic groups in the electorate, young voters aged 18–29, saw their turnout plummet from 19 percent of the total in 2012 to 13 percent in 2014. Heavily Democratic African Americans and Hispanics dropped from 13 percent and 10 percent of the national turnout in 2008, respectively, to 12 percent and 8 percent in 2014. These percentage changes are small but they amount to many net votes subtracted from the Democratic column.

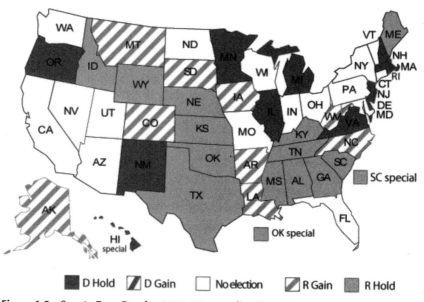

Figure 1.5 Senate Race Results, 2014. *Map credit:* **Tim Robinson, U.Va. Center for Politics**

Meanwhile, the most Republican-friendly voters were participating in much larger numbers. Those aged 65 and over skyrocketed from 16 percent of the electorate in 2012 to 22 percent in 2014. White voters jumped from 72 percent in 2012 to 75 percent of the 2014 electorate.

These marginal changes add up to several million more GOP votes. (Table 1.10, which you will find at the end of this chapter, gives all the key exit poll breakdowns, including some not commented upon directly in the text. It is well worth a read.) Whites voted Republican by 60 percent to 38 percent in 2014, a slight increase over their GOP edge of 59 percent to 39 percent in 2012. The same change is visible among older voters, with a 12 percent GOP margin in 2012 swelling to 16 percent in 2014. As usual, men of all races and ages were more Republican, 57 percent to 41 percent—quite a contrast with the closer 52 percent to 45 percent in 2012. The surprise was women, who voted Democratic by 55 percent to 44 percent in 2012 but just 51 percent to 47 percent in 2014. Unmarried women continued their allegiance to the Democrats by a wide (though diminished) margin; unmarried men were split in their party allegiance; and married men and women (by 61 percent and 54 percent, respectively) backed the GOP. Married voters with children supported Republicans by an 18 percent margin. About three-quarters of gays and lesbians voted Democratic, one-quarter chose Republicans—more or less the standard split in this segment of the electorate.

Table 1.6. Governors' Races, 2014

State	Candidate	Percentage	Total
Alabama	Robert Bentley (R)*	64	750,231
	Parker Griffith (D)	36	427,787
Alaska	Bill Walker (I)	48	134,658
	Sean Parnell (R)*	46	128,435
Arizona	Doug Ducey (R)	53	805,062
	Fred DuVal (D)	42	626,921
Arkansas	Asa Hutchinson (R)	55	470,429
	Mike Ross (D)	41	352,115
California	Jerry Brown (D)*	60	4,388,368
	Neel Kashkari (R)	40	2,929,213
Colorado	John Hickenlooper (D)*	49	1,006,433
	Bob Beauprez (R)	46	938,195
Connecticut	Dan Malloy (D)*	51	554,314
	Tom Foley (R)	48	526,295
Florida	Rick Scott (R)*	48	2,865,343
	Charlie Crist (D)	47	2,801,198
Georgia	Nathan Deal (R)*	53	1,345,237
	Jason Carter (D)	45	1,144,794
Hawaii	David Ige (D)	49	181,106
	Duke Aiona (R)	37	135,775
	Mufi Hannemann (I)	12	42,934
Idaho	Butch Otter (R)*	54	235,405
	A.J. Balukoff (D)	39	169,556
Illinois	Bruce Rauner (R)	50	1,823,627
	Pat Quinn (D)*	46	1,681,343
Iowa	Terry Branstad (R)*	59	666,023
	Jack Hatch (D)	37	420,778
Kansas	Sam Brownback (R)*	50	433,196
	Paul Davis (D)	46	401,100
Maine	Paul LePage (R)*	48	294,533
	Michael Michaud (D)	43	265,125

Table 1.6.   (Continued)

State	Candidate	Percentage	Total
Maryland	Larry Hogan (R)	51	884,400
	Anthony Brown (D)	47	818,890
Massachusetts	Charlie Baker (R)	48	1,044,573
	Martha Coakley (D)	47	1,004,408
Michigan	Rick Snyder (R)*	51	1,607,399
	Mark Schauer (D)	47	1,479,057
Minnesota	Mark Dayton (D)*	50	989,113
	Jeff Johnson (R)	45	879,257
Nebraska	Pete Ricketts (R)	57	308,751
	Chuck Hassebrook (D)	39	211,905
Nevada	Brian Sandoval (R)*	71	386,340
	Robert Goodman (D)	24	130,722
New Hampshire	Maggie Hassan (D)*	52	254,666
	Walt Havenstein (R)	47	230,610
New Mexico	Susana Martinez (R)*	57	293,443
	Gary King (D)	43	219,362
New York	Andrew Cuomo (D)*	54	2,069,480
	Rob Astorino (R)	40	1,536,879
Ohio	John Kasich (R)*	64	1,944,848
	Edward FitzGerald (D)	33	1,009,359
Oklahoma	Mary Fallin (R)*	56	460,298
	Joe Dorman (D)	41	338,239
Oregon	John Kitzhaber (D)*	50	733,230
	Dennis Richardson (R)	44	648,542
Pennsylvania	Tom Wolf (D)	55	1,920,355
	Tom Corbett (R)*	45	1,575,511
Rhode Island	Gina Raimondo (D)	41	131,899
	Allan Fung (R)	36	117,428
	Robert Healey (M)	21	69,278
South Carolina	Nikki Haley (R)*	56	696,645
	Vincent Sheheen (D)	41	516,166

Table 1.6. (Continued)

State	Candidate	Percentage	Total
South Dakota	Dennis Daugaard (R)*	70	195,477
	Susan Wismer (D)	25	70,549
Tennessee	Bill Haslam (R)*	70	951,796
	Charlie Brown (D)	23	309,237
Texas	Greg Abbott (R)	59	2,796,274
	Wendy Davis (D)	39	1,835,896
Vermont	Peter Shumlin (D)*	46	89,509
	Scott Milne (R)	45	87,075
Wisconsin	Scott Walker (R)*	52	1,259,706
	Mary Burke (D)	47	1,122,913
Wyoming	Matt Mead (R)*	59	99,700
	Pete Gosar (D)	27	45,752

Source: Official Sources
* Indicates incumbent.

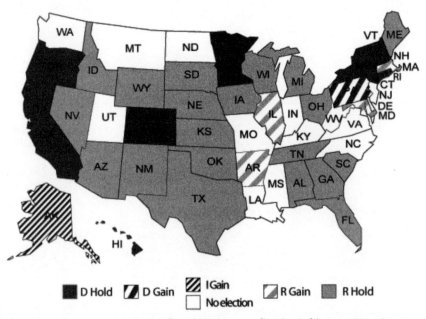

Figure 1.6 Governors' Race Results, 2014. *Map credit:* **Tim Robinson, U.Va. Center for Politics**

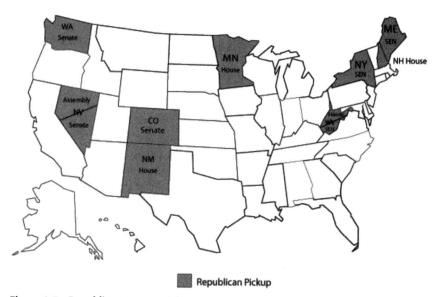

Republican Pickup

Figure 1.7   Republican State Legislature Pick-Ups, 2014. *Map credit:* **Tim Robinson, U.Va. Center for Politics**

Table 1.7.   Voter Turnout in Midterm Elections

Year	Turnout of Voting Eligible Population (VEP)
1962	47.7%
1966	48.7
1970	47.3
1974	39.1
1978	39.0
1982	42.1
1986	38.1
1990	38.4
1994	41.1
1998	38.1
2002	39.5
2006	40.4
2010	40.9
2014	35.9

Note: Voting eligible population (VEP) means the voting age population (adults age 21 and over from 1962–1970, and age 18 and over from 1974 until present) minus those ineligible to vote, such as noncitizens, felons, and mentally incapacitated persons, but adding persons in the military or civilians living overseas who are eligible to cast ballots in U.S. elections.

Sources: United States Elections Project, http://www.electproject.org/; *Vital Statistics on American Politics 2011–2012.*

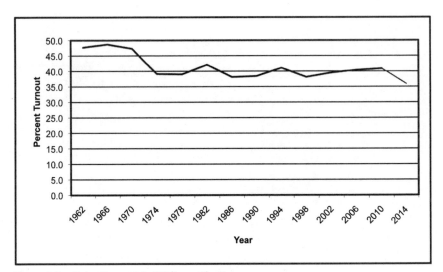

Figure 1.8   Voter Turnout in Midterm Elections

As with women, other usually Democratic groups showed some slippage to Republicans. The Democratic edge among Latinos fell from 44 percent in 2012 to 22 percent in 2014. At least according to the exit poll, Asian Americans went from 47 percent pro-Democratic in 2012 to about evenly split in 2014; other research contradicts this, suggesting that Asian Americans cast approximately two-thirds of their votes for Democrats in 2014 (still down from 73 percent Democratic in 2012).[5] The most loyal Democratic demographic of all, African Americans, also displayed a very slight Republican trend, increasing its backing of GOP candidates from 6 percent

Table 1.8.   Party Identification among Voters Who Cast a Ballot, 1998–2014

Party ID	Percent of the Electorate								
	2014	*2012*	*2010*	*2008*	*2006*	*2004*	*2002*	*2000*	*1998*
Republican	36	32	35	32	36	38	40	32	33
Democratic	35	38	35	39	38	38	31	37	34
Independent	28	29	29	29	26	25	23	27	30

Sources: 2004, 2006, 2008, 2010, 2012, and 2014: Conducted Election Day by Edison Media Research for the Nat'l Election Pool; surveyed 19,441 voters as they left the polls or early voters who said they had already voted via phone; margin of error +/−1% (CNN.com, 11/4/2014).

2002: Exit poll conducted November 6–7, 2002 and released on November 18, 2002, by Ayres, McHenry and Associates (R) for the American Association of Health Plans. The company surveyed 1,000 voters and had a margin of error +/−3 percent. This is the only exit poll available for 2002, since the Voter News Service network consortium had an organizational meltdown on Election Day and was unable to provide verifiable polling data for 2002.

Table 1.9. Total Votes by Party, 2014

Party	Number of Votes	Percentage
Governors		
Republicans	32,351,951	50.3
Democrats	29,721,645	46.2
Independents/Others	2,217,378	3.4
Total	64,290,974	
Senate		
Republicans	23,794,122	51.7
Democrats	20,250,842	44.0
Independents/Others	1,975,913	4.3
Total	46,020,877	
House		
Republicans	40,080,861	51.4
Democrats	35,622,551	45.7
Independents/Others	2,244,353	2.9
Total	77,947,765	

Sources: Governor and Senate calculations by author. House data as of January 22, 2015, from David Wasserman, Loren Fulton, and Ashton Barry, "2014 National House Popular Vote Tracker," Cook Political Report, https://docs.google.com/spreadsheet/ccc?key=0AjYj9mXElO_QdHVsbnNNdXRoaUE5QThHclNWaTgzb2c&usp=drive_web#gid=0. Percentages may not total 100 percent because of rounding.

in 2012 to 10 percent in 2014. Much the same thing can be observed in every category of voter, as one would expect in a "wave" election like 2014 where disproportionately Republican and conservative voters were more motivated to cast a ballot. The same phenomenon was observed in 2010. Democrats were especially weak with white men, who gave the party's candidates only 33 percent of their votes.

While Republican margins grew everywhere, the normal divisions of American politics were still visible, and not just among the races, genders, and age groupings. Democrats handily won voters making less than $50,000 a year, with Republicans carrying those over $50,000 with an even larger majority. Voters making an annual income of $200,000 or more chose the GOP by a 57 percent to 42 percent margin. Democrats were favored by the least well-educated (no high school diploma) and the most well-educated (those with postgraduate training), while Republicans won the in-between categories. Union households were Democratic; those with no union connection were Republican. The GOP won Protestants and Catholics alike (especially white, evangelical Christians), but Democrats were heavily preferred by those belonging to other religions or having no religion. The more often one attends church, the more likely one is to vote Republican. We have seen these patterns repeatedly in recent decades. It is worth noting that the Catholic vote, which can swing from election to election, voted Republican by 9 percent in 2014 after having favored the Democrats by 2 percent in 2012.

As would be expected in this polarized era, Democrats won almost all Democratic Party identifiers in the electorate (92 percent), and the Republicans swept the GOP voters (94 percent). It was among independents that preferences changed from 2012 to 2014. Republicans won independents in both elections, but by 5 points in 2012 versus 12 points in 2014. (Obama had won independents by 8 points in 2008.) Of course, once again, those independents choosing to vote in the midterm election were, on the whole, more conservative and closely aligned with the GOP than those who voted in 2008 or 2012.

The Republican identity of the 2014 electorate is revealed in the job approval numbers for President Obama: 44 percent approve, 55 percent disapprove. Moreover, those strongly disapproving (42 percent) were more than double the group of voters strongly approving (20 percent). Fully 59 percent of voters described themselves as either "dissatisfied" or "angry" about the Obama administration; 68 percent of the former group and 93 percent of the latter group voted Republican.

CONNECTING THE DOTS—OR NOT

Elections are nuanced, and in a diverse country, they can be analyzed from a thousand perspectives. Yet they are thematic too, especially in decisive years like the last four contests, 2008 to 2014. Barack Obama's first election was as much about the unpopularity of the outgoing president as it was Obama's uniqueness. President Obama and his own record have dominated his two midterms and his reelection. When it counted for him, the president was able to bring out overwhelming numbers of his supporters to secure a second term. Just like most presidents, he was unsuccessful in duplicating his electorate in the 2010 and 2014 midterms.

The next election will be decided by a much larger electorate than the one that showed up last November. But President Obama's record and job approval rating will still matter a great deal. We fully address the 2016 possibilities in the final chapters of this volume.

Yet it is vital to remember that every election follows a different drum beat, created by the special combination of issues and candidates in a particular year. None of this is especially predictable two years in advance; the next White House contest viewed solely through the lens of its previous midterm results is distorted, sometimes severely.

Be careful about connecting the dots too quickly. The Democratic near-landslide of 2008 could never have immediately foretold the thumping

Democrats took in 2010. Nor did the Republican tsunami of 2010 tell us very much about the eventual outcome in 2012. So a reasonable guess is that the 2014 midterm won't be determinative in any way about the forthcoming White House campaign, regardless of which party captures the presidency in the end.

It is only natural to take what we see as true today and project it forward. But who can say what President Obama's approval level will be in 2016? Obama may have great difficulty in climbing above 50 percent again—an important benchmark to keep him from being dead weight for his party's presidential candidate. On the other hand, presidential popularity can be affected by a wide range of unseen domestic and foreign developments that even a soothsayer would be hard pressed to conjure up.

Where will the economy go in the next two years? As this is written, a solid recovery appears to be in the offing at last, and it could help Democrats recover their balance. Yet long-term economic forecasting is one of the least reliable social sciences, and the economy's strength or weakness in the actual election year is far more telling than GDP growth years in advance. Then there is terrorism, many international hot spots, scandal, social issues, future Supreme Court decisions, and—lest we forget—the strengths and weaknesses of the actual 2016 major-party (and other) presidential nominees that might alter the political landscape.

The past is worth analyzing at length as retrospectives grounded in hard data are fascinating and illuminating. But the future is endlessly unknowable, and we should be hesitant to project a reality beyond our knowledge. Events not in anyone's immediate control, and trends that can only be guessed at, will be in the saddle two years hence.

Table 1.10.   Exit Polls, 2014

Vote by Gender (Percentage of Total)	Democrat	Republican
Male (49%)	41% [45%]*	57% [52%]**
Female (51%)	51% [55%]	47% [44%]

Vote by Age (Percentage of Total)	Democrat	Republican
18–24 (7%)	54% [60%]	44% [36%]
25–29 (6%)	54% [60%]	43% [38%]
30–39 (13%)	51% [55%]	47% [42%]
40–49 (19%)	44% [48%]	54% [50%]
50–64 (33%)	46% [47%]	52% [52%]
65 + (22%)	41% [44%]	57% [56%]

Table 1.10.   (Continued)

Vote by Race

(Percentage of Total)	Democrat	Republican
White (75%)	38% [39%]	60% [59%]
African-American (12%)	89% [93%]	10% [6%]
Latino (8%)	62% [71%]	36% [27%]
Asian (3%)	49% [73%]	50% [26%]
Other (2%)	49% [58%]	47% [38%]

Vote by Gender and Race

(Percentage of Total)	Democrat	Republican
White Men (37%)	33% [35%]	64% [62%]
White Women (38%)	42% [42%]	56% [56%]
Black Men (5%)	86% [87%]	13% [11%]
Black Women (7%)	91% [96%]	8% [3%]
Latino Men (4%)	57% [65%]	41% [33%]
Latino Women (4%)	66% [76%]	32% [23%]
All Other Races (5%)	49% [66%]	48% [31%]

Vote by Age and Race

(Percentage of Total)	Democrat	Republican
White 18–29 (8%)	43% [44%]	54% [51%]
White 30–44 (15%)	40% [38%]	58% [59%]
White 45–64 (32%)	36% [38%]	62% [61%]
White 65+ (19%)	36% [39%]	62% [61%]
Black 18–29 (2%)	88% [91%]	11% [8%]
Black 30–44 (3%)	86% [94%]	12% [5%]
Black 45–64 (5%)	90% [93%]	9% [7%]
Black 65+ (2%)	92% [93%]	7% [6%]
Latino 18–29 (2%)	68% [74%]	28% [23%]
Latino 30–44 (2%)	56% [71%]	42% [28%]
Latino 45–64 (3%)	62% [68%]	37% [31%]
Latino 65+ (1%)	64% [65%]	34% [35%]
All Others (5%)	49% [67%]	49% [31%]

Vote by Ideology

(Percentage of Total)	Democrat	Republican
Liberal (23%)	87% [86%]	11% [11%]
Moderate (40%)	53% [56%]	45% [41%]
Conservative (37%)	13% [17%]	85% [82%]

Vote by Party ID

(Percentage of Total)	Democrat	Republican
Democrats (35%)	92% [92%]	7% [7%]
Republicans (36%)	5% [6%]	94% [93%]
Independents (28%)	42% [45%]	54% [50%]

Table 1.10. (Continued)

Vote by Gender and Party		
(Percentage of Total)	Democrat	Republican
Democratic Men (14%)	92%	7%
Democratic Women (21%)	92%	7%
Republican Men (19%)	5%	94%
Republican Women (18%)	5%	94%
Independent Men (17%)	38%	57%
Independent Women (12%)	46%	50%

Vote by Education		
(Percentage of Total)	Democrat	Republican
No High School (2%)	54% [64%]	44% [35%]
High School Graduate (18%)	45% [51%]	53% [48%]
Some College (29%)	44% [49%]	54% [48%]
College Graduate (31%)	44% [47%]	54% [51%]
Postgraduate (20%)	53% [55%]	45% [42%]

Are You a College Graduate?		
(Percentage of Total)	Democrat	Republican
Yes (51%)	47% [50%]	50% [48%]
No (49%)	45% [51%]	53% [47%]

Did You Attend College?		
(Percentage of Total)	Democrat	Republican
Yes (80%)	46% [50%]	52% [48%]
No (20%)	46% [52%]	52% [46%]

Vote by Race and Education		
(Percentage of Total)	Democrat	Republican
White College Graduates (39%)	41%	57%
White/No College Degree (36%)	34%	64%
Non-White College Graduates (11%)	70%	28%
Non-White/No College Degree (14%)	74%	25%

Vote by Income		
(Percentage of Total)	Democrat	Republican
Under $30K (16%)	59%	39%
$30–50K (20%)	51%	47%
$50–100K (34%)	44%	55%
$100–200K (23%)	41%	57%
Over $200K (7%)	42%	57%

Vote by Income		
(Percentage of Total)	Democrat	Republican
Less Than $50K (36%)	54% [60%]	43% [38%]
$50–100K (24%)	44% [46%]	55% [52%]
$100K or More (30%)	41% [44%]	57% [54%]

Table 1.10.   (Continued)

Vote by Religion (Percentage of Total)	Democrat	Republican
Protestant (53%)	37% [42%]	61% [57%]
Catholic (24%)	45% [50%]	54% [48%]
Jewish (3%)	66% [69%]	33% [30%]
Other (8%)	67% [74%]	31% [23%]
None (12%)	69% [70%]	29% [26%]

Vote by Religion and Race (Percentage of Total)	Democrat	Republican
White Protestant (39%)	26% [30%]	72% [69%]
White Catholic (19%)	38% [40%]	60% [59%]
White Jewish (3%)	65% [71%]	34% [29%]
White/Other Religions (4%)	61% [61%]	36% [35%]
White/No Religion (9%)	66% [63%]	32% [31%]
Non-Whites (26%)	71% [80%]	27% [18%]

How Often Do You Attend Religious Services? (Percentage of Total)	Democrat	Republican
More Than Weekly (13%)	40%	59%
Weekly (27%)	40% [39%]	58% [59%]
Monthly (14%)	43%	55%
Few Times a Year (26%)	48% [55%]	51% [43%]
Never (18%)	62% [62%]	36% [34%]

Vote by Church Attendance and Religion (Percentage of Total)	Democrat	Republican
Protestant/Attend Weekly (15%)	31% [29%]	67% [70%]
Protestant/Attend Less (14%)	37% [44%]	61% [55%]
Catholic/Attend Weekly (11%)	43% [42%]	55% [57%]
Catholic/Attend Less (13%)	50% [56%]	49% [42%]
All Other Religions (46%)	55% [58%]	43% [39%]

Are You White Evangelical or Born-Again Christian? (Percentage of Total)	Democrat	Republican
Yes (26%)	20% [21%]	78% [78%]
No (74%)	55% [60%]	43% [37%]

Country Is Going in . . . (Percentage of Total)	Democrat	Republican
Right Direction (31%)	82% [93%]	17% [6%]
Wrong Track (65%)	28% [13%]	69% [84%]

Your View of Government (Percentage of Total)	Democrat	Republican
Government Should Do More (41%)	78% [81%]	21% [17%]
Government Doing Too Much (54%)	21% [24%]	77% [74%]

Table 1.10.   (Continued)

Are You Worried about Economic Conditions?		
(Percentage of Total)	Democrat	Republican
Very Worried (38%)	30%	68%
Somewhat Worried (41%)	48%	50%
Not Too Worried (17%)	72%	27%
Not At All Worried (4%)	79%	19%

National Economic Conditions		
(Percentage of Total)	Democrat	Republican
Excellent (1%)	N/A [N/A]	N/A [N/A]
Good (28%)	74% [90%]	24% [9%]
Not So Good (48%)	41% [55%]	58% [42%]
Poor (22%)	18% [12%]	79% [85%]

U.S. Economy Is . . .		
(Percentage of Total)	Democrat	Republican
Getting Better (32%)	75% [88%]	23% [9%]
Getting Worse (32%)	20% [9%]	77% [90%]
Staying About the Same (34%)	41% [40%]	57% [57%]

Economic Conditions Are . . .		
(Percentage of Total)	Democrat	Republican
Getting Better (32%)	75% [88%]	23% [9%]
Good and Staying the Same (6%)	70% [71%]	28% [27%]
Poor and Staying the Same (27%)	34% [35%]	65% [62%]
Getting Worse (32%)	20% [9%]	77% [90%]

Your Family's Financial Situation		
(Percentage of Total)	Democrat	Republican
Better (28%)	57% [84%]	41% [15%]
Worse (25%)	30% [18%]	67% [80%]
Same (45%)	49% [58%]	49% [40%]

US Economic System Generally . . .		
(Percentage of Total)	Democrat	Republican
Favors the Wealthy (63%)	64% [71%]	35% [26%]
Is Fair to Most Americans (32%)	17% [22%]	81% [77%]

Life for the Next Generation of Americans Will Be . . .		
(Percentage of Total)	Democrat	Republican
Better Than Today (22%)	68%	31%
Worse Than Today (48%)	29%	69%
Same as Today (27%)	60%	38%

Table 1.10. (Continued)

Trust Government in Washington?		
(Percentage of Total)	Democrat	Republican
Just About Always (3%)	72%	28%
Most of the Time (17%)	71%	28%
Only Some of the Time (60%)	44%	54%
Never (18%)	27%	70%

Your House Vote Meant to Express . . .		
(Percentage of Total)	Democrat	Republican
Support for Obama (19%)	93%	6%
Opposition to Obama (33%)	5%	92%
Obama Not a Factor (45%)	55%	43%

How Obama Is Handling His Job		
(Percentage of Total)	Democrat	Republican
Strongly Approve (20%)	91% [97%]	8% [2%]
Somewhat Approve (24%)	84% [80%]	15% [18%]
Somewhat Disapprove (13%)	37% [9%]	59% [88%]
Strongly Disapprove (42%)	8% [1%]	90% [96%]

How Congress Is Handling Its Job		
(Percentage of Total)	Democrat	Republican
Strongly Approve (3%)	56%	43%
Somewhat Approve (17%)	53%	46%
Somewhat Disapprove (30%)	42%	56%
Strongly Disapprove (48%)	48%	50%

Opinion of Obama Administration		
(Percentage of Total)	Democrat	Republican
Enthusiastic (10%)	93% [98%]	5% [2%]
Satisfied (29%)	84% [87%]	15% [11%]
Dissatisfied (32%)	29% [9%]	68% [86%]
Angry (27%)	5% [1%]	93% [97%]

Opinion of GOP Leaders in Congress		
(Percentage of Total)	Democrat	Republican
Enthusiastic (7%)	12%	86%
Satisfied (32%)	17%	81%
Dissatisfied (37%)	53%	45%
Angry (22%)	84%	13%

Opinion of Democratic Party		
(Percentage of Total)	Democrat	Republican
Favorable (43%)	90% [93%]	8% [6%]
Unfavorable (55%)	12% [3%]	86% [94%]

Table 1.10.   (Continued)

Opinion of Republican Party		
(Percentage of Total)	Democrat	Republican
Favorable (42%)	10% [6%]	88% [93%]
Unfavorable (54%)	74% [92%]	24% [5%]
Opinion of Tea Party		
(Percentage of Total)	Democrat	Republican
Strongly Support (13%)	9%	89%
Somewhat Support (19%)	16%	81%
Neutral (28%)	41%	57%
Somewhat Oppose (10%)	58%	40%
Strongly Oppose (26%)	87%	11%
Most Important Issue Facing Country Today		
(Percentage of Total)	Democrat	Republican
Foreign Policy (13%)	42% [56%]	56% [33%]
Health Care (25%)	59% [75%]	39% [24%]
Economy (45%)	48% [47%]	50% [51%]
Illegal Immigration (14%)	24%	74%
2010 Federal Health Care Law . . .		
(Percentage of Total)	Democrat	Republican
Did Not Go Far Enough (25%)	78%	19%
Was About Right (21%)	80%	19%
Went Too Far (49%)	14%	84%
U.S. Military Action Against ISIS		
(Percentage of Total)	Democrat	Republican
Approve (58%)	49%	49%
Disapprove (35%)	41%	56%
Should Same-Sex Marriages Be Legal In Your State?		
(Percentage of Total)	Democrat	Republican
Yes (48%)	67% [73%]	31% [25%]
No (48%)	27% [25%]	72% [74%]
Legalize Marijuana in Your State?		
(Percentage of Total)	Democrat	Republican
Favor (49%)	60%	38%
Oppose (47%)	31%	67%
Most Illegal Immigrants Working in U.S. Should Be . . .		
(Percentage of Total)	Democrat	Republican
Offered Legal Status (57%)	64% [61%]	35% [37%]
Deported (39%)	23% [24%]	75% [73%]

Table 1.10.   (Continued)

Abortion Should Be . . .

(Percentage of Total)	Democrat	Republican
Always Legal (23%)	74% [76%]	24% [22%]
Mostly Legal (29%)	57% [58%]	41% [40%]
Mostly Illegal (27%)	23% [22%]	75% [76%]
Always Illegal (17%)	28% [19%]	71% [79%]

Worried about Major Terrorist Attack in
United States?

(Percentage of Total)	Democrat	Republican
Very Worried (28%)	32%	66%
Somewhat Worried (43%)	44%	55%
Not Too Worried (22%)	67%	31%
Not at All Worried (6%)	74%	23%

Race Relations in U.S. Have . . .

(Percentage of Total)	Democrat	Republican
Gotten Better (20%)	54%	44%
Stayed the Same (40%)	53%	46%
Gotten Worse (38%)	36%	62%

Federal Government Response to Ebola

(Percentage of Total)	Democrat	Republican
Approve (42%)	68%	30%
Disapprove (52%)	26%	72%

Is Global Warming a Serious Problem?

(Percentage of Total)	Democrat	Republican
Yes (57%)	70%	29%
No (41%)	14%	84%

Vote by Marital Status

(Percentage of Total)	Democrat	Republican
Married (63%)	40% [42%]	58% [56%]
Unmarried (37%)	55% [62%]	42% [35%]

Vote by Gender and Marital Status

(Percentage of Total)	Democrat	Republican
Married Men (33%)	37% [38%]	61% [60%]
Married Women (30%)	44% [46%]	54% [53%]
Unmarried Men (16%)	49% [56%]	48% [40%]
Unmarried Women (21%)	60% [67%]	38% [31%]

Any Children Under 18 Living in Your Home?

(Percentage of Total)	Democrat	Republican
Yes (34%)	46% [51%]	52% [47%]
No (66%)	47% [50%]	51% [47%]

Table 1.10.   (Continued)

Do You Have Children Under 18?		
(Percentage of Total)	Democrat	Republican
Fathers (17%)	41%	57%
Mothers (17%)	50%	48%
Men with No Children (33%)	43%	55%
Women with No Children (34%)	51%	47%

Vote by Marital Status and Children		
(Percentage of Total)	Democrat	Republican
Married Voters with Kids (25%)	40% [45%]	58% [54%]
All Other Voters (75%)	49% [53%]	49% [45%]

Ever Served in the U.S. Military?		
(Percentage of Total)	Democrat	Republican
Yes (17%)	44%	54%
No (83%)	48%	50%

Is Anyone in Household a Union Member?		
(Percentage of Total)	Democrat	Republican
Yes (17%)	60% [58%]	38% [40%]
No (83%)	44% [49%]	54% [48%]

Do You Work Full-Time for Pay?		
(Percentage of Total)	Democrat	Republican
Yes (60%)	44% [49%]	54% [49%]
No (59%)	48% [53%]	50% [45%]

Followed This Year's Political Campaigns . . .		
(Percentage of Total)	Democrat	Republican
Extremely Closely (18%)	38%	60%
Very Closely (32%)	44%	54%
Somewhat Closely (36%)	48%	50%
Not Too Closely (12%)	54%	43%

Are You Gay, Lesbian, or Bisexual?		
(Percentage of Total)	Democrat	Republican
Yes (4%)	75% [76%]	24% [22%]
No (96%)	45% [49%]	53% [49%]

Vote by Size of Place		
(Percentage of Total)	Democrat	Republican
Urban (32%)	56%	42%
Suburban (52%)	43%	55%
Rural (16%)	38%	59%

Table 1.10.   (Continued)

Vote by Region (Percentage of Total)	Democrat	Republican
East (20%)	55%	43%
Midwest (25%)	45%	53%
South (33%)	38%	59%
West (22%)	50%	48%

Source: http://www.cnn.com/election/2014/results/race/house#exit-polls

* Bracketed percentages in "Democrat" column indicate percentages received by President Barack Obama in 2012.

** Bracketed percentages in "Republican" column indicate percentages received by Governor Mitt Romney in 2012.

NOTES

1. *The Sixth Year Itch*, ed. Larry J. Sabato (New York: Longman, 2007).

2. Larry J. Sabato, "What a Drag: Why a Party May Well Be Better Off Losing the White House," *Politico Magazine*, December 1, 2014, http://www.politico.com/magazine/story/2014/12/presidents-bad-for-their-parties-113241.html#.VIYP6D HF98E (accessed December 8, 2014). Numbers updated as of December 12, 2014, from National Conference of State Legislatures data, http://www.ncsl.org/research/elections-and-campaigns/statevote-2014-post-election-analysis635508614.aspx.

3. Interestingly, in 1942's low turnout, Republicans won a majority of the vote for U.S. House of Representatives (50.6%), though because of district alignments and the Democratic Solid South, Democrats still won a 222 to 209 majority of seats (there were also four third-party members).

4. National Exit Poll: http://www.cnn.com/election/2014/results/exit-polls.

5. Asian American Decisions' election eve survey found that group intended to support Democrats by about a two-to-one margin (66 percent to 34 percent) over Republicans in U.S. House elections. Survey results can be found at http://asian americandecisions.com/wp-content/uploads/2014/11/AAPI-Poll-Results-for-web1 .pdf.

2

The Primaries of 2014

More Than Meets the Eye

Rhodes Cook

How might the 2014 primary season ultimately be remembered?

There was the shocking defeat of Virginia's Eric Cantor, the majority leader in the House of Representatives, who appeared to be on course to be House speaker one day.

There was the Tea Party-flavored challenges to a half-dozen veteran Republican senators, none of which was successful but all of which drew some political "blood."

And there was the reinforcement of the basic reality, the Senate challenges aside, that the vast majority of incumbents were able to win renomination without breaking a sweat. Only four House members, one governor, and nary a senator were defeated by intraparty competition in 2014. There were more casualties in the previous midterm election four years earlier, when four representatives, three senators, and one governor were primary losers.[1]

Yet in the long run, the 2014 primary season may be remembered more than anything else for its place in the evolution of the American electorate, as for the second straight midterm election cycle, more votes were cast in Republican than Democratic primaries.

It has not always been that way. From the advent of the New Deal in the 1930s until essentially the end of the twentieth century, the Democrats boasted more adherents than the Republicans at the grassroots level even when they were regularly losing presidential elections.

To be sure, there are still more registered Democrats than Republicans in the thirty or so states that register voters by party. But that is a lagging indicator of the true nature of the political landscape.[2]

The nation is now in a different era. In 2010, 19.3 million voters participated in Republican primaries, compared to 15.9 million who cast Democratic primary ballots—a GOP advantage of 3.4 million. In 2014, 15.3 million Republican primary votes were cast, compared to 13.0 million Democratic ballots—a GOP advantage of 2.3 million.[3]

It might be a stretch just yet to call the Republicans the nation's majority party, as the Democrats appear to still hold the upper hand in presidential elections. But with the GOP's recent edge in the "battle of the primary ballots," combined with Republican dominance at the state level, where they emerged from the 2014 election with control of 31 governorships and 68 of 98 state legislative chambers (Nebraska's is unicameral and nonpartisan), Republicans might well be viewed as the reigning champions of America's grassroots.[4]

MOST PRIMARY ACTION ON REPUBLICAN SIDE

The 2014 primaries and the general election that followed played out on two different stages. In the latter, the nature of the midterm election put the Democrats on the defensive. In the primaries, though, intraparty friction was focused on the Republican side. Of the twenty House members in 2014 who drew less than 60 percent of their party's primary vote, seventeen were Republicans. Of the six senators who received less than 60 percent, five were Republicans. And of the three sub-60 percent governors in the 2014 primaries, two were Republicans (see Table 2.1).[5]

Close primary contests are often a function of local factors—such as an incumbent's age and ethics, personal rivalries, and changing demographics within his or her state or district. But in 2014, there was the national overlay of grassroots conservative activists (often identified as the "Tea Party") challenging the GOP establishment on basic issues such as the value of federal spending and the desirability of long-time congressional service. The infighting roiled Republican primaries as the Vietnam War bedeviled the Democrats decades ago.

The spirited, sometimes harsh competition was nothing new for the GOP. There were conspicuous Tea Party candidacies in 2010 and 2012. But in 2014, the challenges were more ambitious in scope. Six veteran Republican senators were targeted—Lamar Alexander of Tennessee, Thad Cochran of Mississippi, John Cornyn of Texas, Lindsey Graham of South Carolina, Mitch McConnell of Kentucky, and Pat Roberts of Kansas. All were renominated, but none won their primary with more than 60 percent of the vote.

Table 2.1. 2014 Congressional Primaries: Incumbent Losers and Modest Winners

The biggest story of the 2014 primary season undoubtedly was the stunning upset of House Majority Leader Eric Cantor, who lost his bid for renomination in his central Virginia district in June to a challenger who was lightly funded (compared to Cantor) and relatively unknown. Other than that, it was a year of chastening for a few incumbents, but hardly any defeats. Of the six Republican and one Democratic senators who were seriously challenged in their party's primary, none lost, although four were nominated with less than a majority of the vote. Only one governor suffered a primary defeat in 2014, and gubernatorial primaries as a whole did not tend to be as close as those for the Senate. Still, there were some noteworthy results, with two nationally prominent governors, Andrew Cuomo of New York and Sam Brownback of Kansas, barely clearing 60 percent against little-known opponents who essentially served as a protest option.

Incumbent Governor	State	Terms	Total Votes in Primary	% of Primary Vote Won	Margin of Victory (or Defeat)
DEFEATED					
Neil Abercrombie (D)	HI	1	233,179	31.5%	(lost to David Ige by 36.0%)
Modest Winners (sub-60%)					
C.L. "Butch" Otter (R)	ID	2	155,310	51.4%	(beat Russ Fulcher by 8%)
Matt Mead (R)	WY	1	97,884	54.8%	(beat Taylor Haynes by 23%)

Incumbent Senator	State	Terms	Total Votes in Primary	% of Primary Vote Won	Margin of Victory
Modest Winners (sub-60%)					
Pat Roberts (R)	KS	3	264,340	48.1%	(beat Milton Wolf by 7%)
Thad Cochran (R)#	MS	6	318,895 (RO) 382,221	49.0% 51.0%	(trailed Chris McDaniel by 0.5%) (beat McDaniel in runoff by 2%)
Brian Schatz (D)	HI	@	233,950	49.3%	(beat Colleen Hanabusa by 0.7%)
Lamar Alexander (R)	TN	2	668,039	49.7%	(beat Joe Carr by 9%)
Lindsey Graham (R)	SC	2	316,989	56.4%	(beat Lee Bright by 41%)
John Cornyn (R)	TX	2	1,314,556	59.4%	(beat Steve Stockman by 40%)

Table 2.1. (Continued)

Incumbent Representative	District	Terms	Total Votes in Primary	% of Primary Vote Won	Margin of Victory (or Defeat)
DEFEATED					
Kerry Bentivolio (R)	MI-11	1	63,262	33.6%	(lost to David Trott by 33%)
John Tierney (D)	MA-06	9	69,144	40.1%	(lost to Seth Moulton by 11%)
Eric Cantor (R)	VA-07	7	65,017	44.5%	(lost to David Brat by 11%)
Ralph Hall (R)#	TX-04	17	65,720 (RO) 42,170	45.4% 47.2%	(led John Ratcliffe by 17%) (lost runoff to Ratcliffe by 6%)
Modest Winners (sub-60%)					
Scott DesJarlais (R)	TN-04	2	77,504	44.9%	(beat Jim Tracy by 0.05%)
Charles Rangel (D)	NY-13	22	49,827	47.8%	(beat Adriano Espaillat by 5%)
Steven Palazzo (R)	MS-04	2	107,389	50.5%	(beat Gene Taylor by 8%)
Chuck Fleischmann (R)	TN-03	2	91,640	50.8%	(beat Weston Wamp by 2%)
Walter Jones (R)	NC-03	10	44,438	50.9%	(beat Taylor Griffin by 6%)
Doug Lamborn (R)	CO-05	4	73,708	52.6%	(beat Bentley Rayburn by 5%)
Bill Shuster (R)	PA-09	6	46,371	52.8%	(beat Arthur Halvorson by 18%)
Lee Terry (R)	NE-02	8	48,782	52.9%	(beat Dan Frei by 6%)
Richard Hanna (R)	NY-22	2	30,119	53.5%	(beat Claudia Tenney by 7%)
Leonard Lance (R)	NJ-07	3	29,208	54.4%	(beat David Larsen by 9%)
Rodney Davis (R)	IL-13	1	50,914	54.6%	(beat Erika Harold by 13%)
Hank Johnson (D)	GA-04	4	48,423	54.8%	(beat Tom Brown by 10%)
Tim Huelskamp (R)	KS-02	2	77,955	55.0%	(beat Alan LaPolice by 10%)
David Joyce (R)	OH-14	1	50,093	55.0%	(beat Matt Lynch by 10%)
Justin Amash (R)	MI-03	2	69,128	57.4%	(beat Brian Ellis by 15%)
Renee Ellmers (R)	NC-02	2	36,457	58.7%	(beat Frank Roche by 17%)

Note: A pound sign (#) indicates that the incumbent was forced into a runoff. "(RO)" stands for runoff. "@" means that the incumbent was appointed to office after the last election. This list does not include results from "top-two," all-party primaries in California and Washington. Nor does it include Rep. Vance McAllister (R), who was defeated in Louisiana's "general primary," an election that took place the same November day as the general election in all other states. In that election in Louisiana's Fifth District), no candidate won a majority, meaning there would be a "general election" in December between the top-two finishers, which is commonly viewed as a runoff election. Because McAllister failed to finish in the top two, he did not advance to the December contest.

Sources: The number of primary ballots cast and incumbent vote percentages are based on official returns posted on state election websites for all states.

At the House level, conservative activists mounted assaults on GOP incumbents from New York to Idaho. The biggest scalp they claimed in 2014 was that of Cantor, who was upset in the June primary in his Richmond-area district by a little-known economics professor from Randolph-Macon College, David Brat. Cantor's loss was widely seen as more of a home-grown revolt than one instigated by national interest groups. To many of his central Virginia constituents, the majority leader had come to reflect Republican interests in Washington rather than those of his district.

A few other GOP congressional leaders did not lose but were chastened at the ballot box, with Senate Minority Leader McConnell losing 40 percent of the Republican primary vote in Kentucky to his opposition and House Speaker John Boehner of Ohio dropping nearly 30 percent in his Ohio district.

NO "TURKEYS"

The Republican Party establishment did get its wish in 2014 that no "turkeys" be nominated as Republican Senate candidates. In both 2010 and 2012, GOP chances of taking over the Senate were undermined by grassroots favorites such as Christine O'Donnell of Delaware, Richard Mourdock of Indiana, and Todd Akin of Missouri, who proved "nominatable" but not electable. Nor did the problems they posed end there, as ill-timed comments from these candidates on issues ranging from rape and abortion (Akin and Mourdock) to the supernatural (O'Donnell) created a media firestorm that was no help to other Republican candidates in swing states. The low point for these controversial candidacies came when O'Donnell felt compelled to run advertising to deny that she was a witch.[6]

In 2014, GOP leaders worked hand and hand with allies in the business community to make sure that the party's nominees for major office were within the political mainstream of their state or district. By and large, they were successful, which left the GOP well positioned for success in the fall.

On the other hand, Democratic primaries in 2014 were not as competitive as their Republican counterparts, either in terms of the quantity of candidates or the intensity of the competition. In many places, the once dominant Democrats seemed to lack much of a "farm team" anymore and had trouble finding decent candidates to fill the ballot.

In Alabama, for the first time in the party's history, Democrats did not run a Senate candidate at all in 2014.[7] In Tennessee, Democratic voters nominated a political unknown for governor who benefitted from a famous cartoon name (Charlie Brown) and top line on the primary ballot. In Texas, the Democratic Senate contest between a dental clinic executive and a follower of Lyndon LaRouche required a runoff before the former won. In

Idaho, William Bryk drew 30 percent of the Democratic primary vote for Senate, even though he lived in New York. And in Nevada, the field of Democratic gubernatorial candidates was apparently so weak that a plurality of the party's primary voters cast their ballots for a line labeled "None of these candidates."[8]

All in all, it was not a good showing for a party that once ruled the roost at the grassroots.

"PRIMARIED"

Over the last few years, a new word has worked its way into the political lexicon: "primaried." It changes a noun to a verb and refers to a significant intraparty challenge that a favored candidate, often an incumbent, draws for reasons that are frequently ideological. With so many states and districts nowadays considered safe for one party or the other, the primary is being widely seen as the only venue in which an incumbent can be effectively challenged.

The advent of the word "primaried" parallels the recent rise of the Tea Party. The conservative, populist grassroots movement has roiled Republican politics since its inception in 2009.

For most of the past few decades, the odds of ousting a sitting senator in a primary have been low. From 1982 through 2008, a total of just four senators were denied renomination (and one, Democrat Joe Lieberman, won the 2006 general election as an independent after losing his primary). With the advent of the Tea Party, though, that total was matched in the 2010 and 2012 election cycles. Republicans Robert Bennett of Utah and Lisa Murkowski of Alaska, plus Democrat Arlen Specter (a long-time Republican before his party switch prior to the 2010 election), lost bids for renomination in 2010. (Murkowski refused to accept her primary defeat as the last word and successfully ran for reelection as a write-in candidate.) Republican Richard Lugar of Indiana landed in the losers' circle in 2012.[9]

SENATE PRIMARIES

In 2014, the Tea Party cast a wider net, mounting challenges to six veteran Republican senators. Alexander, Cornyn, and Graham were finishing their second term in the Senate; Roberts was wrapping up his third; McConnell his fifth; and Cochran his sixth term.

A number of them were long-time powers on Capitol Hill. McConnell was Senate Minority Leader (en route to becoming majority leader with the

GOP's takeover of the Senate that fall). Cornyn was his number two in the Republican leadership. Cochran had served as chairman of the Senate Appropriations Committee.

Five of the six were from the South, the base of the Republican Party nowadays. (The lone non-Southern senator in the group was Kansas' Roberts, who hails from a historically Republican state.)

Four of the six were septuagenarians (Alexander, Cochran, McConnell, and Roberts).

None had faced a significant primary challenge since first winning their Senate seat. But all their intraparty success had been pre-Tea Party. To their conservative critics, they were part and parcel of a federal government they did not like.

With the backing of the party establishment and its interest group allies, the Republican "six" were well counseled and well funded. In addition, they faced primary opposition that was not well known when their campaigns began. But in a number of the states, their opponents were able essentially to act as a "none of the above" line and capitalized on that to capture 40 percent or more of the vote against each of the six GOP senators (see Table 2.2).

Two, in particular, drew the national spotlight: McConnell, who would arguably have been the biggest scalp the Tea Party ever bagged; and Cochran, who proved to be the most vulnerable of the Republican Senate incumbents in the 2014 primaries.

McConnell Dominates

McConnell had long been an anomaly in Kentucky politics. He had high negatives among voters in his home state but still had been able to comfortably win elections. His formula for success: well-organized and funded campaigns, coupled with a willingness to play political hardball. His primary challenger, businessman Matt Bevin, basically served as a vehicle of protest for those who saw the Senate minority leader as a deal-making enabler of big government.

Conservative groups such as the Senate Conservatives Fund spent heavily on Bevin's behalf. But McConnell and his supporters spent even more to drive home the message that McConnell's clout was indispensable to Kentucky and that Bevin's nomination would put the Republican seat in jeopardy. The incumbent also ran a number of negative attacks against Bevin, basically challenging his trustworthiness. But arguably McConnell's greatest asset was the backing of the state's junior senator, Republican Rand Paul, a Tea Party favorite who had crushed McConnell's preferred candidate in Kentucky's 2010 Senate primary.[10]

Table 2.2. Republican Senate Incumbents under Primary Fire

Six veteran Republican senators in 2014 were challenged in primaries by conservative activists, many affiliated with the grassroots-oriented Tea Party. None of the incumbents lost. But to one degree or another, all had to break a sweat. Three of the GOP senators drew less than a majority of the primary vote—Pat Roberts of Kansas, Lamar Alexander of Tennessee, and Thad Cochran of Mississippi (though Cochran won a bare majority in a runoff). Two others—Lindsey Graham of South Carolina and John Cornyn of Texas—were in the 50 to 59.9 percent range. One and only one, Mitch McConnell of Kentucky, reached 60 percent of the primary vote. And in McConnell's case, just barely (60.2 percent). (The only other senator to be held to less than 60 percent of the vote in his party's primary in 2014 was Democrat Brian Schatz of Hawaii, who won with 49 percent.)

In the aggregate, the six Republican incumbents collected 1.79 million votes in their primary races, while their opponents garnered 1.45 million votes. Put another way, the half-dozen GOP senators who drew significant intraparty challenges in 2014 won 55 percent of the aggregate GOP primary vote in their states, while their opposition received 45 percent.

Incumbent	State	Primary Date	Incumbent Vote Total	Other Votes	Inc. %	Other %	Inc. Counties	Others' Counties	Leading Challenger
John Cornyn	TX	March 4	781,259	533,297	59%	41%	243	1	Steve Stockman—19%
Mitch McConnell	KY	May 20	213,753	141,363	60%	40%	118	2	Matt Bevin—35%
Thad Cochran#	MS	June 3	156,313	162,582	49%	51%	52	30	Chris McDaniel—49.5%
Lindsey Graham	SC	June 10	178,833	138,156	56%	44%	46	0	Lee Bright—15%
Pat Roberts	KS	Aug. 5	127,089	137,251	48%	52%	92	13	Milton Wolf—41%
Lamar Alexander	TN	Aug. 7	331,705	336,334	49.7%	50.3%	66	29	Joe Carr—41%
Total			1,788,952	1,448,983	55%	45%	617	75	

Note: A pound sign (#) indicates that Thad Cochran of Mississippi was forced into a runoff June 24, which he won with 51 percent of the vote. Only the primary results, though, are included in this chart. In Texas, eight of the 254 counties did not report any vote in this year's Republican primary. One fairly small county (Hardin) was carried by Sen. John Cornyn's leading rival, Rep. Steve Stockman. In another very small county (Culberson), there was a tie between Cornyn and Stockman, six votes apiece. And in Newton County, there was an apparent error in the tabulation of the vote. Cornyn was credited with only six of the 487 votes cast in the Republican Senate primary (barely 1 percent of the county total) and was listed in sixth place behind Stockman and a slew of minor candidates. Of these counties, only Hardin is included in the tally above.
Sources: Official 2014 primary results from the election websites of Kansas, Kentucky, Mississippi, South Carolina, Tennessee and Texas.

Against the incumbent's aggressive campaign, Bevin was able to gain little traction. And on primary day, McConnell exhibited near-total domination. He prevailed by 25 percentage points and swept all but two of Kentucky's 120 counties.

Cochran Survives

The 2014 Mississippi Republican Senate primary was a classic confrontation between different generations and political philosophies.

The genteel, seventy-six-year-old Cochran was a card-carrying member of the party establishment, having served more than half his adult life in Congress. His opponent, state Senator Chris McDaniel, was barely half of Cochran's age and bore the standard of the Tea Party.

Cochran boasted of his ability to steer federal largesse to the impoverished Magnolia State, anathema to Tea Partiers. McDaniel proclaimed the virtues of small government.

Cochran drew the backing of GOP establishment stalwarts such as former Mississippi Governor Haley Barbour, Senator John McCain, and the U.S. Chamber of Commerce. McDaniel had support from anti-establishment figures, including Sarah Palin, Rick Santorum, and the Club for Growth.

McDaniel finished narrowly ahead in the early June primary by one-half of a percentage point (49.5 percent to 49.0 percent, with the remaining votes cast for a minor candidate). Cochran won the closely contested runoff later that month by two percentage points (51.0 percent to 49.0 percent), an election that was required because neither candidate won a majority of the initial vote.

Coming out of the primary, it looked as though McDaniel had the momentum and might cruise to victory in the runoff. But Cochran ultimately won by executing the historically difficult task of expanding the electorate. Usually turnout shrinks for overtime contests. But that was not the case in this one. The number of ballots cast increased from less than 320,000 for the primary to over 380,000 for the runoff, as the incumbent pitched his candidacy to independents and Democrats, especially African Americans, who comprise more than one-third of Mississippi's population. The only caveat: Any voter who had participated in the Democratic primary could not vote in the Republican runoff.

But there were barely 85,000 of the latter, which left plenty of non-Republican voters for Cochran to woo. Of the state's 25 counties with an African American majority, Cochran carried 22 of them in the runoff. The remaining 57 counties without an African American majority were split roughly evenly between Cochran and McDaniel.[11]

What Might Have Been

The lone Democratic Senate primary of note in 2014 took place in Hawaii between the appointed incumbent, Brian Schatz, and Representative Colleen Hanabusa. It was a contest with racial and generational overtones. Schatz was forty-one years old at the time of the August primary; Hanabusa was sixty-three. The latter was Japanese American and reportedly was the late Senator Daniel Inouye's choice to succeed him when he died in late 2012. But Democratic Governor Neil Abercrombie, who had his moments of friction with Inouye, chose his Michigan-born lieutenant governor (Schatz) instead.[12]

Supported in the primary by President Barack Obama, a native son of Hawaii, Schatz prevailed narrowly (49.3 percent to 48.6 percent). But Abercrombie, who had made the controversial appointment of Schatz, was swamped in the Democratic gubernatorial primary by a margin of better than two to one. He was the only sitting governor in 2014 to lose his bid for renomination.[13]

Scratched from the list of Senate primaries in 2014 was one that could have been the most colorful of all. It would have pitted three-term incumbent Republican Senator Mike Enzi against Liz Cheney, the daughter of the former vice president. Cheney actually entered the race in the summer of 2013, raised several million dollars, and had fashioned a message citing the need for younger, more vociferously conservative leadership within the GOP. (Enzi was seventy at the time of the August primary.)

But Cheney drew criticism as a carpetbagger who only recently had rediscovered Wyoming as a launching pad for her political ambitions. Polls were not kind to her candidacy. And in early January 2014, she dropped her primary challenge, citing "serious health issues" within her family.[14]

HOUSE PRIMARIES

In 1992, nineteen House members were defeated in their primaries; in 2002, the number was eight; in 2012, thirteen lost their bids for renomination. But elections in years that end with "2" are quite different from the rest. Congressional district lines are redrawn at the beginning of each decade, forcing several pairs of incumbents to run against each other in the election held immediately after redistricting, as well as necessitating that virtually all representatives introduce themselves to some new constituents. The result is a degree of turbulence in "2" years that is not present in other election years, in which the number of House primary casualties over the last quarter century has never exceeded four (see Table 2.3).[15]

Table 2.3. Incumbents Defeated in Senate, House, and Gubernatorial Primaries Since 2000

The 2014 primary season will not be one that is remembered for its incumbent carnage. Only four House members, one governor, and no senators were defeated. That matches the number of House members and governors that lost primaries in the previous midterm election cycle in 2010, and represents three less senators that lost intraparty nominating contests.

Election	Number of Incumbents Denied Renomination			Senators	Terms	Governors	Terms
	House	Senate	Govs.				
2000	3	0	0	—	—	—	—
2002	8	1	0	Robert Smith (R-NH) (lost to John E. Sununu)	2	—	—
2004	2	0	2	—		Bob Holden (D-MO) (lost to Claire McCaskill)	1
						Olene Walker (R-UT)* (lost to Jon Huntsman)	@
2006	2	1	1	Joe Lieberman (D-CT)# (lost to Ned Lamont)	3	Frank Murkowski (R-AK) (lost to Sarah Palin)	1

Table 2.3. (Continued)

Election	Number of Incumbents Denied Renomination			Senators	Terms	Governors	Terms
	House	Senate	Govs.				
2008	4	0	0	—	—	—	—
2010	4	3	1	Robert Bennett (R-UT)* (lost to Mike Lee)	3	Jim Gibbons (R-NV) (lost to Brian Sandoval)	1
				Lisa Murkowski (R-AK)# (lost to Joe Miller)	1	—	—
				Arlen Specter (D-PA) (lost to Joe Sestak)	5	—	—
2012	13	1	0	Richard Lugar (R-IN) (lost to Richard Mourdock)	6	—	—
2014	4	0	1	—	—	Neil Abercrombie (D-HI) (lost to David Ige)	1

Note: An asterisk (*) indicates that Governor Olene Walker in 2004 and Senator Robert Bennett in 2010 sought election but were eliminated at the Utah Republican state convention and failed to qualify for the primary ballot. A pound sign (#) denotes that Senators Joe Lieberman of Connecticut in 2006 and Lisa Murkowski of Alaska in 2010 both lost their party's primary but won reelection as an independent (or in Murkowski's case, as a write-in candidate). The icon "@" means that Utah's Walker assumed the governorship in 2003 from the lieutenant governorship post.
Sources: Editions of America Votes (CQ Press) from 2000 to 2012. Official results from state election websites for 2014.

Nonetheless, every two years there is widespread speculation that voters are in an "anti-incumbent" mood and ready to "throw the bums out." But with the exception of the post-redistricting year, the handful of House members that actually lose a primary usually do so for individual reasons. This year, there were four defeated congressional incumbents and four different reasons.

For Kerry Bentivolio, a freshman Republican from Michigan, it was a question of competence. Described by *The Almanac of American Politics 2014* as a "former high school teacher and part-time reindeer rancher," he won in 2012 only because GOP incumbent Thaddeus McCotter abruptly quit the race on the eve of the primary after trouble arose over how his campaign had carried out the normally routine process of collecting signatures to qualify for the ballot. Once in Congress, Bentivolio showed at times that he was out of his element.[16]

For Ralph Hall, a Republican from Texas, age was a major factor. He was the oldest member of the House at age ninety-one, with seventeen terms in Congress under his belt.[17]

For John Tierney, a Democrat from Massachusetts, it was a matter of ethics. His wife was sentenced to jail time a few years earlier after being caught in a family gambling scandal.

For Eric Cantor, a Republican from Virginia, it was "going national," while appearing to take his constituents for granted. Evidence that the House majority leader's defeat was "Cantor-centric" was evident in the Virginia returns. While he was losing his primary to a little-known economics professor from Randolph-Macon by eleven points, Republican Representative Rob Wittman was cruising to renomination with 76 percent of the vote in a neighboring district.

No one saw Cantor's loss coming. He was expected to coast to renomination in the GOP primary in Virginia's Richmond-area Seventh District. Instead, he became the first House majority leader to be defeated in a primary since the position was created in 1899.

The "why" of Cantor's upset loss was very much a matter of conjecture. He had experience, fame, and was seemingly on track to become House speaker someday. Cantor had never been seriously tested at the polls in his decidedly Republican district since he first won his House seat in 2000. On the other hand, his challenger, David Brat, was essentially unknown, had little national support other than elements of conservative talk radio, and had a fraction of the money that Cantor did.[18]

Yet the perception of a mismatch worked to Brat's advantage. While Cantor mounted a "top-down" campaign heavy on TV advertising, the challenger's effort was more "bottom-up," reliant on energy and grassroots activism that was basically overlooked by the media and Cantor alike. Brat's message: The incumbent had gone "national" and lost touch with his district, especially on the issues of immigration reform and amnesty.

CLUES TO VOTER TURNOUT

Due in part to the advent of the Tea Party, Republicans in the last few years have tended to be more passionate about their primaries than Democrats. That, in turn, has essentially meant more competition and larger turnouts on the GOP side.

Another major reason for the GOP's recent primary turnout advantage has been the total transformation of the South, from solidly Democratic a generation ago to a region that is now overwhelmingly Republican. In each state across the Deep South from South Carolina to Mississippi (with Alabama and Georgia in between), at least 200,000 more votes were cast in GOP primaries this year than Democratic ones. In Tennessee, the Republican margin was more than 400,000 votes, and in Texas, nearly 800,000.

Altogether, more Republican than Democratic votes were cast this primary season in twenty-eight of the forty-four states where a direct comparison between the two parties was readily possible. Of these, eight were states that President Barack Obama carried in 2012, including such major megastate prizes as Florida, Illinois, Michigan, and Ohio.

Meanwhile, of the sixteen states where Democrats had the primary turnout advantage this year, only two (Kentucky and West Virginia) were carried by GOP standard-bearer Mitt Romney in the last presidential election. In both of these states, Democrats continue to have a substantial registration edge, even though voters in Kentucky and West Virginia have painted the states bright red in recent presidential elections.

Yet comparing the combined number of Democratic and Republican ballots cast in 2014 with 2010, the aggregate nationwide primary turnout was down by more than 5 million—from 33.7 million to 28.1 million (in states where a direct comparison of turnout could be made). To be sure, circumstances can change from one election to another. There may be an embattled incumbent or an exciting open-seat race in a state one year, and a dull renomination contest for major office in another year. But whatever the reason, roughly one of every six voters who had cast a primary ballot in 2010 did not return in 2014.[19]

Both sets of numbers proved prescient for the fall election. Republicans won more votes in November 2014 than the Democrats, enabling the GOP to take control of the Senate and build their majority in the House of Representatives. Yet the voter turnout rate for the 2014 general election—35.9 percent of eligible voters—fell to the lowest point since 1942, when many potential voters were off fighting World War II.[20]

WHAT'S NEXT

Congressional and state primaries in 2014 extended across the calendar from early March to early September, with the largest clusters in May, June, and August. In 2016, there will also be a host of presidential primaries, running from February to June. The early presidential primaries and caucuses held in February are traditionally stand-alone events. But once the calendar flips to March, it is normal for most states voting from then until June to hold their presidential and congressional/state primaries on the same date.

A big question moving forward is whether more states will adopt the "top-two" format currently used in California and Washington. Under this system, candidates from all parties run together on a single primary ballot, with the top two vote-getters, regardless of party, advancing to the November general election. Proponents of the top-two primary contend that it aids mainstream candidates over those on the fringes, since the two candidates that advance presumably are the most electable. It also means there is not always a Democrat versus a Republican in every general election race, as is the case in almost every other state.

The top-two primary has not been a particular boon for turnout in California. In 2010, the last year that the state held separate Democratic and Republican primaries, a total of nearly 4.8 million ballots were cast for gubernatorial candidates of the two major parties. In 2014, the total primary vote for *all* candidates for the California governorship barely exceeded 4.3 million. Still, the top-two primary is widely viewed as an intriguing option that a few other states may adopt before 2016.[21]

And then there is the Tea Party and what role it might play in 2016 Republican politics. Will it still seek to reshape the GOP through the party's primaries, or might it back away in favor of some other way to reshape government to its liking? And might other grassroots movements be born that would seek to impact Democratic politics? At this point, all are very open questions. But it would be no surprise if the dynamics of the 2016 primaries are quite different than 2014, in ways that are yet unknown.

NOTES

1. Harold W. Stanley and Richard G. Niemi, *Vital Statistics on American Politics 2011–2012* (Thousand Oaks, CA: CQ Press, an Imprint of SAGE, 2011), 43–44.

2. Richard Winger, "Libertarian Registration Up by 11% Since 2012," *Ballot Access News*, April 2014, http://www.ballot-access.org/2014/04/april-2014-ballot-access-news-print-edition/. As of March 2014, the aggregate voter registration totals for the 30 states (plus the District of Columbia) that register voters by party were:

Democrats, 42,468,708 (41.45%); Republicans, 30,615,503 (29.88%); Independents, 26,996,241 (26.35%); Third Parties, 718,522 (0.70%); Other, 1,653,409 (1.61%); Total, 102,452,383.

3. Rhodes Cook, *The Rhodes Cook Letter*, September 2014, 5. The comparative 2010 and 2014 primary vote totals were based on the ballots cast in each party's Senate or gubernatorial contest (whichever office produced the highest number of votes in a particular state). In a few states, the partisan comparison had to be based on the House vote. And in several other states, no comparison of the Democratic and Republican primary vote was readily possible. Altogether, 45 states were included in the 2010 primary tally and 44 states in its 2014 counterpart.

4. Tim Storey, "StateVote 2014: Election Results," National Conference of State Legislatures, November 19, 2014, accessed December 15, 2014, http://www.ncsl .org/research/elections-and-campaigns/statevote-2014-post-election-analysis6355 08614.aspx.

5. Cook, *The Rhodes Cook Letter*, September 2014, 9, 11.

6. Michael Barone and Chuck McCutcheon, *The Almanac of American Politics 2014* (Chicago: University of Chicago Press, 2013), 354–55.

7. Richard Winger, "For First Time in History, Democrats Won't Run Anyone for U.S. Senate in Alabama," *Ballot Access News*, February 17, 2014, accessed December 12, 2014, http://www.ballot-access.org/2014/02/for-first-time-in-history-demo crats-wont-run-anyone-for-u-s-senate-in-alabama/.

8. William Bryk, "Bay Ridge Lawyer Runs for U.S. Senate in Idaho, Alaska and Oregon," *New York Daily News*, April 17, 2014.

9. Stanley and Niemi, 44.

10. Barone and McCutcheon, 696.

11. Cook, *The Rhodes Cook Letter*, June 2014, 13.

12. Adam Nagourney, "A Disregarded Request from a Beloved Senator Shakes Up Hawaii's Primary," *New York Times*, June 30, 2014.

13. Ian Lovett, "Hawaiian Governor Loses Primary by Wide Margin; Senate Race Is Undecided," *New York Times*, August 11, 2014.

14. Neil King Jr., "Cheney's Exit Spares GOP a Divisive Race," *Wall Street Journal*, January 7, 2014.

15. Stanley and Niemi, 43.

16. Barone and McCutcheon, 884.

17. Cameron Joseph, "Rep. Ralph Hall Fights for Final Term," *The Hill*, March 4, 2014.

18. Peggy Noonan, "Cantor Bows Out with Grace," *Wall Street Journal*, June 14, 2014.

19. Cook, *The Rhodes Cook Letter*, September 2014, 3–6, 31.

20. Editorial Board, "The Worst Voter Turnout in 72 Years," *New York Times*, November 12, 2014, accessed December 15, 2014, http://www.nytimes.com/2014/ 11/12/opinion/the-worst-voter-turnout-in-72-years.html?_r = 0; "2014 November General Election Turnout Rates," U.S. Elections Project, last updated December 5, 2014, http://www.electproject.org/2014g.

21. Richard Winger, "Oregon Voters Defeat Top-Two 68%-32%," *Ballot Access News*, December 2014.

3

The 2014 Senate Elections— and Beyond

James Hohmann

Republicans winning control of the Senate in 2014 appears inevitable in hindsight, but it did not feel that way for much of the two-year election cycle.

On paper, it's easy to see how the GOP picked up nine seats. Since World War II, a president's party has lost an average of six Senate seats during his sixth-year midterm elections—exactly the number the GOP needed to pick up.[1] Democrats also had to defend seven seats in states that Barack Obama lost back in 2012—before his national approval rating started to tank.

But, two years ago, no insiders believed Republicans would sweep all seven of those states Mitt Romney won, plus claim an open seat in Iowa and knock off an incumbent in Colorado.

Obama deserves a big share of the blame, but national Republicans also should get credit for capitalizing on red state Democratic retirements, recruiting top-flight candidates to expand the playing field into purple states, and ensuring that the most electable candidate won in every competitive primary.

For much of the preceding 2012 cycle, Republicans had been favorites to take back the Senate. But they lost two net seats after blowing winnable contests in red states such as Indiana, Missouri, Montana, and North Dakota. Mitt Romney got whipped in the Electoral College, setting off a dark period of soul searching and emboldening Democrats to become cocky. Incensed major GOP donors kept their checkbooks closed through 2013, feeling burned by all the rosy promises from the previous cycle and then agitated by the party's complicity in shutting down the federal government that fall. Most rank-and-file Republican senators believed the party had blown its opportunity and resigned themselves to an extended period in the wilderness.

Instead of focusing on favorable historical precedents, official Washington tended to dwell on other statistics. Only three sitting Democratic senators had lost in the previous decade. Republicans had not defeated more than two Democratic incumbents in the same election since 1980.[2] The 2012 results showcased the GOP's dire demographic problems with single women, Hispanics, and younger voters. Republicans also had an undeniable talent problem; the ghosts of terrible candidates like Todd Akin, Richard Mourdock, Ken Buck, Christine O'Donnell, and Sharron Angle hung like dark clouds over flourishing hopes of a comeback.

As late as Labor Day of 2014, the top strategists on each side truly believed the race for Senate control was a jump ball and that several contests that polls put inside the margin of error could go either way. Republicans remained nervous through the final weeks that they could lose seats they were defending in Kentucky and Georgia. Even in October, there was genuine fear that weak GOP candidates in ruby-red Kansas and South Dakota would cost the party its dream.

Basically every race broke late and hard for the Republicans. They won all but one of the contests that polls showed were close—New Hampshire was the exception—and almost won a stunning upset in Virginia, a race that drew little attention and no outside money. Louisiana Republican Bill Cassidy defeated three-term Democratic Senator Mary Landrieu by double digits in a December runoff, which he described as "an exclamation point" to end the midterms.[3]

Democrats tried hard to localize each Senate race. They wanted to disqualify the GOP candidates with an early onslaught of attack ads. North Carolina ads attacked GOP challenger Thom Tillis over K–12 class sizes and for not firing an aide who had an affair with a lobbyist, for example. Alaska ads attacked Republican Dan Sullivan for supporting a controversial mining project and giving lenient sentences to sex criminals. Both challengers relentlessly linked incumbents to Obama.

THE OBAMA REFERENDUM

The midterms ultimately became a national referendum on the president, which spelled doom for his party.

Obama could not catch a break in 2014. The long stretch of bad news began with the disastrous rollout of healthcare.gov, the web site to sign up for coverage under the Affordable Care Act. It made the administration look incompetent and raised fresh questions about the virtue of the president's signature achievement. Not long after the site was up and running, a scandal blew up at the Department of Veterans Affairs. With public outcry about vets who died before they could get care, the president eventually relented and asked for Secretary Eric Shinseki's resignation.

Obama lost a stretch of the summer to a "border crisis," as tens of thousands of parents in Central America paid "coyotes" to smuggle their children into the United States so they could escape terrible gang violence. These migrant kids brought immigration back to the fore, inflaming conservative concerns about border security.

The situation overseas was even worse. Voters very rarely cast ballots on international issues, but the chaotic world looked like a tinderbox about to explode. Obama looked unable to control the course of events. He could do little but impose sanctions when Russia invaded Ukraine. He poohpoohed the rise of the Islamic State in the Middle East—calling it "a J.V. team."[4] Then, as the country grappled with videos of the group beheading westerners, the president said during a press conference that he did not have a strategy to deal with them. Ultimately, he sent soldiers back into Iraq and ordered airstrikes in the region. Remember, this is the guy elected in 2008 on the promise of bringing the boys home from the Middle East.

In the closest thing to an October Surprise, the Centers for Disease Control and Prevention announced September 30 that a patient has been diagnosed with Ebola on American soil.[5] This created widespread panic about a pandemic spreading from Africa, and it was followed by weeks of stories about others testing positive for the virus. The president took heat for naming Democratic fixer Ron Klain, someone with no medical or scientific experience, as the Ebola czar. On the advice of experts, Obama also refused to impose a travel ban with West Africa. That idea polled very well across the country, and with voters in the battleground states anxious about Ebola, Republicans attacked Democrats non-stop on the issue.[6]

Under pressure from Hispanics, a key Democratic constituency, Obama planned to issue an executive order delaying deportation of those who came to the country illegally. The push grew out of the House's failure to pass comprehensive immigration reform. But such action tested so poorly among crucial persuadable voters in battlegrounds like Iowa and Arkansas that, presented with internal Democratic polling, the White House postponed action until after the election.[7] Obama made his announcement in late November, which quickly appeared in ads attacking Landrieu, but the specter of the coming order undoubtedly hurt Democratic candidates elsewhere during the fall.

All of these issues kept Obama front and center in the news through the year, forcing Democratic incumbents in states where he'd never been very popular to say if they agreed with his approach on this or that. In many

states, Democrats were nervous about turning off their base voters, especially African Americans and liberals, so they treaded very carefully. But not
one Senate candidate in a truly competitive race wanted Obama to come
campaign with them.

The president was personally frustrated to be sidelined, especially in the
states he carried in 2012 and where he thought he still could make a difference. When he came to Colorado for a fundraiser to help Democratic Senator Mark Udall, the incumbent stayed back in D.C. to avoid him. Through
the fall, the most active Democratic surrogates were Hillary Clinton and
Bill Clinton, neither of whom was tainted politically by the unpopular
White House. Candidates in Kentucky, West Virginia, and Iowa even wel-
comed liberal firebrand Elizabeth Warren to stump with them—but not
Obama. First Lady Michelle Obama was an exception because she could
draw large crowds without being as polarizing as her husband. When she
went to Iowa, though, she made news for all the wrong reasons: repeatedly
referring to Democratic candidate Bruce Braley as "Bruce Bailey."[8]

Many Democrats ham-handedly distanced themselves from Obama. In
Kentucky, Democratic Senate candidate Alison Lundergan Grimes steadfastly refused to acknowledge that she voted for him—even though she was
a delegate at the 2012 Democratic National Convention.[9] In North Carolina, freshman Democratic Senator Kay Hagan ran television ads that said
she stood up to Obama but, at the same time, ran radio ads on urban
stations aimed at African Americans that starred the president endorsing
her.[10] Landrieu often criticized the president's record, especially on energy,
when speaking to white audiences, but she ran ads on urban stations that
assured African Americans she stood with him.[11]

The one area many Democrats wanted the president to play a more active
role was in talking about the economy. His party actually had a good story
to tell, with a rising stock market, falling unemployment, and rebounding
home prices. On October 2, Obama delivered a speech at Northwestern
University intended to do just that. But he only made matters worse when
he declared, "I am not on the ballot this fall. . . . But make no mistake—
these policies are on the ballot, every single one of them." It took less than
24 hours for the clip to start appearing in Republican ads across the map.[12]

No matter how much the candidate actually on the ballot talked about
Obama, or how often they had actually supported his agenda, Republicans
saturated the airwaves with ads portraying them as a rubber stamp. It was
their overarching message. By Election Day, more than 300,000 advertisements aired in all the Senate races linking the Democratic candidate with
the president, according to a Kantar Media analysis.[13]

Exit polls on Election Day showed just how bad things had gotten for
Obama. His national approval rating was 44 percent. But it was more than
just frustration; it was fear about the future. Two-thirds of those who voted
believed the country was on the wrong track, only 22 percent believed their

children will be better off than them in the next generation, and 71 percent worried about a terrorist attack on American soil. History will probably judge America's first African American president very differently than the voters did in these midterms, but it's hard to see how November 2014 is not a nadir in future biographical narratives of the forty-fourth president.

An unpopular president was not enough for Republicans to win control of the Senate, though. Obama was not super popular himself in 2012, but he won reelection by making the election as much about Romney—his business background, his comment that 47 percent of voters are takers, and so on—as a referendum on his own performance. Democrats failed to define the terms of the 2014 election, and Republicans broke with recent history by not again pulling defeat from the jaws of victory.

RETIREMENTS, RECRUITING, AND RUNOFFS: THE GOP GETS SOME BREAKS

Rob Collins, the man most responsible for GOP strategy as executive director of the National Republican Senatorial Committee, believed there were five key steps to making sure that his party did not blow it. As he put it after the election, he needed to recruit top-notch candidates who could win in their states; convince donors that the mistakes of the past would not be repeated; navigate potentially problematic primaries; expand the map into purple and blue states; and modernize turnout operations to be competitive with the other side.

Democratic retirements created big openings. Senate Majority Leader Harry Reid urged his members thinking about leaving to announce early so the party would have time to find replacements who could raise money.

A number of major figures in the Democratic caucus announced their retirements during the first months of 2013. West Virginia Senator Jay Rockefeller, who won reelection by twenty-seven points in 2008, retired on January 11 rather than seek a sixth term.[14] Obama had just lost all 55 of the Mountain State's counties, carrying just 35 percent of the vote. Two weeks later, another five-termer, Iowa Senator Tom Harkin, followed suit.[15] He had won by twenty-five points last time and could have easily held the seat. South Dakota Senator Tim Johnson, who easily won in 2008 despite a medical crisis that left him in a wheelchair, retired in March rather than seek a fourth term.[16] Romney had won the state by eighteen points. In April, Montana Senator Max Baucus announced he would retire too. He won by forty-six points in 2008 and had $5 million cash in his campaign account; Obama lost the state by fourteen points.[17]

All of these incumbents chaired Senate committees and could easily have raised a lot of money. Some, like Harkin, would have cruised to reelection.

Others, like Rockefeller or Johnson, might have had tough races. But it's hard to think of a single Democrat in any of the four states who could have been more competitive than the incumbent.

Republicans wound up winning all four of these states. Representative Shelley Moore Capito won Rockefeller's seat by twenty-eight points. Representative Steve Daines picked up the Montana seat by eighteen points after the Democrat appointed to replace Baucus when he became ambassador to China, John Walsh, dropped out in the face of revelations that he plagiarized an Army War College paper. Former South Dakota Governor Mike Rounds wound up winning by twenty-one points to get Johnson's seat. Iowa Republican state Senator Joni Ernst surged from a crowded primary field with the help of a provocative ad about castrating hogs as a kid. Her Democratic opponent, a former trial lawyer, made a series of unforced errors, including threatening to sue a neighbor over her chickens wandering onto his yard and dumping on the state's Republican senator, Chuck Grassley, as "a farmer from Iowa who never went to law school" during a caught-on-camera fundraiser.[18] The GOP may not have won the Senate without these retirements.

Long-time Michigan Democratic Senator Carl Levin also retired after six terms. He would have easily won reelection. The party, through Democratic Representative Gary Peters, wound up holding this seat, but for months it looked like this could become one of the more competitive fights of 2014. National Republicans were bullish on former Secretary of State Terri Lynn Land, who had the ability to self-fund, but she ran an inept campaign, had to replace her manager, and was totally inarticulate when talking to reporters. Though it slipped off the map after Labor Day, when the NRSC canceled its advertising buys, more than $50 million was still spent on the Michigan contest.[19]

Republicans also had retirements, to be sure. Georgia Senator Saxby Chambliss's retirement created a messy primary and headaches for the party, but they held the seat. Nebraska Senator Mike Johanns, a former governor and U.S. agriculture secretary, retired after one term, but it was an easy hold in a bright-red state.

An important part of the Senate story, addressed more fully in Rhodes Cook's chapter, is that for the first time since 2008 no Republican Senate incumbent seeking reelection lost a primary. Just as Democrats announced their retirements early, most GOP incumbents geared up early—building campaign teams, raising money, and working to scare off the most formidable challengers. The result was a clean sweep in the primaries, starting with Texas Senator John Cornyn in March and ending with Tennessee Senator Lamar Alexander in August. Some of the best news stories of the cycle grew out of these primaries, including Liz Cheney's short-lived bid against Wyoming Senator Mike Enzi and South Carolina Senator Lindsey Graham's ability to avoid a hotly anticipated runoff.

The closest call came in Mississippi, where Republican Senator Thad Cochran almost lost to state Senator Chris McDaniel. McDaniel had support from outside groups like the Senate Conservatives Fund, but the NRSC was terrified about his history of incendiary comments. As a radio host, he had talked about Mexican women as "mamacitas" and made racially inflammatory comments. Party strategists feared he would be the Todd Akin of 2014. Akin's comment that the female body had ways of not getting impregnated if a rape was "legitimate" didn't just cost him a Missouri Senate seat the previous election; it also created headaches for other GOP candidates asked about the boneheaded remarks. So the national party and the establishment-friendly groups went all in to stop him. The U.S. Chamber of Commerce even ran an ad starring football legend Brett Favre praising Cochran. The seventy-six-year-old incumbent received fewer votes than McDaniel, forty-one, in the first round of voting but prevailed in a runoff with higher turnout.

In other efforts to avoid more Akin-like nominees, the NRSC invested heavily in candidate training programs. Operatives set up a series of two-day sessions in D.C. where candidates would get ambushed at the airport by experienced trackers who taped their every move. (This has become routine on the campaign trail.) Then the candidates would come to committee headquarters to watch tapes of gaffes by failed Republicans like Akin and do practice drills to answer tough media questions.

As these sessions went on, NRSC operatives tried to recruit additional candidates to jump into tougher-to-win races. Ambitious politicians did not want to hurt their careers by running in races they could not realistically win. The president's declining popularity was essential to wooing and fielding top-tier candidates later in 2013 and into 2014.[20]

One of the biggest breaks of the cycle for Republicans came in February of 2014 in Colorado. Ken Buck, who lost a totally winnable 2010 Senate race after running a disastrous campaign, was running again against freshman Democratic Senator Mark Udall. No establishment Republican thought he could win, so they had written the state off. Representative Cory Gardner, a conservative who had been a leader in the state legislature and knocked out a Democratic House incumbent in 2010, was the dream candidate of party insiders. Gardner was ambitious, but he didn't think Udall was beatable—until the party presented him with internal polling that showed him in striking distance of Udall. With the help of the national party, Buck agreed to drop out of the Senate race to run for Gardner's open House seat—avoiding a messy primary and giving the GOP a shrewd candidate who would raise tons of money—and ultimately win.

Another recruiting coup for Republicans came in New Hampshire, where they convinced former Senator Scott Brown to run. Brown picked up the late Ted Kennedy's Senate seat in a January 2010 special election in Massachusetts, driven by a rising tide of opposition to Obamacare. Despite high personal popularity, Brown could not survive in 2012 against Democrat Elizabeth Warren amidst presidential-level turnout in a deeply blue state. After taking a pass on running in another Massachusetts special election, to replace John Kerry after he was appointed Secretary of State, Brown moved permanently to his vacation home in neighboring New Hampshire.

Brown engaged in a prolonged, somewhat-public, months-long dance with the national party. As he hit the rubber-chicken dinner circuit around the Granite State, he insisted on promises that he would get massive assistance and the best staff. The party brass commissioned several polls to show him that Democratic Senator Jeanne Shaheen, the only woman in U.S. history elected both governor and senator, was vulnerable and her support for Obamacare was toxic. Still, Brown hesitated. He didn't want to lose. He was making a lot of money on boards, as an adviser at the Boston office of Nixon Peabody, and as a Fox News contributor. He took a lot of heat from the right over his support for abortion rights and an assault-weapons ban, among other apostasies.

Finally, in March 2014, Brown pulled the trigger after being presented with internal polling that showed Obama's New Hampshire approval rating in the low 40s. The president had carried the state by six points in 2012, but the notoriously fickle voters had historically shown a willingness to throw out incumbents and swim with the national tide. Brown had to fend off a September primary challenge and eventually lost in the general election—but only by three points. The race, which would cost over $56 million, proved that the GOP was serious about competing in states Obama carried twice.[21]

The president's unpopularity also doomed Democratic hopes of playing offense.

Senate Minority Leader Mitch McConnell had a tough reelection fight in 2008 in Kentucky, and his low approval rating put him in a real danger zone. The three-decade incumbent had pronounced himself a guardian of gridlock and famously said he saw his role as making Obama a one-term president. Bluegrass State voters saw him as part of D.C. and thus part of the problem.

Actress Ashley Judd initially wanted to run and made that clear publicly, but national Democrats told her she would not have their support and was too liberal to win. Eventually party leaders recruited Kentucky Secretary of State Alison Lundergan Grimes, the thirty-four-year-old daughter of a former state party chair. She would be the best fundraiser of any challenger all cycle, leading in some early polling as McConnell fended off a primary challenge from Tea Party businessman Matt Bevin.

Polls showed a relatively tight race through the fall, but McConnell won by fifteen points as undecided voters broke his way late. They concluded that they disliked Obama more than they disliked McConnell. Voters in Kentucky were particularly angry at what they perceived as the administration's anti-coal agenda and job-killing regulations pushed by the Environmental Protection Agency. Grimes ran ads that featured her skeet shooting and saying to the camera, "I'm not Barack Obama!"[22] But even though she did not have a voting record, McConnell won by convincing voters that she would be a rubber stamp for the president's agenda.

Politics, like sports, is a game of absolutes. You either win or lose when you run for office. Those who prevail tend to look like geniuses, even if they are not, and those who lose are forced to live with second-guessing about their mistakes. In 2014, there were three important races where the Republican victor was deeply flawed but won because of Obama's deep unpopularity. Each of these three candidates very well could have lost in a different national atmosphere.

In Georgia, star Democratic recruit Michelle Nunn had no voting record, which made it harder for opposition admakers to link her with Obama. The daughter of popular, moderate former Senator Sam Nunn, she had run the nonprofit volunteerism foundation inspired by George H.W. Bush and run by his son Neil. Nunn did not have a competitive primary, so there was no need to tack to the left. The biggest mistake of her campaign was the fault of staff: They accidentally posted a detailed campaign plan on the Internet that made her look inauthentic and laid out her biggest weaknesses.

Republicans nominated former Fortune 500 CEO David Perdue after a testy runoff with Jack Kingston, who had represented southeastern Georgia in the House for two decades. Perdue was certainly more electable than a few of the candidates who had run in the primary; Representatives Paul Broun and Phil Gingrey had both made comments about abortion that heightened GOP fears of another Akin. But Perdue had a thick opposition research file as well. He said during a 2005 deposition that he spent most of his career outsourcing. When the story blew up, he publicly defended his controversial business dealings in a way that made it worse. Perdue, a first-time candidate, even managed to anger the U.S. Chamber of Commerce, showing up late to an endorsement meeting and then being very rude. He was also vulnerable over a class-action gender discrimination lawsuit filed against Dollar General that covered the period he was CEO.[23]

But the "D" after Nunn's name trumped all of Perdue's weaknesses as a candidate. Republicans ran attack ads against her for saying "I defer to the president's judgment" when answering a question about whether Shinseki should resign as VA secretary. The context didn't matter.[24] She had also said she supported the comprehensive immigration bill that passed the Senate in 2013, which the GOP used to justify ads saying she supported "amnesty." Democratic objections that the bill in question was co-sponsored by Republican Senators Marco Rubio of Florida and John McCain of Arizona did little to lessen the potency of the attack.[25] She lost by eight points.

In Kansas, Republican Senator Pat Roberts did not aggressively prepare for a campaign. He won an August primary with less than 50 percent of the vote only because it came out that his challenger, radiologist Milton Wolf, posted patient X-rays to Facebook with disgustingly coarse comments. National operatives warned Roberts in early 2013 that he was vulnerable on attacks over his residency (or lack thereof); Indiana Senator Richard Lugar lost his primary the year before because he did not have a home in the state. But Roberts angrily dismissed these concerns; he rented a room at the home of two donors and later told a reporter he had easy access to their La-Z-Boy. After winning the unexpectedly close primary, Roberts's campaign manager told local reporters that he was going home to rest up—home, as in the Virginia suburbs . . .[26]

If not for a September intervention by McConnell, the senator would have lost. Democratic nominee Chad Taylor dropped out to clear the way for independent candidate Greg Orman, a successful entrepreneur, who refused to say which party he would caucus with. Orman had donated to Obama, and Senate Majority PAC—Reid's outside group—quietly funneled money to a pro-Orman super PAC. McConnell forced Roberts to fire his manager, a close friend who was a retired college professor, and bring in a former Marine known for taking no prisoners. After an NBC/Marist poll one month out showed Orman ahead by ten points, the new operatives spent every day trying to link him with Obama one way or another. They relied heavily on surrogates like Bob Dole, himself a former Kansas senator, and Mitt Romney to drive the message. Roberts kept his mouth shut and won by eleven points.[27]

In South Dakota, former Republican Governor Mike Rounds should have had an easy time picking up the Senate seat. National Democrats had blown the recruiting process; Harry Reid wanted former Representative Stephanie Herseth Sandlin and convinced U.S. Attorney Brendan Johnson, son of retiring Senator Tim Johnson, not to get in. Then former Senate Majority Leader Tom Daschle encouraged former staffer Rick Weiland to get in, which dissuaded Herseth Sandlin from running. Reid was furious and refused to support Weiland, who he believed (correctly) was too liberal to win.[28]

Rounds was a terrible fundraiser, refused to run any negative ads, and ignored advice from professional operatives. He found himself caught up in a scandal surrounding the awarding of EB-5 visas to foreigners during his tenure as governor. Suddenly, with a four-way race, polls showed Rounds as vulnerable.[29] The Democratic Senatorial Campaign Committee said it would spend $1 million trying to help Weiland. This forced Republicans to spend in what should have been a safe seat. They poured a few hundred thousand dollars into the state for pretty standard ads linking Weiland and independent candidate Larry Pressler to Obama. Pressler had lost the seat to Johnson in 1996 as a Republican incumbent but acknowledged voting for Obama, a fellow Harvard alumnus, in 2008 and 2012. The Obama attacks worked: the polls moved, Democrats pulled out, and Rounds handily won.[30]

REPUBLICANS EXTEND THEIR DOMINANCE OF THE SOUTH

Obama was, of course, a major factor behind Democratic incumbents losing in Arkansas, Louisiana, and North Carolina. But the country's geographic polarization is nothing new.

Powerful political dynasties in the region proved no match for the much larger tectonic forces at play. In Arkansas, Democratic Senator Mark Pryor won his seat in 2002 in part because of the popularity of his father, David, who preceded Bill Clinton as governor and served three terms in the Senate. Pryor did not even have a Republican opponent in 2008. But the conservative state has lost its patience with national Democrats. The temperamentally moderate Pryor had backed most big-ticket Obama agenda items and lost by seventeen points to Representative Tom Cotton, a freshman Republican who served in Iraq and Afghanistan. Democrats threw the kitchen sink at Cotton: They attacked him for opposing the farm bill, which the state's junior Republican senator had supported. They attacked him for voting against the reauthorization of the Violence Against Women Act, including a watered-down Republican substitute. When the Ebola outbreak happened, Pryor ran an alarmist ad accusing his opponent of wanting to slash funding for pandemic research.[31] Cotton, whose fiscal conservatism earned him strong backing from outside groups like the Club for Growth, won without backing away from any of these positions.

In Louisiana, Senator Mary Landrieu had proven herself as a survivor by beating the odds since 1996. She ran ads starring her dad, Moon, who as mayor of New Orleans integrated city hall in the 1970s and served as Jimmy Carter's Secretary of Housing and Urban Development. Her brother, Mitch, is the current mayor of New Orleans. She talked about bringing home the bacon for the state and her clout as chair of the Senate Energy Committee. Private polling showed this message, which once worked so well in the state that gave the country Huey Long, had lost its resonance.

National Democrats left her for dead in a runoff, believing she had no path to victory. She lost by twelve points.[32]

It didn't matter whether Democratic incumbents came from families with deep roots in their states. North Carolina Senator Kay Hagan, who beat Elizabeth Dole in 2008 when Obama carried the state, lost to the Republican speaker of the state House. Virginia Senator Mark Warner, a popular former governor who won his seat by thirty-one points in 2008, is the richest member of the Senate. He had spent a decade cultivating a reputation as a moderate and far outspent his challenger, former Republican National Committee Chairman Ed Gillespie. Even internal GOP polls showed Gillespie down in the high single digits, but a late surge driven by anti-Obama sentiment meant that he lost by less than one point, about 18,000 votes out of more than 2.1 million cast.

Democrats said throughout 2014 that they knew the climate was tough but expressed a high degree of confidence because of an unprecedented investment in get-out-the-vote operations. The DSCC spent $60 million on what it codenamed the Bannock Street Project. The idea was that a good enough field program could drive people to the polls who typically vote in presidential elections but not midterms. Because Democrats controlled the Senate majority and had Obama to help fundraise, they maintained a significant hard money fundraising advantage through the year. This allowed them to invest more than the other side in hiring paid canvassers to register new voters.[33]

At the end of the day, a get-out-the-vote operation is like a special teams unit in football. It can win close games, but it cannot overcompensate for an injured quarterback. The national turnout rate was a dismal 35.9 percent, the lowest since 1942, when in the midst of World War II turnout was 33.9 percent.[34]

Turnout was much higher in targeted states. Take Alaska, where 54.4 percent of eligible voters participated, the third best rate in the country.[35] Television airwaves were saturated with advertisements for months. The $60.7 million spent in the sparsely populated state means that more than $120 was spent for each vote cast, making it the most expensive per capita U.S. Senate race in American history.[36] Even Republicans were impressed by Democratic Senator Mark Begich's investment in a field program to get Alaska Natives who had never before voted to support him. But Obama had lost the state by fourteen points two years prior, and Begich could not escape his drag, losing by two points.

Democratic operatives are adamant that their losses would have been worse without the Bannock Street Project. Indeed, Jeanne Shaheen would likely have lost in New Hampshire if not for her field program. Democrats also note that Virginia's closeness was an extension of the party not spending heavily to turn out African Americans and other drop-off voters.

It was not necessarily the field program, but Republicans did not win any seats in traditionally blue states that are competitive during presidential year. Democrats believed the wave might have washed away more of their senators had they not prepared early to withstand one. Republicans got what they thought was a top recruit in Oregon against freshman Senator Jeff Merkley, pediatric neurosurgeon Monica Wehby, but he wound up beating her by 18.5 percent after it came out that an ex-boyfriend called the police to say she was "stalking" him. Minnesota Senator Al Franken barely won in 2008 after a prolonged recount and legal battle. But the former "Saturday Night Live" star kept a low profile and easily dispatched Republican candidate Mike McFadden by using his fundraising advantage to attack his business career.

CAN DEMOCRATS WIN BACK THE SENATE IN 2016?

The Senate map next election cycle is as bad for Republicans as it was for Democrats in 2014, with the GOP forced to defend seven seats in states Obama carried twice. Republican incumbents are also up in North Carolina and Indiana, which he carried in 2008. The only states where Democratic incumbents could face tough races are Nevada and Colorado. Turnout will also be higher because it's a presidential election, which benefits Democrats.

Republicans have a cushion. In the fall of 2014, as Republicans looked increasingly likely to seize the Senate, Democrats took solace in the idea that it would be a very narrow majority—meaning they could easily take the chamber back next time. But Republicans wound up picking up nine seats, leaving them with fifty-four. That means that they can afford to lose three seats—and four if the GOP takes back the presidency, which gives them the vice president's tie-breaking vote.

It seems inevitable that a few Republicans will lose reelection. After all, the candidates up in 2016 won their seats during the much more favorable 2010 Tea Party wave. Three sitting Republican senators start the new cycle as possible underdogs: Wisconsin's Ron Johnson, Illinois's Mark Kirk, and Pennsylvania's Pat Toomey. Obama won each state by at least five points in 2012, and there are strong potential Democratic recruits in each one.

Wisconsin's Johnson is probably in for a rematch with former Democratic Senator Russ Feingold. The wealthy businessman spent $9 million of his own fortune on the 2010 campaign but this time could benefit from his popularity within the Koch brothers' donor network. Feingold could clear the field and avoid a primary. If he doesn't run, Representative Ron Kind may try. Despite being in a Democratic-leaning state, Johnson has hardly moderated on a single issue. He's an outspoken conservative, including unsuccessfully filing suit to block the federal government from implementing Obamacare.

Pennsylvania's Toomey is also likely to get a rematch against former Democratic Representative Joe Sestak, who has basically been running nonstop since he lost in 2010. Sestak, who beat party-switcher Arlen Specter in the 2010 Democratic primary, has been working to shore up his standing with party insiders. Toomey, who previously ran the very conservative Club for Growth, has been trying to position himself more toward the center, cosponsoring a gun background check bill in 2013, for example. He knows that the Democratic presidential nominee is likely to carry the state, so he's thinking about what he can do to get voters to split their tickets.

Illinois's Kirk, elected as a moderate after representing a suburban Chicago House district for a decade, narrowly won his seat in 2010. Despite ongoing rehab for a massive stroke, he made clear early that he's going to run. Just days after the midterms, Kirk announced that his state director was stepping down to focus on the reelection effort. The Democrat mentioned most as a potential challenger is state Attorney General Lisa Madigan, but she might decide to challenge GOP Governor Bruce Rauner in 2018. The best recruit for Democrats may be Representative Tammy Duckworth, an Iraq War veteran and Purple Heart recipient who served as an assistant secretary of the Veterans Affairs Department before winning her House seat in 2012. There is a long list of other names below that.

The only truly endangered Democratic incumbent is Senate Minority Leader Harry Reid of Nevada. Like McConnell did in 2014, he will be able to raise vast sums of money, hire the best staff, and use his powerful perch to help his reelection campaign. Reid survived in 2010 against all odds by annihilating his flawed challenger and turning out unprecedented numbers of Hispanics in a midterm. Should Reid run again in 2016, he'll be up during a presidential election—with a sizably larger Hispanic population. The big question mark is whether popular Republican Governor Brian Sandoval, who won his 2014 reelection in a landslide, will decide to challenge him. He's the most coveted GOP recruit in any race nationally.

That Republicans now control the majority for the first time in eight years seems certain to dissuade some members who have been contemplating retirement. These old bulls now chair committees and have bigger staffs after being in the wilderness. Someone like Chuck Grassley, the veteran Iowa senator, is much less likely to throw in the towel now that he's chairman of the Senate Judiciary Committee. But even the junior members facing tough reelection fights will also now get leadership perches that they can use to raise money and tout their influence. Johnson of Wisconsin, for example, is the new chair of the Homeland Security committee.

Other Republicans from more purple states could be vulnerable in 2016 if it turns into a big year for Democrats. New Hampshire Republican freshman Senator Kelly Ayotte, the former state attorney general, gets talked about as a rising national star and potential vice presidential material. But the state has trended more Democratic over the last decade; Democratic senior Senator Jeanne Shaheen just survived in 2014 over Scott Brown despite the national wave. The big question is whether Democratic Governor Maggie Hassan, elected to a second term in 2014, decides to challenge her. Hassan would have to be on the ballot again in 2016 anyway because New Hampshire governors only get two-year terms. If she passed, there are a host of other Democrats who could potentially run, though Hassan would be the biggest get for her party.

In Florida, Senator Marco Rubio announced he will not run for reelection to a second term if he runs for president. But at the end of 2014, he was watching and waiting on Jeb Bush. If his mentor, the former Florida governor, decides to run for president, he may decide to stay in the Senate. Rubio would be favored to win another term in 2016, even if the Democratic presidential nominee carried the state, because of the power of incumbency. But he's also staked out a series of conservative positions with the Iowa caucus electorate in mind over the last few years that could be politically unpopular in the swingy Sunshine State. If Rubio does not run for another term, the race will be wide open. It's not clear who Democrats might field.

Ohio Republican Senator Rob Portman announced the month after the midterms that he would not run for president so that he could focus on winning a second term. The former White House budget director has carved out a niche as a pro-gay marriage, socially moderate, pragmatic deal maker. His approval rating shows he could be vulnerable. But, as one of the best fundraisers in politics, he set out quickly after 2014 to build a massive war chest to deter potentially formidable Democratic rivals from taking him on.

With the Buckeye State sure to be targeted in the presidential election, it seems inevitable that there will still be a race. Former Governor Ted Strickland, a Democrat, could put the race in play, though he's already seventy-three years old. Another possible challenger is Richard Cordray, the director of the Consumer Financial Protection Bureau. There are also several current and former members of the House delegation who might take the chance.

The only other Democrat beside Reid who could find himself in a real 2016 dogfight is Colorado Democratic Senator Michael Bennet. As DSCC chair last cycle, he became the first party committee chair to have a home-state colleague lose since the 1970s.[37] But unlike Mark Udall, Bennet will not be caught off-guard. He will raise a lot of money and started to moderate in late 2014, coming out in favor of an unsuccessful push by Mary Landrieu during the lame duck session to build the Keystone XL Pipeline. Like Reid in Nevada, Bennet will benefit from higher turnout of core Democratic voters such as Hispanics and young people in a presidential election.

Arizona Senator John McCain, who turns eighty in 2016, will run again. He'll undoubtedly face a primary challenge, and if he wins that, he'll win the general election. Representative David Schweikert would probably be the biggest threat on McCain's right. Tea Party activists who control the Arizona state party censured McCain in early 2014 over his support for immigration reform and backing the White House on other issues. But former Representative J.D. Hayworth learned the hard way what it's like to take on McCain, receiving only 32 percent of the vote in their 2010 primary. If McCain retired, the race to succeed him would be a marquee contest of the cycle, with lots of Democrats chomping to run.

Other Republican incumbents who are likely to face potentially legitimate primary challengers are Senators Richard Shelby of Alabama, Mike Crapo of Idaho, and Jerry Moran of Kansas. Less likely but still possible are Utah Senator Mike Lee (who may still need to win at a convention, or in a primary, depending on new state rules) or North Carolina Senator Richard Burr. Watch for unsuccessful 2014 primary candidates to run again, such as Milton Wolf in Kansas or Greg Brannon in North Carolina.

Shortly after the 2014 election, Senate Republicans picked Mississippi Senator Roger Wicker to lead their committee and Democrats tapped Montana Senator Jon Tester. Wicker beat out Nevada Senator Dean Heller because Republican colleagues feared he did not have the backbone to take on Reid, his state's senior senator. With the quiet support of McConnell, they also appreciated Wicker's efforts on behalf of his Mississippi colleague Thad Cochran. Tester beat the odds to win a tough reelection in 2012 after knocking off an incumbent in 2006. Fresh off their big wins, Wicker sought continuity: He promoted the NRSC's 2014 political director, Ward Baker, to executive director and kept senior adviser Kevin McLaughlin as the new deputy director. Tester populated the committee's senior staff with operatives who have worked on his previous races, installing his chief of staff, Tom Lopach, as executive director.

If Democrats do not win the Senate in 2016, they will have a much tougher time in 2018. Democrats will need to defend 25 seats, including independents in Vermont and Maine, while Republicans must defend just eight incumbents. Nevada's Heller is the only Republican who seems possibly vulnerable this far out. For Republicans, there are obvious Democratic targets: Indiana freshman Senator Joe Donnelly, who won because Republican Richard Mourdock self-imploded with comments about rape in 2012; Missouri Senator Claire McCaskill, who spent money to help Todd Akin win the GOP primary last time and got another term because of it; Montana's Tester; and North Dakota's Heidi Heitkamp, who ran an incredible campaign and took advantage of a lazy opponent. No one has done more to distance himself from the Democratic caucus than West Virginia Senator Joe Manchin, who is up in 2018. But Manchin, who remains popular, seems unhappy and may decide to leave so he can run for governor. If he gave up the seat, it would be a certain Republican pickup. If he stays, Democrats will be favored to keep it.

One big factor in the 2018 elections will be who wins the 2016 presidential election. The president's party often loses seats in his—or her—first midterm election. If Republicans lost the Senate after two years, they could win it again in 2018. If Hillary Clinton won the presidency, for instance, it's very easy to see Democrats losing some of these seats in places like North Dakota. But four years is an eternity in politics.

NO MATTER WHICH PARTY IS IN CONTROL, THE INSTITUTION ITSELF IS CHANGING

Partisan gridlock seems the norm; it's hard to imagine the Senate "working" again as it did in the old days. Harry Reid invoked the so-called "nuclear option" in 2013 to make it easier to confirm Obama's nominees. It is unclear as of this writing if the new Republican majority will undo his controversial changes. Republicans complained loudly that Reid did not allow what's called Regular Order, moving bills through the traditional process and allowing amendments from any member during debate on the floor. They promised to change the way business is done, but it's unclear whether they will honor those campaign promises.

The Senate is becoming the House. It is a long-term trend that has only been accelerated by the latest results. In 2015, an all-time high of fifty-three senators will have previously served in the House. Arkansas's Tom Cotton and Montana's Steve Daines just won Senate seats as freshman members of Congress. These members are used to the rules and norms of the lower chamber, which has historically been more chaotic, less deliberative, and more majoritarian. Longtime Senate hands worry about the body moving this direction.

It will be interesting to watch how Republicans handle being in charge again; there are implications for 2016 but also, of course, for the country's future. Only twenty Republican senators, in a caucus of fifty-four, were around when the party last held the Senate in 2006. The Democratic caucus has changed; through retirements, appointments, deaths and defeats, 30 of the 60 senators who voted to pass Obamacare in 2009 are gone in 2015.

The 2014 elections will have a lasting impact on the complexion of the Senate. A surprising number of the new members are relatively young. Four members of the new class were born in the 1960s. Another four were born after 1970: Iowa's Joni Ernst is forty-four; Nebraska's Ben Sasse is forty-two; Colorado's Cory Gardner is forty; and Arkansas' Tom Cotton is thirty-seven. Unless they mess up in a big way, the new faces from safe Republican states should be able to stick around as long as they want.

NOTES

1. Harold W. Stanley and Richard G. Niemi, *Vital Statistics on American Politics 2011–2012* (Thousand Oaks, CA: CQ Press, 2011), 30–31.

2. Kyle Kondik, "The Hidden Barrier to a Republican Senate Majority," *Sabato's Crystal Ball*, July 17, 2014, accessed December 16, 2014, http://www.centerforpoli tics.org/crystalball/articles/the-hidden-barrier-to-a-republican-senate-majority/.

3. Bernie Becker, "Newest GOP Senator: Victory an 'Exclamation Mark,'" *The Hill*, December 7, 2014, accessed December 16, 2014, http://thehill.com/blogs/bal lot-box/senate-races/226242-newest-gop-senator-victory-an-exclamation-mark.

4. David Remnick, "Going the Distance," *New Yorker*, January 27, 2014, 57.

5. Denise Grady, "Ebola Is Diagnosed in Texas, First Case Found in the U.S.," *New York Times*, September 30, 2014, accessed December 16, 2014, http://www.ny times.com/2014/10/01/health/airline-passenger-with-ebola-is-under-treatment-in -dallas.html.

6. Scott Hensley, "Poll: Broad Support in U.S. for Ebola Travel Ban," NPR, October 22, 2014, accessed December 16, 2014, http://www.npr.org/blogs/health/ 2014/10/22/358095163/poll-broad-support-in-u-s-for-ebola-travel-ban; Alexander Burns, "Politico Poll: Alarm, Anxiety as Election Looms," *Politico*, October 20, 2014, accessed December 16, 2014, http://www.politico.com/story/2014/10/politico -poll-2014-elections-112016.html.

7. Evan McMorris-Santoro and Adrian Carrasquillo, "Inside President Obama's Decision to Delay Immigration Actions," *BuzzFeed*, September 6, 2014, accessed December 16, 2014, http://www.buzzfeed.com/evanmcsan/inside-president-oba mas-decision-to-delay-im migration-action.

8. Lucy McCalmont, "Michelle Obama Muffs Braley's Name," *Politico*, October 10, 2014, accessed December 16, 2014, http://www.politico.com/story/2014/10/ michelle-obama-bruce-braley-111798.html.

9. Sam Youngman, "Alison Lundergan Grimes Refuses to Say Whether She Voted for Obama," *Lexington Herald-Leader*, October 9, 2014, accessed December 16, 2014, http://www.kentucky.com/2014/10/09/3472697/bluegrass-politics-the -question.html.

10. Rebecca Berg, "Obama Endorses Hagan in Radio Ad," *Washington Examiner*, November 3, 2014, accessed December 16, 2014, http://www.washingtonexaminer .com/obama-endorses-hagan-in-radio-ad/article/2555656.

11. James Hohmann, "Mary Landrieu Stands with Obama—Or Hardly Knows Him," *Politico*, December 1, 2014, accessed December 16, 2014, http://www.politi co.com/story/2014/12/mary-landrieu-barack-obama-113242.html.

12. Kirsten Appleton, "The Obama Quote Republicans Can't Stop Repeating," *ABC News*, October 10, 2014, accessed December 16, 2014, http://abcnews.go.com/ Politics/obama-quote-republicans-stop-repeating/story?id=26086760.

13. Ben Wieder, "Obama Takes Star Turn in State Political Ads," Center for Public Integrity, October 2, 2014, accessed December 16, 2014, http://www.publicintegri ty.org/2014/10/02/15829/obama-takes-star-turn-state-political-ads.

14. John Raby and Vicki Smith, "Jay Rockefeller Retiring: West Virginia Senator Won't Run Again When Term Ends in 2014," *Huffington Post* (AP), January 11, 2013,

accessed December 16, 2014, http://www.huffingtonpost.com/2013/01/11/jay-rock efeller-resigns_n_2455812.html.

15. Jeff Zeleny, "Tom Harkin of Iowa Won't Seek Re-election to Senate," *New York Times*, January 26, 2013, accessed December 16, 2014, http://www.nytimes .com/2013/01/27/us/politics/tom-harkin-of-iowa-wont-seek-re-election-to-senate .html.

16. Rachel Weiner, "South Dakota Sen. Tim Johnson Announces Retirement," *Washington Post*, March 26, 2013, accessed December 16, 2014, http://www.washing tonpost.com/blogs/post-politics/wp/2013/03/26/south-dakota-sen-tim-johnson -retiring-gop-split-on-candidate/.

17. Alexander Burns, "Max Baucus Retiring," *Politico*, April 23, 2013, accessed December 16, 2014, http://www.politico.com/story/2013/04/max-baucus-retiring -2014-90491.html.

18. Emily Schultheis, "Bruce Braley on Chuck Grassley: A 'Farmer' with No Law Degree," *Politico*, March 25, 2014, accessed December 16, 2014, http://www.politi co.com/story/2014/03/bruce-braley-chuck-grassley-farmer-with-no-law-degree-10 5010.html.

19. "Michigan Senate Race, Summary Data," Center for Responsive Politics, accessed December 16, 2014, https://www.opensecrets.org/races/summary.php?id = MIS1&cycle = 2014.

20. Edward Isaac-Dovere, Manu Raju, and John Bresnahan, "How the Democrats Lost the Senate," *Politico*, November 6, 2014, accessed December 16, 2014, http:// www.politico.com/story/2014/11/democrats-lose-2014-midterms-112581.html.

21. James Hohmann, "Scott Brown, Man of Mystery," *Politico*, February 23, 2014, accessed December 16, 2014, http://www.politico.com/story/2014/02/scott-brown -keeps-everyone-guessing-103807.html; James Hohmann and Alexander Burns, "Scott Brown Makes Moves in New Hampshire," *Politico*, March 13, 2014, accessed December 16, 2014, http://www.politico.com/story/2014/03/scott-brown-2014 -senate-new-hampshire-104651.html; "New Hampshire Senate Race, Summary Data," Center for Responsive Politics, accessed December 16, 2014, https://www .opensecrets.org/races/summary.php?id = NHS2&cycle = 2014.

22. James Hohmann, "Alison Lundergan Grimes Goes Shooting in New Ad," *Politico*, September 15, 2014, accessed December 16, 2014, http://www.politico .com/story/2014/09/alison-lundergan-grimes-shooting-ad-110954.html.

23. Cameron McWhirter, "Republican David Perdue Wins Georgia Senate Race," *Wall Street Journal*, November 4, 2014, accessed December 16, 2014, http://blogs .wsj.com/washwire/2014/11/04/republican-david-perdue-wins-georgia-senate-race/.

24. Alexandra Jaffe, "Embattled Shinseki Becomes Lightning Rod in Fight for Senate," *The Hill*, May 22, 2014, accessed December 16, 2014, http://thehill.com/ blogs/ballot-box/senate-races/207039-shinseki-becomes-lightning-rod-in-battle -for-senate.

25. Laura Meckler, "GOP Ad Attacking Michelle Nunn Underscores Immigration Shift," *Wall Street Journal*, September 9, 2014, accessed December 16, 2014, http:// blogs.wsj.com/washwire/2014/09/09/gop-ad-attacking-michelle-nunn-underscores -immigration-shift/.

26. Jonathan Martin, "Lacking a House, a Senator Is Renewing His Ties in Kansas," *New York Times*, February 7, 2014, accessed December 16, 2014, http://www

.nytimes.com/2014/02/08/us/senator-races-to-show-ties-including-an-address-in
-kansas.html; Molly Ball, "The Mystery Candidate Shaking Up Kansas Politics," *The Atlantic*, September 27, 2014, accessed December 16, 2014, http://www.theatlantic
.com/politics/archive/2014/09/the-mystery-candidate-shaking-up-kansas-politics/
380856/.

27. Byron York, "Yes, Dems Did Funnel Money to 'Independent' in Kansas Senate Race," *Washington Examiner*, December 8, 2014, accessed December 16, 2014, http://www.washingtonexaminer.com/yes-dems-did-funnel-money-to-independent
-in-kansas-senate-race/article/2557116.

28. John Bresnahan and Manu Raju, "Harry Reid, Tom Daschle Feud Over S.D. Senate Seat," *Politico*, May 20, 2013, accessed December 16, 2014, http://www.poli
tico.com/story/2013/05/harry-reid-tom-daschle-south-dakota-senate-91646.html.

29. Ryan Casey, "Would Rounds Indictment Leave South Dakota Without a Senator?" *Huffington Post*, October 21, 2014, accessed December 16, 2014, http://www
.huffingtonpost.com/ryancasey/would-rounds-indictment-l_b_6013346.html.

30. David Montgomery, "National Parties Cut Back South Dakota Investment," *Argus Leader*, October 28, 2014, accessed December 16, 2014, http://www.argus
leader.com/story/davidmontgomery/2014/10/28/national-parties-cut-investment/
18076689/.

31. Cameron Joseph, "Senate Dem Stumbles in Arkansas Race," *The Hill*, October 17, 2014, accessed December 16, 2014, http://thehill.com/blogs/ballot-box/senate
-races/221047-stumbles-put-pryor-on-defense.

32. Jason Berry, "Mary and the Landrieus," *Politico Magazine*, December 7, 2014, accessed December 16, 2014, http://www.politico.com/magazine/story/2014/12/
mary-and-the-landrieus-113368.html.

33. Ashley Parker, "Democrats Aim for a 2014 More Like 2012 and 2008," *New York Times*, February 6, 2014, accessed December 16, 2014, http://www.nytimes
.com/2014/02/07/us/politics/democrats-aim-to-make-2014-more-like-2012-and
-2008.html.

34. Jennifer Burnett, "Voter Turnout: 1940–2014," The Council of State Governments, November 19, 2014, accessed December 11, 2014, http://knowledgecenter
.csg.org/kc/content/voter-turnout-1940-2014; Michael McDonald, "2014 November General Election Turnout Rates," last updated December 16, 2014, accessed December 16, 2014, http://www.electproject.org/2014g.

35. "2014 November General Election Turnout Rates," U.S. Elections Project, last updated December 16, 2014, accessed December 16, 2014, http://www.electproject
.org/2014g.

36. Fredreka Schouten, "Study: Alaska Senate Battle Tanks No. 1 in Per-Voter Spending," *USA Today*, November 7, 2014, accessed December 16, 2014, http://on
politics.usatoday.com/2014/11/07/brookings-study-shows-alaska-battle-between
-begich-and-sullivan-most-costly-per-voter/.

37. Nathan Gonzales, "Senate Chairmen Try to Avoid Historic Home-State Losses," *Roll Call*, September 24, 2014, accessed December 16, 2014, http://blogs
.rollcall.com/rothenblog/senate-campaign-committee-chairmen-trying-to-avoid
-historic-home-state-losses/.

4

The State of the House

The Midterm's Presidential Penalty Strikes Again

Kyle Kondik

While it's not as constant as the sun rising in the east or a broken clock being correct twice a day, there's a longstanding trend in American midterm elections that's been very consistent for at least a century and a half: The party that controls the White House loses House seats in midterm elections.

Going back to the first federal election conducted after the start of the Civil War in 1862, there have been thirty-nine midterm elections, including 2014. In thirty-six of those elections, the president's party has lost ground in the U.S. House of Representatives.[1] Those losses are typically not small, either: As the *New York Times* noted right before the midterm election, over the last one hundred years (going back to 1914's midterm), the president's party lost an average of "32 House seats in their first midterm and 29 in their second."[2]

The three elections where the president's party did net seats in the House show the remarkably positive conditions required to buck this otherwise consistent trend. The exceptions are as follows:

- 1934, when President Franklin Roosevelt and the Democrats netted nine House seats thanks to Roosevelt's tremendous popularity in fighting the Great Depression and the discrediting of the Republican Party following the onset of the economic catastrophe during Herbert Hoover's ill-fated presidency.
- 1998, when a booming economy and Republican overreach in the impeachment of popular President Bill Clinton allowed the Democrats

73

to net a modest four seats. Clinton's approval was 66 percent at the time of that midterm, according to Gallup.[3]

- 2002, which was dominated by the shadow of the September 11 terrorist attacks and the looming war in Iraq. Issues of national security boosted popular President George W. Bush and the Republicans, helping them gain eight net seats.

That's it.

The short list of presidential midterm success stories clearly shows that a combination of factors—a booming economy, a popular president, other outside events like war and controversy—is necessary to beat back the midterm trend. Even popular presidents can't overcome the midterm handicap, although they can mitigate it. For instance, Presidents John F. Kennedy (D) and Ronald Reagan (R) both had Gallup approval ratings over 60 percent right before the 1962 and 1986 midterms, respectively, but their parties still lost five net seats apiece in those midterms.

As the 2014 midterm unfolded, it became clear that this midterm was going to be more rule than exception: Unlike in 1934, 1998, or 2002, there were no special circumstances indicating that the Democrats would perform outside the midterm norm.

Like many reelected presidents, Barack Obama had a brief honeymoon period where his approval rating went over 50 percent at the end of 2012 and into early 2013, according to *HuffPost* Pollster's polling average.[4] However, by the middle of May 2013, Obama's disapproval became higher than his approval, and for the rest of the election cycle, his approval rating was mired in the low to mid-forties. Historically speaking, Obama's average approval right before the midterm (about 42.5 percent approval in the polling average) was quite similar to the following post–World War II presidents right before their midterms (all approval figures are from Gallup): Harry Truman in 1950 (41 percent), Lyndon Johnson in 1966 (44 percent), Ronald Reagan in 1982 (42 percent), and Obama himself before the 2010 midterm (45 percent). In each of these cases, the president's party suffered midterm losses: forty-one seats per midterm on average.[5]

Additionally, there were no special issues or outside factors, like issues of war and peace or scandal, that dramatically impacted the election. The United States, despite limited ongoing actions in the Middle East and Afghanistan, was not fighting a major land war overseas during the midterm. Unlike in 1998, when Republican overreach on impeachment probably aided Democratic hopes, the Republicans generally did not suffer any self-inflicted wounds, with the exception of a government shutdown in October 2013. The shutdown briefly sent Democratic numbers soaring: Democrats took a four-point lead in the generic ballot average, a national poll that measures which party respondents would vote for in their local House race.[6]

After the shutdown ended, the poor rollout of the Affordable Care Act website dominated the news, and the generic ballot settled back into a small Republican lead, which the GOP would maintain for most of the rest of the year before the election.

In other words: Nothing happened during the 2014 House election cycle to suggest that President Obama and his Democrats would provide another rare exception to the midterm curse. And they did not.

The Republicans netted thirteen House seats on Election Day, giving them a 247–188 majority, eclipsing the post-1946 Republican caucus of 246 for their party's biggest House majority since the one they won in 1928. The total was five seats higher than the 242 the Republicans won in the 2010 midterm, when the party netted sixty-three seats to retake the House after four years of Democratic control.

While the midterm curse helps explain a lot of what happened, the reasons that led to the biggest GOP majority in the lifetime of nearly every American are more legion than that.

THE GOP'S STRUCTURAL HOUSE ADVANTAGES

For much of the twentieth century, Democrats routinely won more House seats than their share of the national House vote would suggest, a phenomenon that can largely be explained through their dominance in the South, which was a mostly one-party Democratic region for much of the twentieth century. But that started to change in 1994, when Republicans started to consistently win a greater percentage of House seats than their share of the national House vote.[7]

The reasons for this structural advantage are many.

First of all, Democratic voters are inefficiently distributed nationally. There is a striking urban/rural split in American politics. After 2014, Democrats will hold just twenty of the one hundred largest districts by land area, down from twenty-seven after the 2012 election. Republicans hold just thirteen of the one hundred smallest districts, which is the same number as they held after 2012. Drilling down further, Democrats hold thirty-nine of the forty smallest districts, and Republicans hold thirty-six of the forty biggest districts.[8]

In the one hundred largest districts, Mitt Romney won an average of 56 percent in each district, or nine percentage points more than his 47 percent national performance in 2012. Meanwhile, in the one hundred smallest districts, Obama won an average of 68 percent of the vote, or seventeen points better than his 2012 share of the national vote, 51 percent. That suggests an inefficient clustering of the Democratic vote in the smallest (urban) districts.

So does this: In 2012, Obama got two-thirds or more of the vote in eighty-one House districts. Romney got two-thirds or more in just thirty-three.

This helps prove a point made by the political scientists Jonathan Rodden of Stanford University and Jowei Chen of the University of Michigan in a recent study, which is that the Democratic vote is inefficiently distributed across the country, and that one would not expect the Democrats to receive 50 percent of all House seats even if they won 50 percent of the national vote.[9]

The other factor worth noting is the decennial redistricting process, which Republicans dominated after their successes in 2010's federal and state elections. Republicans controlled the drawing of 213 districts, while Democrats controlled just forty-four (the other 178 districts were either at-large statewide districts or they were drawn by either independent bodies or with the input of both parties).[10] Experts debate how important redistricting is, but the mass concentration of Democratic voters in heavily Democratic urban districts paired with GOP-controlled redistricting in a far greater number of districts than Democrats has undoubtedly given the Republicans at least a small leg up in the House.

After all, Mitt Romney lost the 2012 election by about four points nationally, but he actually won a clear majority of individual congressional districts, 226 to Barack Obama's 209.

Indeed, much was made of the Democrats winning just 46 percent of all House seats in 2012 despite narrowly winning the national popular House vote. As it was in 2014, Republicans won 51 percent of all House votes cast, but won 57 percent of the seats. Democrats won 46 percent of the votes but only 43 percent of the seats (the remaining votes went to non-major-party candidates, and every single member of the House is either a Democrat or a Republican).[11]

THE LEAD-UP TO THE CAMPAIGN

The structural factors noted above—the inability of almost every president to deliver gains to their party in the midterm combined with the natural Republican tilt of the current House environment—were clear even as the cycle started. However, Democrats were coming off a decent 2012 election in which they netted eight seats and, as previously noted, won the national popular House vote.

Despite the perilous historical odds, Democrats hoped that Republican mistakes would create a political miracle that would deliver them the

House. In early 2013, Representative Steve Israel of New York, the chairman of the Democratic Congressional Campaign Committee, wanted 2014 to be a "referendum" on "tea party extremism," as the *Washington Post* reported at the time.[12] Democrats got a tantalizing vision of how quickly the numbers could move in their favor during the government shutdown of October 2013, but that proved to be a political mirage.

Early in the cycle, the National Republican Congressional Committee announced the creation of its Red Zone program, a focus on seven districts held by Democrats that Republican presidential candidates had won in the previous three presidential elections.[13] Coming into the cycle, Republicans did not have an overwhelming number of natural targets: Just nine Democrats sat in districts won by Mitt Romney in 2012. But Republicans knew that if they could grab some of these districts, which in some cases are overwhelmingly Republican at the presidential level, they would be relatively easy to defend in future elections.

The Republicans got a few early breaks in these districts when Democratic Representatives Mike McIntyre of North Carolina and Jim Matheson of Utah decided to retire. Matheson and McIntyre held, respectively, the first and third-most Republican districts held by any Democrat—Romney won 67 and 59 percent of the vote in each district, respectively—and both had won very narrow reelection victories in 2012. The GOP ended up winning both districts, though Republican Mia Love's margin of victory in Utah ended up being a surprisingly small five points.

Matheson and McIntyre were two of the twenty-four members of the House—ten Democrats and fourteen Republicans—who decided to retire before the 2014 elections. Those retirements seemingly provided the Democrats with some opportunities, too. Republican Representatives Gary Miller of California, Mike Rogers of Michigan, Jon Runyan of New Jersey, Jim Gerlach of Pennsylvania, and Frank Wolf of Virginia all announced they were leaving the House, and each of their districts was hypothetically competitive enough to be vulnerable to a strong Democratic challenge.

Ultimately, 392 incumbents elected to run for reelection in 2014 (beyond the retirees, others opted to run for other offices or otherwise did not stand for reelection). Of those, only four failed to win renomination in primaries.[14]

Democrats got an early opportunity when Republican Representative Bill Young of Florida, a long-time member from a Tampa Bay-area seat narrowly won by Obama in 2012, announced his retirement and later died in office. That led to a March 2014 special election. While Democrats quickly recruited a high-profile candidate, 2010 Florida gubernatorial nominee Alex Sink, Republicans were unable to secure a top candidate. David Jolly, a lobbyist and former Young staffer, ultimately won the GOP nomination.

Sink entered the race against Jolly as a favorite, but the poor national environment and local issues, like questions about Sink's residency, took their toll, and Jolly won a two-point upset.

This was, to put it mildly, a poor sign for Democratic hopes. "The Florida special election Tuesday was supposed to be an ideal chance for Democrats to show that 2014 isn't a lost year," wrote Alex Isenstadt of *Politico*. "Instead, they were dealt another body blow, further weakening their prospects for this year's midterms."[15]

In order to win the House in 2014, Democrats needed to net seventeen seats. That's the same number of seats carried by Obama that Republican representatives won in the 2012 election, a group that included Young. Special elections are often not predictive of the general election outcome— Democrats, for instance, won three high-profile and competitive special elections in the 2010 cycle only to lose big in the actual midterm election— but this was a bad development for the Democrats, anyway. To add insult to injury, Democrats botched the recruitment for the general election and ended up failing to field a candidate to run against Jolly in November.

THE NOVEMBER RESULTS

Republicans netted thirteen seats on Election Night, a slightly bigger gain than most analysts predicted. (The author of this chapter picked the GOP to net nine seats.[16]) Tables 4.1 and 4.2 show the seats that changed hands.

Ultimately, and predictably because of the Republican-tilting environment, Democrats ended up being unable to seriously contest many Republican districts in 2014. Of the aforementioned Republican districts that came open because of retirements, Democrats only won one, Gary Miller's Thirty-first District in California. Going into the 2014 election, this was the most Democratic district held by any Republican (57 percent Obama in 2012), and Miller had previously won it in a fluky way. In advance of the 2012 elections, California had gone to a "top-two" primary system, where every candidate runs against each other in the primary, and the top two

Table 4.1. Republican-Held House Districts Captured by Democrats in 2014

District	Winner	Results in Percentage Points	2012 Presidential Result in Percentage Points	Beat Incumbent?
CA-31	Pete Aguilar	52–48	57–41 Obama	No
FL-2	Gwen Graham	50–49	52–47 Romney	Yes
NE-2	Brad Ashford	49–46	53–46 Romney	Yes

Table 4.2. Democratic-Held House Districts Captured by Republicans in 2014

District	Winner	Results in Percentage Points	2012 Presidential Result in Percentage Points	Beat Incumbent?
AZ-2	Martha McSally	50-50	50-48 Romney	Yes
FL-26	Carlos Curbelo	51-49	53-46 Obama	Yes
GA-12	Rick Allen	55-45	55-44 Romney	Yes
IL-10	Robert Dold	51-49	58-41 Obama	Yes
IL-12	Mike Bost	52-42	50-48 Obama	Yes
IA-1	Rod Blum	51-49	56-42 Obama	No
ME-2	Bruce Poliquin	47-42	53-44 Obama	No
NV-4	Cresent Hardy	49-46	54-44 Obama	Yes
NH-1	Frank Guinta	52-48	50-48 Obama	Yes
NY-1	Lee Zeldin	54-46	50-49 Obama	Yes
NY-21	Elise Stefanik	55-34	52-46 Obama	No
NY-24	John Katko	60-40	57-41 Obama	Yes
NC-7	David Rouzer	59-37	59-40 Romney	No
TX-23	Will Hurd	50-48	51-48 Romney	Yes
UT-4	Mia Love	51-46	68-30 Romney	No
WV-3	Evan Jenkins	55-45	65-33 Romney	Yes

Source: Election results from the *Cook Political Report*'s 2014 National House Popular Vote Tracker. 2012 Obama/Romney results by district from the *Almanac of American Politics*.

vote-getters advance to the general election. In 2012, a big group of Democratic candidates allowed two Republicans to advance to the general election, and something similar almost happened in the 2014 primary. But Democrat Pete Aguilar advanced to November and narrowly defeated Republican Paul Chabot to capture the seat.

Only two Republican incumbents lost, and both hurt themselves with self-inflicted mistakes. Representative Lee Terry of Nebraska, who frequently had difficult races despite residing in a district that is a few points more Republican than the nation as a whole, steadfastly refused to consider not taking a paycheck during the October 2013 shutdown. His reasoning? "I've got a nice house and a kid in college, and I'll tell you we cannot handle it. Giving our paycheck away when you still worked and earned it? That's just not going to fly."[17] He lost to Democratic state Senator Brad Ashford, who entered the race after a more heralded national Democratic recruit, Omaha City Councilman Pete Festersen, bailed on a previously announced run for the seat in late 2013.

The other GOP loser was Representative Steve Southerland of Florida. Southerland had a strong challenger—Democrat Gwen Graham, daughter of Bob Graham, the former Florida governor and senator—but he also ran a poor race, highlighted by a "men-only" fundraiser that only fueled Democratic attacks that Southerland was out of touch with women.

That concludes the Democratic highlights from Election Night 2014 in the House. Besides the two defeated incumbents, just two other Republican incumbents failed to win by less than ten percentage points, according to Nathan Gonzales of the *Rothenberg Political Report*.[18] Every other incumbent won by more than that. Among the double-digit winners was Representative Michael Grimm of New York City's Staten Island, who was the lone Republican to win one of the nation's forty smallest districts by land area and who won despite being under indictment on federal fraud charges (after pleading guilty, he resigned before the opening of the new Congress).

All in all, even vulnerable Republicans largely coasted to reelection.

Republicans flipped sixteen seats from the Democrats. That included five of the seven Red Zone seats mentioned above, the Republican-leaning seats with Democratic incumbents. In addition to winning the open seats vacated by Matheson of Utah and McIntyre of North Carolina, Republicans defeated Representatives Ron Barber of Arizona, John Barrow of Georgia, and Nick Rahall of West Virginia. The Barrow and Rahall losses are worth noting because, in many ways, they represent the last of a dying breed. Barrow was the last white, male Democratic House member from the Deep South, and Rahall was the last true Appalachian Democrat from rural Coal Country. In the age of Obama, both of these regions have trended hard against the president and his party, and it's unclear when Democrats will next be able to compete in districts such as these. Of these seven red-district targets, only two Democratic incumbents survived: Representatives Ann Kirkpatrick of Arizona and Collin Peterson of Minnesota.

Republicans had perhaps their best performance in New York, where they netted three seats, beating Democratic incumbents Tim Bishop in a swingy district on the eastern end of Long Island and Dan Maffei in a Democratic upstate district. Maffei's loss was eye-opening, given that Republican John Katko won the 57 percent Obama district by twenty points over the incumbent. Republicans almost won another upstate district, the one held by long-time Democratic Representative Louise Slaughter, but she narrowly hung on by less than half a point against an unknown Republican challenger. Democratic turnout problems, acute across the country, were felt in New York in part because there were no competitive races at the top of the ticket to motivate voters.

Speaking of poor turnout, Democrats' failure to run a credible challenger to Republican Nevada Governor Brian Sandoval contributed to a down-ballot drubbing that surprisingly included freshman Democratic Representative Steven Horsford, who was knocked off by Republican Assemblyman Cresent Hardy. Before his win, Hardy was a fringe candidate best known for making outlandish comments.[19]

Republicans netted another two seats in Illinois, proving that redistricting —controlled here by Democrats—is not always fool-proof, particularly in a one-sided political environment.

On Election Night, it appeared that Republican gains would be even bigger. But in the days and weeks following the election, Democrats won nearly every close race, including several in California, where vote-counting can be slow and laborious. The only truly close race the Republicans officially won late in the game was Barber's seat in Arizona, which Republican Martha McSally finally captured in December after a recount.

Despite the GOP successes, incumbents who sought reelection generally won, which is the historical norm. Roughly 95 percent of House members who sought reelection won it in 2014, which is actually higher than the post–World War II average of 92 percent.[20] While Congress continues to suffer from very low approval ratings, a generic distaste for the body has yet to translate into true vulnerability for the lion's share of members of Congress.

THE FUTURE: DO DEMOCRATS HAVE TO LOSE TO WIN?

With a 247-188 advantage in the House, Republicans can afford some losses in 2016 and still maintain control. Democrats would need to net thirty seats to retake the chamber. There's plenty of historical precedent for such a gain by a victorious party in a presidential election year. Perhaps the best example would be 1928, when the Republicans won the White House for the third straight time and netted thirty House seats. Democrats, in both the race for the presidency and the House, have a goal to do exactly the same in 2016.

Republicans go into the 2016 cycle at least somewhat overextended, a natural consequence of winning such a large majority. They now control twenty-six seats in districts that Obama won in 2012. Meanwhile, Democrats control just five districts won by Romney in 2012. Those districts are shown in Tables 4.3 and 4.4.

However, many of these Obama-seat Republicans are not really all that vulnerable. Several of these seats are held by long-term incumbents who

Table 4.3. Democratic House Members in Districts Won by Mitt Romney in 2012

Member	District	2012 Romney victory in percentage points
Ann Kirkpatrick	AZ-1	50-48
Gwen Graham	FL-2	52-47
Patrick Murphy	FL-18	52-48
Collin Peterson	MN-7	54-44
Brad Ashford	NE-2	53-46

Source: Almanac of American Politics for 2012 Obama/Romney results by district.

Table 4.4. Republican House Members in Districts Won by Barack Obama in 2012

Member	District	2012 Obama victory in percentage points
Jeff Denham	CA-10	51-47
David Valadao	CA-21	55-44
Mike Coffman	CO-6	52-47
Carlos Curbelo	FL-26	53-46
David Jolly	FL-13	50-49
Ileana Ros-Lehtinen	FL-27	53-47
Rod Blum	IA-1	56-42
David Young	IA-3	51-47
Mike Bost	IL-12	50-48
Robert Dold	IL-10	58-41
Bruce Poliquin	ME-2	53-44
John Kline	MN-2	49-49
Erik Paulsen	MN-3	50-49
Frank Guinta	NH-1	50-48
Frank LoBiondo	NJ-2	54-46
Tom MacArthur	NJ-3	52-48
Cresent Hardy	NV-4	54-44
Joe Heck	NV-3	49-49
Chris Gibson	NY-19	52-46
Michael Grimm	NY-11	52-47
John Katko	NY-24	57-41
Peter King	NY-2	52-47
Elise Stefanik	NY-21	52-46
Lee Zeldin	NY-1	50-49
Scott Rigell	VA-2	50-49
Dave Reichert	WA-8	50-48

Source: Almanac of American Politics for 2012 Obama/Romney results by district.

will be very difficult for Democrats to defeat in 2016 or beyond, like Representatives Ileana Ros-Lehtinen of Florida, Frank LoBiondo of New Jersey, and Peter King of New York. Also, while some of these districts are clearly more Democratic than the country as a whole, in 16 of these 26 districts Romney matched or exceeded his 2012 national performance of 47 percent.

Also, Republicans will almost certainly run credible challenges against all five of the Romney-district Democrats in 2016, and there are a handful of other marginal, Obama-won districts that the GOP failed to capture in 2014 that it might be able to plausibly target again.

A reasonable, early projection for 2016 is probably that the Democrats will gain seats so long as the presidential race is close and competitive, if only because the Republicans are exposed in some Democratic-leaning districts. It's also not impossible to imagine the Democrats retaking the House in 2016 if the party also wins a sizable presidential victory and if Republicans make a lot of mistakes and also lose many incumbents through primaries or retirements. A combination of such factors would amount to a Democratic miracle. That's unlikely in the extreme, but not impossible.

Practically speaking, though, House Democrats might have to root for the other party in the 2016 presidential race. Why? Because given what we know about midterm elections almost always going against the president's party in the House, perhaps the next best chance for the Democrats to win the House will be in 2018—*if* a Republican is in the White House.

After all, while we can be 100 percent certain that when the sun sets on Election Day 2018 it will do so in the west, we can be 92 percent certain, based on the statistics since the Civil War, that the party that controls the presidency will lose House seats that very same day. And the number of seats that party is likely to lose is likelier to be more than just a few.

NOTES

1. All statistics on historical House seat gains and losses in this chapter come from "Table 1–10, House and Senate Election Results, by Congress, 1788–2010," *Vital Statistics on American Politics 2011–2012* (Thousand Oaks, CA: CQ Press, 2011).

2. Juliet Lapidos, "The President's Party Will Probably Lose Seats—That's Often How It Goes," *New York Times*, November 4, 2014, accessed December 8, 2014, http://takingnote.blogs.nytimes.com/2014/11/04/the-presidents-party-will-probably-lose-seatsthats-often-how-it-goes/.

3. All Gallup approval information comes from the "Gallup Presidential Job Approval Center," Gallup, accessed December 8, 2014, http://www.gallup.com/poll/124922/presidential-approval-center.aspx.

4. "HuffPost Pollster Obama Job Approval," *The Huffington Post*, accessed December 8, 2014, http://elections.huffingtonpost.com/pollster/obama-job-approval.

5. "Seats in Congress Gained/Lost by the President's Party in Mid-Term Elections," The American Presidency Project, accessed December 8, 2014, http://www.presidency.ucsb.edu/data/mid-term_elections.php.

6. "HuffPost Pollster 2014 National House Race," *The Huffington Post*, accessed December 8, 2014, http://elections.huffingtonpost.com/pollster/2014-national-house-race.

7. "Table 1–12, Popular Vote and Seats in House Elections, by Party, 1896–2010," *Vital Statistics on American Politics 2011–2012* (Thousand Oaks, CA: CQ Press, 2011).

8. Kyle Kondik, "Size Matters," *Sabato's Crystal Ball,* May 23, 2013, accessed December 8, 2014, http://www.centerforpolitics.org/crystalball/articles/size-matters/. Figures from article updated with 2014 election results.

9. Jowei Chen and Jonathan Rodden, "Unintentional Gerrymandering: Political Geography and Electoral Bias in Legislatures," *Quarterly Journal of Political Science,* Vol. 8, No. 3: 239–269, accessed December 8, 2014, http://www-personal .umich.edu/~jowei/florida.pdf.

10. Sundeep Iyer and Keesha Gaskins, "Redistricting and Congressional Control: A First Look," Brennan Center for Justice, accessed December 8, 2014, http://www .brennancenter.org/sites/default/files/legacy/publications/Redistricting_Congres sional_Control.pdf.

11. David Wasserman, Loren Fulton, and Ashton Barry, "2014 National House Popular Vote Tracker," *Cook Political Report,* accessed December 8, 2014, https:// docs.google.com/spreadsheet/ccc?key=0AjYj9mXElO_QdHVsbnNNdXRoaUE5QT hHclNWaTgzb2c&usp=drive_web#gid=0. Other results cited in this chapter are also from this document.

12. Sean Sullivan, "Steve Israel 'Pretty Comfortable' Rahall and Barrow Won't Bolt for Senate," *Washington Post,* March 13, 2013, accessed December 8, 2014, http://www.washingtonpost.com/blogs/post-politics/wp/2013/03/13/steve-israel -pretty-comfortable-rahall-and-barrow-wont-bolt-for-senate/.

13. Alex Isenstadt, "GOP Draws Red Zone over 7 House Dem Seats," *Politico,* May 9, 2013, accessed December 8, 2014, http://www.politico.com/story/2013/05/ gop-draws-red-zone-over-7-house-dem-seats-91103.html.

14. "Roll Call Casualty List: 113th Congress (2013–2014)," *Roll Call,* accessed December 8, 2014, http://www.rollcall.com/politics/casualtylist.html/. This count does not include Representative Vance McAllister (R), who was defeated in Louisiana's "general primary," an election that took place on the same November day as the general election in all other states. In that election (in Louisiana's Fifth District), no candidate won a majority, necessitating a "general election" in December between the top-two finishers, which is commonly viewed as a runoff election. Because McAllister failed to finish in the top two, he did not advance to the December contest.

15. Alex Isenstadt, "Florida Loss Big Blow to Democrats' 2014 Hopes," *Politico,* March 11, 2014, accessed December 8, 2014, http://www.politico.com/story/2014/ 03/david-jolly-alex-sink-florida-special-election-2014-democrats-104560.html.

16. Kyle Kondik, "House 2014: Calling the Toss-ups, Take 1," *Sabato's Crystal Ball,* October 30, 2014, http://www.centerforpolitics.org/crystalball/articles/house -2014-calling-the-toss-ups-take-1/.

17. Joseph Morton, "Lee Terry Says He 'Cannot Handle' Giving Up Own Paycheck During Shutdown," Omaha.com, October 4, 2013, accessed December 8, 2013, http://www.omaha.com/news/lee-terry-says-he-cannot-handle-giving-up-own -paycheck/article_06c17b2b-84ac-54f9-ad38-248b4ffbd423.html.

18. Nathan Gonzales, "Don't Call 2014 an Anti-Incumbent Election," Five ThirtyEight.com, November 25, 2014, accessed December 8, 2014, http://five thirtyeight.com/datalab/dont-call-2014-an-anti-incumbent-election/.

19. Steve Sebelius, "Top 5 Worst Cresent Hardy Quotes—and by 'Worst' I Mean 'Best,'" *Las Vegas Review-Journal,* September 24, 2014, accessed December 8, 2014,

http://www.reviewjournal.com/columns-blogs/politics/slash-politics/top-5-worst
-cresent-hardy-quotes-and-worst-i-mean-best.

20. Kyle Kondik and Geoffrey Skelley, "14 from '14: Quick Takes on the Midterm," *Sabato's Crystal Ball*, November 13, 2014, accessed December 8, 2014, http://
www.centerforpolitics.org/crystalball/articles/14-from-14-quick-takes-on-the-mid
term/.

5

It's Good to Be a Republican

The Governors' Edition

Geoffrey Skelley

For all the focus on the U.S. Senate during the 2014 cycle, thirty-six states also went about choosing their next governor. With the federal government in a likely state of paralysis at least until the 2016 election, if not beyond, governors and their state legislatures are left in an even more powerful position to offer policy prescriptions for what ails us. The "laboratories of democracy" are hard at work while Washington remains in limbo.

The outcome of the 2014 cycle further cemented Republican domination of the nation's governorships. Following the 2013 off-year elections in Virginia and New Jersey, Republicans held a twenty-nine to twenty-one edge in state governorships. On November 4, 2014, Republicans achieved a net gain of two seats, Democrats suffered a net loss of three, and independents gained one. Thus, Republicans' overall advantage has grown to thirty-one versus the eighteen of their major-party rivals, with independents holding one. The thirty-one seat total matches Republicans' second-highest mark in the post–World War II era. The GOP's zenith remains thirty-two governorships, which it held before the 1998 and 1970 elections. It's very possible that Republicans could match that mark by 2015 and perhaps pass it in 2016.

Republican success in 2014 can be assigned to two principal factors. The first is unquestionably the midterm election atmosphere. As mentioned throughout this book, the president's party almost always struggles to some degree in midterm elections, particularly in "sixth-year itch" election cycles (i.e., a president's second midterm). Gubernatorial contests are no different in this respect, as shown by Table 5.1. Between entering office and the sixth-year election, the president's party has typically lost ground in terms of its share of governorships in the post–World War II period.

Over the past seventy years of two-term presidencies (including some combined ones due to death or resignation), the president's party has, on average, lost control of about 20 percent of the nation's governorships by the conclusion of the sixth-year election. With the exception of Ronald Reagan, every president in this time period has suffered losses. Barack Obama's result is mostly par for the course. After November 2008, Democrats controlled twenty-nine governorships (58 percent). But following the November 2014 election, Democrats now just hold eighteen (36 percent), meaning that since Obama took office Democrats have lost control of more than one-fifth of the nation's total governorships

The other key ingredient to Republican success was incumbency, which helped the GOP preserve its large advantage. Incumbency is a key factor in elections, as current officeholders tend to win a high percentage of elections. Table 5.2 lays out incumbent gubernatorial election data for every presidential and midterm election since 1946. In twenty-two of the thirty-five cycles, at least 70 percent of incumbent governors won a return to office. When we focus on just general elections, as many one-party dominated states have seen successful primary challenges (particularly in the old Democratic Solid South of yesteryear), at least 70 percent have won in twenty-eight of thirty-five cycles.

Table 5.1. Post–World War II Change in President's Party's Share of Governorships after Sixth-Year Election

Presidency	Total State Governors	Pres. Party Governors at Start of Term	Starting % Held	Pres. Party Governors after 6th Year	6th Year % Held	Change
FDR/Truman (D)	48	25	52%	23	48%	−4%
Eisenhower (R)	48/49	30	63%	14	29%	−34%
JFK/LBJ (D)	50	34	68%	25	50%	−18%
Nixon/Ford (R)	50	31	62%	13	26%	−36%
Reagan (R)	50	24	48%	24	48%	0%
Clinton (D)	50	30	60%	17	34%	−26%
G.W. Bush (R)	50	29	58%	22	44%	−14%
Obama (D)	50	29*	58%	18	36%	−22%
Average	N/A	29.0	59%	19.5	39%	−19%

Note: *Includes Gov. Janet Napolitano (D-AZ), who was appointed secretary of homeland security in January 2009. Percentages are rounded post-arithmetic.

Source: CQ Guide to U.S. Elections, vol. ii, 6th ed., 1558; *Crystal Ball* research.

Table 5.2. Post–World War II Election Performance by Incumbent Governors

Year	Inc. Running Again	Lost Primary	Lost General	Won	Inc. Success Rate	General Election Rate
1946	20	3	3	14	70.0%	82.4%
1948	24	4	8	12	50.0%	60.0%
1950	20	1	4	15	75.0%	78.9%
1952	21	2	3	16	76.2%	84.2%
1954	19	3	4	12	63.2%	75.0%
1956	20	2	4*	15	75.0%	78.9%
1958	20	0	9	11	55.0%	55.0%
1960	14	0	6	8	57.1%	57.1%
1962	28	2	11	15	53.6%	57.7%
1964	15	1	2	12	80.0%	85.7%
1966	24	2	7	15	62.5%	68.2%
1968	14	0	4	10	71.4%	71.4%
1970	25	1	7	17	68.0%	70.8%
1972	11	2	2	7	63.6%	77.8%
1974	21	0	5	16	76.2%	76.2%
1976	8	1	2	5	62.5%	71.4%
1978	23	2	5	16	69.6%	76.2%
1980	11	1	3	7	63.6%	70.0%
1982	25	1	5	19	76.0%	79.2%
1984	6	0	2	4	66.7%	66.7%
1986	18	1	2	15	83.3%	88.2%
1988	9	0	1	8	88.9%	88.9%
1990	23	0	6	17	73.9%	73.9%
1992	4	0	0	4	100.0%	100.0%
1994	23	2	4	17	73.9%	81.0%
1996	7	0	0	7	100.0%	100.0%
1998	25	0	2	23	92.0%	92.0%
2000	6	0	1	5	83.3%	83.3%
2002	16	0	4	12	75.0%	75.0%
2004	7	1	2	4	57.1%	66.7%
2006	27	1	1	25	92.6%	96.2%
2008	8	0	0	8	100.0%	100.0%
2010	14	1	2	11	78.6%	84.6%
2012	6	0	0	6	100.0%	100.0%
2014	29	1	3	25	86.2%	89.3%
Total	591	35	124	433	73.3%	77.7%

Note: *In 1956, Gov. J. Bracken Lee (R-UT) lost renomination in the GOP primary but then ran as an independent in the general election, which he also lost.

Sources: CQ Guide to U.S. Elections, vol. ii, 6th ed.; *Crystal Ball* research.

The 2014 election proved to be a record-breaking cycle for incumbent governors. The highest number in the post–World War II period, twenty-nine, attempted to retain their office. Put another way, about four out of every five gubernatorial contests featured an incumbent in 2014. Twenty-five succeeded in winning reelection in 2014, tying the 2006 high-water mark. By party, seventeen of nineteen Republicans and eight of ten Democrats won reelection. One incumbent, Democrat Neil Abercrombie of Hawaii, lost renomination in his party primary, while three others—Republican Sean Parnell of Alaska, Democrat Pat Quinn of Illinois, and Republican Tom Corbett of Pennsylvania—met defeat at the November polls. Despite having almost twice as many incumbents in the mix, Republicans had the same number of losses as Democrats. Having won fifteen of twenty-three open gubernatorial contests in the strong GOP wave of 2010, Republicans consolidated their gains in 2014, holding onto most of their 2010 wins.

Conversely, the lack of incumbency in some races also aided the GOP in 2014. In incumbent-less contests, the GOP took advantage of the favorable midterm environment, strong Republican campaigns, and weak Democratic candidacies to make gains. The GOP won six of the eight open seats in play, and half of Republicans' open-seat victories were in states that Democrats previously controlled: Arkansas, Maryland, and Massachusetts. These three contests provided Republicans with three of their four takeovers on Election Night, along with Illinois, where they defeated Quinn. Victory in these open-seat battles was pivotal to their two-seat net gain for the cycle. As the state-by-state capsules below will show, it was undoubtedly a banner night for Republicans.

THE UNCERTAIN CONTESTS

The University of Virginia Center for Politics' *Crystal Ball* newsletter calls every race by Election Day, leaving no "toss-up" contests. By November 4, we handicapped fourteen gubernatorial races as "leaning" toward one candidate, the most competitive rating, signaling a higher level of uncertainty in the outcome. Tellingly, Republicans won nine of these fourteen elections, including three of their takeovers on Election Night. Election results for these contests are laid out in Table 5.3, with discussion of each race below.

Republicans capitalized on the favorable environment to seize three open-seat governorships. The results in two of those states, Maryland and Massachusetts, came at least as something of a surprise given the traditionally strong Democratic leanings of both states. But it was the Old Line State that particularly stunned everyone on Election Night.

Table 5.3. Election Results in the Uncertain Gubernatorial Contests

State	Winner	Votes	%	Main Opponent	Votes	%	Margin
AK	Bill Walker (I)	134,658	48.1	Sean Parnell (R)*	128,435	45.9	2.2
CO	John Hickenlooper (D)*	1,006,433	49.3	Bob Beauprez (R)	938,195	46.0	3.3
CT	Dan Malloy (D)*	554,314	50.7	Tom Foley (R)	526,295	48.2	2.6
FL	Rick Scott (R)*	2,865,343	48.1	Charlie Crist (D)	2,801,198	47.1	1.1
GA	Nathan Deal (R)*	1,345,237	52.7	Jason Carter (D)	1,144,794	44.9	7.9
IL	Bruce Rauner (R)	1,823,627	50.3	Pat Quinn (D)*	1,681,343	46.3	3.9
KS	Sam Brownback (R)*	433,196	49.8	Paul Davis (D)	401,100	46.1	3.7
MA	Charlie Baker (R)	1,044,573	48.4	Martha Coakley (D)	1,004,408	46.5	1.9
MD	Larry Hogan (R)	884,400	51.0	Anthony Brown (D)	818,890	47.2	3.8
ME	Paul LePage (R)*	294,533	48.2	Mike Michaud (D)	265,125	43.4	4.8
MI	Rick Snyder (R)*	1,607,399	50.9	Mark Schauer (D)	1,479,057	46.9	4.1
NH	Maggie Hassan (D)*	254,666	52.4	Walter Havenstein (R)	230,610	47.4	4.9
RI	Gina Raimondo (D)	131,899	40.7	Allan Fung (R)	117,428	36.2	4.5
WI	Scott Walker (R)*	1,259,706	52.3	Mary Burke (D)	1,122,913	46.6	5.7

Notes: *Signifies an incumbent. Percentages and margins are rounded.
Sources: Official state election results.

After Republican Spiro Agnew became vice president on January 20, 1969, the Maryland legislature elected the state House speaker, Democrat Marvin Mandel, to become the new governor (at that time, the state had no lieutenant governor position).[1] Over the next four decades, only one Republican would win the Maryland governorship, Bob Ehrlich in 2002, and he lost reelection to Democrat Martin O'Malley in 2006 (O'Malley won reelection against Ehrlich in 2010 and was prevented by term limits from running for another term in 2014). This history seemed to augur well for Lieutenant Governor Anthony Brown, the Democratic nominee seeking to succeed O'Malley and in the process become the state's first African American governor. But unpopular tax increases, O'Malley's focus on his presidential ambitions, and the disastrous launch of Maryland's state-run health insurance exchange as a part of the Affordable Care Act (Obamacare) weighed down Brown. The rollout of the exchange was among Brown's key responsibilities, and it failed so badly that the state had to completely rebuild the portal.[2] Still, despite the drag created by O'Malley, Brown's reportedly sputtering campaign, and the generally bad environment for Democrats, few analysts believed that the Republican nominee, former Ehrlich cabinet secretary Larry Hogan, could win. The final major public poll from *New York Times/CBS News*/YouGov showed Brown ahead by thirteen points. In the final two weeks, the only additional polls were two commissioned by Republicans, one that showed Brown up two points and another that found Hogan leading by five.[3] Considering they were partisan polls, few were inclined to take the surveys at full value, but it turned out observers should have given them more credence: Hogan won, edging Brown by 3.8 points. The Republican win shocked the political establishment and analysts alike, proving once again that one cannot predict with certainty what will happen on Election Day.

Less surprising but still noteworthy was the outcome of the gubernatorial contest in Massachusetts between Republican Charlie Baker, his party's 2010 nominee, and Democratic state Attorney General Martha Coakley to succeed retiring Democratic Governor Deval Patrick. Following her embarrassing defeat in the 2010 special U.S. Senate election to Republican Scott Brown—where she lost "the Kennedy seat," long held by the late Ted Kennedy and, before him, John F. Kennedy—Coakley went back to work, rejuvenating her image to the point that National Journal ran an article in July 2014 titled "The Rehabilitation of Martha Coakley."[4] However, the campaign trail tripped Coakley up once again. In September, she won the Democratic nomination with only 42 percent of the vote, and her primary opponents criticized her for running an overly general campaign lacking precise policy goals.[5] These complaints followed her to the general election, where in a post-election analysis the Boston Globe opined that Coakley ran a safe campaign appropriate for a frontrunner, which she never was. Moreover, as a pro-choice and pro-same-sex marriage Republican, Baker couldn't be framed as a "dangerous right-winger," and his policy planks were more tangible than Coakley's.[6] Baker and his allies also outspent Coakley and her associates—the Republican Governors Association spent $12.4 million on behalf of Baker, nearly nine times what the Democratic Governors Association invested—providing an extra bit of oomph for the Republican, who narrowly beat Coakley by about two points.[7] To some extent, no one should be that surprised that a Republican won a Bay State gubernatorial race: Despite the state's deep blue hue at the presidential level, the GOP has held the governorship for 26 of the past 50 years.

The other close contest that saw a Republican takeover was in Illinois, where Republican businessman Bruce Rauner defeated Democratic Governor Pat Quinn, the lone Democratic incumbent to lose in November. Quinn had long been viewed as vulnerable. Having come to the office in 2009 following ex-Governor Rod Blagojevich's removal from office for corruption, the incumbent barely won reelection in 2010. Quinn was troubled by the state's fiscal problems as well as ethics complaints about an anti-violence grant program that some believed was actually a political slush fund; tellingly, a September 2014 Chicago Tribune poll found Quinn's approval at 36 percent.[8] Nonetheless, Quinn's campaign attempted to use the same strategy Obama employed against Mitt Romney in the 2012 presidential campaign, attacking Rauner as a wealthy individual who had done little to actually create jobs. Rauner, a private equity investor who earned over $60 million in 2013, opposed the state referendum that would raise the minimum wage (it passed on November 4), feeding into Quinn's portrayal.[9] Polls found Quinn had seemingly recovered his footing by the early fall, making the race neck and neck. But Rauner proved too much for the damaged Quinn, winning by about four points.

Among the *Crystal Ball's* "leans" contests, polling suggested that Republican incumbents in Florida, Georgia, Kansas, Maine, Michigan, and Wisconsin were all in very close races. But while some only squeaked by, all six incumbents won reelection, holding the line for Republicans in some states where Democrats tend to be stronger (e.g., Maine, Michigan), as well as in states where the GOP has no business losing (e.g., Georgia, Kansas).

A brutal bout took place in Florida between Republican Governor Rick Scott and ex-Governor Charlie Crist, a former Republican running as the Democratic nominee. For example, Scott attempted to connect Crist to a Ponzi-scheme criminal, while Crist ran ads claiming Scott vetoed funding for rape crisis centers. Both charges were shot down by *PolitiFact Florida*.[10] Perhaps reflecting the ugliness of the campaign, each candidate was underwater in favorability heading into Election Day: The last Quinnipiac University poll of the race found both had unfavorable ratings seven points higher than their favorables.[11] The race also proved to be the most expensive gubernatorial contest in Florida history, with campaign spending totaling at least $150 million. Scott and groups supporting him accounted for about two-thirds of that sum, an edge that may have made just enough difference for the incumbent in the end.[12] Going into Election Day, Crist led by only a few tenths of a point in both the *HuffPost* Pollster and *RealClearPolitics* poll averages.[13] In a coin-flip race, Scott eked out a win by 1.1 points, the closest call for any incumbent who survived in 2014.

The grandson of former President Jimmy Carter, Democratic state Senator Jason Carter, took on Republican Governor Nathan Deal in the Georgia gubernatorial race. Although Georgia has been a reliably Republican state for some time in top-level statewide elections (a Democrat last won a Senate or gubernatorial race in Georgia in 2000), Deal had experienced a fair bit of turbulence during the election year. First, a winter storm hit the southeast in January 2014, causing chaos on the highways around metropolitan Atlanta. Deal took a great deal of criticism for the state's ill preparedness.[14] Then came new developments in an ethics case that had plagued Deal since his 2010 gubernatorial campaign. A former ethics commission official launched a whistleblower lawsuit against the state, arguing she was forced out for overly pursuing the case, and that the governor's office had intimidated and threatened her agency.[15] Despite his apparent troubles, Deal defeated Carter by about eight points. In winning over 50 percent of the vote, the incumbent also avoided a runoff election that would have taken place in December, as Georgia law requires the winner to garner a majority of the vote.

Normally ruby-red Kansas proved to be surprisingly competitive in 2014, with its gubernatorial and Senate races both receiving heavy media coverage in the wake of tight pre-election polls. Republican Governor Sam Brownback had a controversial first term in office, creating a rift in the state GOP; as a result, the once-popular conservative only won 63 percent of the vote against a no-name opponent in the Republican primary. Brownback's time in office featured major tax and spending cuts, moves that became viewed by many as chief causes for a huge budget shortfall and a downgrade of the state's bond rating. His November opponent, Democratic state House Minority Leader Paul Davis, particularly attacked the incumbent for education spending cuts.[16] Heading into Election Day, Davis led Brownback by about two points in the polling averages.[17] But although Kansas Republicans didn't strongly back their standard bearer, Brownback received just enough support to hang on, defeating Davis by a little less than four points.

Known for his combative personality, Republican Governor Paul LePage of Maine was a top target for Democrats going into 2014. Elected in the 2010 Republican wave, LePage won only 38 percent of the vote but narrowly edged independent Eliot Cutler in a three-way race (the Democrat won 19 percent). Having seen LePage win in part because of a split field, in 2014 Democrats rallied behind Representative Mike Michaud, who represented the state's Second Congressional District and has a blue-collar background. LePage appeared very vulnerable because of his history of controversial remarks—LePage once called the Internal Revenue Service the "new Gestapo"—sub-40 percent approval ratings, and the nature of his 2010 win.[18] Moreover, polls suggested Cutler, who was running again, would not win nearly the same level of support as he did in 2010. But Michaud proved to be a mediocre campaigner, unable to seriously eat into LePage's support in rural and milltown communities in the interior of the state. LePage also avoided making serious gaffes in the closing months of the campaign while stressing a conservative social and economic message that turned out his base.[19] Although Cutler told his voters he couldn't win in a half-exit from the race right before the election, the move wasn't enough to help Michaud.[20] Confounding pundits who had left him for dead politically, LePage beat Michaud by about five points, 48.2 percent to 43.4 percent, with Cutler winning 8.4 percent.

In Michigan and Wisconsin, incumbent Republican Governors Rick Snyder and Scott Walker each faced close races in states that, at least in recent presidential elections, leaned toward Democrats. Both governors, particularly Walker, had drawn the ire of the left for going after laws that protected labor groups. Snyder had branded himself "One Tough Nerd" in 2010, when he first won, and he largely pursued a pragmatically conservative course during his time in office. But when he signed off on "right-to-work" legislation in late 2012, it set off a firestorm in a state with a long history of union strength in the automotive industry.[21] Walker caused even more controversy when he cut the benefits and collective bargaining power of state employees in 2011. The new law incited so much opposition that Walker wound up facing a recall election in 2012, which he won in a major defeat for labor groups.[22] Snyder and Walker both looked to be in danger at times during the fall campaign in 2014. In mid-September, Democrat Mark Schauer, a former U.S. House member, found himself in a near-tie with Snyder according to the *RealClearPolitics* average, perhaps as a result of Schauer's early advertising efforts, to which observers said the incumbent's campaign didn't react quickly.[23] In the Badger State, Democrat Mary Burke, a former executive with Trek Bicycle Corporation (also daughter of the company's founder), found herself holding a very slight lead over Walker in the *RealClearPolitics* average just a couple weeks before Election Day.[24] But on November 4, both incumbents won more comfortably than some anticipated. Snyder survived his state's sharper Democratic lean (Obama won the state by nearly ten points in 2012), while Walker again proved his electoral mettle, winning his third election in four years and positioning himself to potentially take a shot at the presidency in 2016.

The one GOP blemish among these very competitive races came in Alaska, where independent Bill Walker triumphed over Republican Governor Sean Parnell. The incumbent, who took over for ex-Governor Sarah Palin when she resigned in 2009 and won a full term in his own right in 2010, looked like a safe bet for reelection at the start of 2014. Walker, Parnell's 2010 GOP primary opponent, initially planned another primary challenge but opted to run as an independent instead. With Democrat Byron Mallott running as well, opposition to Parnell appeared to be split. But the race turned upside down when Walker and Mallott announced they were forming a unity ticket in September, with Mallott dropping to the lieutenant governor slot on the ballot.[25] With his opposition now unified, Parnell's troubles—a struggling economy in the wake of lower oil revenues, a $2 billion budget deficit, and a late-breaking scandal involving allegations of sexual assault and other misconduct in Alaska's National Guard—held him back.[26] Walker won by two points and became the country's lone independent governor.

Despite the generally favorable Republican climate, Democratic incumbents survived in Colorado, Connecticut, and New Hampshire. In the Centennial State, Democratic Governor John Hickenlooper faced criticism over his decision to grant a temporary reprieve to a man sentenced to death for murdering four people. The move was quite unpopular—a June 2013

Quinnipiac survey showed two-thirds of the public opposed it—and Republican nominee Bob Beauprez, a former congressman, went after "Hick" for it.[27] The Democratic brand in Colorado was also hampered by gun control measures that the legislature passed and the governor signed into law in 2013, which prompted a conservative recall effort that led to the defeat of two Democrats in the state senate.[28] But while Republicans managed to topple incumbent Democratic Senator Mark Udall in the state's concurrent Senate election, Hickenlooper held on by about three points.

The Connecticut race featured a rematch of the state's 2010 gubernatorial contest between now-Democratic Governor Dan Malloy and former Republican U.S. Ambassador Tom Foley. Malloy appeared vulnerable from day one, never reaching 50 percent approval and struggling with a budget gap that led to a $1.5 billion tax hike early in his tenure.[29] Foley excoriated the incumbent's fiscal record and the increased taxes. But Foley may have hurt himself by criticizing gun control legislation passed after the Sandy Hook tragedy. Meanwhile, Malloy touted his liberal record on gun control and others, keeping him afloat in the fairly Democratic Nutmeg State.[30] In the end, the incumbent won by 2.6 points, a slightly more comfortable victory than his 0.6-point win in 2010.

Elsewhere in the northeast, Democratic Governor Maggie Hassan's race against Republican businessman Walt Havenstein in New Hampshire remained under the national radar until just a few weeks out. New Hampshire is one of the only two states (along with Vermont) that has two-year terms for governor, meaning Hassan had to run again after winning her first term in 2012. Though the race narrowed in the politically fickle Granite State, Hassan had history on her side: Only once since the 1920s had a first-term governor who sought reelection failed to succeed, the single case being Republican Craig Benson, who lost in 2004.[31] Hassan avoided Benson's fate, winning by about five points to earn a second term. In nearby Rhode Island, Democratic state Treasurer Gina Raimondo held onto the seat of retiring Governor Lincoln Chafee, who had entered office in 2010 as an independent before becoming a Democrat (he had also previously served as a Republican in the U.S. Senate). Raimondo won a sharply divided primary and never managed to unify Democrats behind her, in part because her efforts to reform the state pension program alienated public unions and other parts of the left.[32] Republican Allan Fung, the mayor of Cranston, made a push despite being vastly outspent by around a twelve-to-one margin and nearly pulled off a win in one of the most Democratic states in the country.[33] Perhaps throwing a wrench into Fung's upset hopes was the performance of Moderate Party nominee Bob Healey, who amazingly spent just $35 in his campaign but garnered a little over 21 percent of the vote.[34] Raimondo only won about 41 percent but still beat Fung by 4.5 points.

ADDITIONAL RACES OF NOTE

Some additional contests, all of which were viewed by the *Crystal Ball* as "likely" or "safe" for one party or the other, also merit examination, particularly the other two party takeovers that occurred in Arkansas and Pennsylvania. The election results for the races explored in this section are shown in Table 5.4.

Republicans captured the Arkansas governorship for only the fourth time since the end of Reconstruction, as former Republican Representative Asa Hutchinson defeated fellow ex-Representative Mike Ross, a Democrat, to win the open-seat contest to succeed term-limited Democratic Governor Mike Beebe. With the president about as unpopular in Arkansas as anywhere in the country, Ross faced a tough task from the get-go. Although the popular Beebe campaigned with his fellow Democrat, the increasingly Republican state soundly rejected the "D" label on Election Day—the GOP claimed every statewide office and every seat in the U.S. House in the Razorback State. Hutchinson led almost all polling throughout the campaign and won by about fourteen points.[35]

Democrats' brightest spot was undoubtedly in Pennsylvania, where Republican Governor Tom Corbett started the cycle as the most endangered incumbent, and at no point during the campaign did he look capable of making a comeback. Corbett's gaffes—for instance, comparing gay marriage to incest—and his firmly conservative positions in a state that Democrats have won in six straight presidential elections imperiled him. The incumbent also wasn't helped by problems associated with his actions during the investigation of the Penn State child molestation case, which began while

Table 5.4. Election Results in the Additional Races of Note

State	Winner	Votes	%	Main Opponent	Votes	%	Margin
AR	Asa Hutchinson (R)	470,429	55.4	Mike Ross (D)	352,115	41.5	13.9
HI	David Ige (D)	181,106	49.5	Duke Aiona (R)	135,775	37.1	12.4
ID	Butch Otter (R)*	235,405	53.5	A.J. Balukoff (D)	169,556	38.6	15.0
NV	Brian Sandoval (R)*	386,340	70.6	Bob Goodman (D)	130,722	23.9	46.7
NY	Andrew Cuomo (D)*	2,069,480	54.2	Rob Astorino (R)	1,536,879	40.2	13.9
OH	John Kasich (R)*	1,944,848	63.6	Ed FitzGerald (D)	1,009,359	33.0	30.6
OR	John Kitzhaber (D)*	733,230	49.9	Dennis Richardson (R)	648,542	44.1	5.8
PA	Tom Wolf (D)	1,920,355	54.9	Tom Corbett (R)*	1,575,511	45.1	9.9
TX	Greg Abbott (R)	2,796,274	59.2	Wendy Davis (D)	1,835,896	38.8	20.3
VT	Peter Shumlin (D)*†	89,509	46.4	Scott Milne (R)	87,075	45.1	1.3

Notes: *Signifies an incumbent. †Signifies that Shumlin was reelected by the Vermont legislature because no candidate received a majority of the vote. Percentages and margins are rounded.
Sources: Official state election results.

he was attorney general and continued into the early years of his gubernatorial tenure. Polls found that all of the potential Democratic challengers could potentially beat Corbett, which naturally attracted a large number of Democrats to the primary field.[36] In the end, businessman Tom Wolf won the Democratic nomination in a surprisingly easy fashion and defeated Corbett by about ten points in November. Corbett's defeat ended a long practice in the Keystone State of the two major parties trading off the governor's mansion every eight years, stretching back to the 1950s.[37]

In Hawaii, Democratic Governor Neil Abercrombie was the only incumbent running for reelection who failed to make it to November. Not only did he lose renomination in the Democratic primary to state Senator David Ige, Abercrombie did so in record-breaking fashion, losing by 36.1 points, the largest primary defeat ever for an incumbent governor seeking renomination.[38] Had Abercrombie won renomination, Republicans might have been able to reclaim the Aloha State governorship through the able candidacy of their nominee, former Lieutenant Governor Duke Aiona, and the potential party-splitting mischief of Mufi Hannemann, a Democrat-turned-independent who might have attracted disaffected Democrats. But Ige's presence on the ballot in place of Abercrombie removed that danger, and the newcomer won by twelve points.

The Idaho gubernatorial race grabbed national attention when two quirky, long-shot candidates included in the lone GOP primary debate acted up on stage. Republican Governor Bruce Otter, who insisted on their inclusion, likely wanted them to distract from his threatened position in a heated race with state Senator Russ Fulcher, a Tea Party candidate running to his right, and they didn't disappoint, turning the event into a circus.[39] Otter went on to win renomination with just 51 percent, allowing him to carry on his quest for a third term in Boise. He then defeated conservative Democrat A.J. Balukoff by 15 points in November.

Some might compare the 2014 election in Nevada to the famous Battle of Cannae, as Silver State Republicans wiped out Democrats in the same manner Hannibal's Carthaginians crushed the Romans. But instead of their army being annihilated, the Democrats just didn't really show up for the battle. The foremost problem for Democrats was popular Republican Governor Brian Sandoval, who had a job approval rating of 68 percent in October 2013. The second was getting anyone to run against him.[40] In the end, Democrats were left with no first-, second-, or even third-tier candidate. Strikingly, the Nevada-only option "None of these candidates" beat out the eight no-namers in the Democratic primary field. The second-place finisher, Bob Goodman, served as the party's nominee and went on to be trounced: Sandoval topped 70 percent, and the absence of a viable Democrat at the top of the ticket coupled with the pro-GOP environment caused Democrats to lose across the state as the party provided essentially no reason for its voters to show up.

New York Governor Andrew Cuomo, a Democrat, may have won the battle, but he almost certainly lost the war, if he hoped a strong 2014 win might position him for a 2016 presidential run. Cuomo defeated Republican Westchester County Executive Rob Astorino by 14 points, but alienated parts of the Democratic base along the way. Whether it was engineering deals with Republicans at the expense of Democrats in the state senate or creating a new women's party with the possible intention of derailing the liberal Working Family's Party, Cuomo made enemies on the left.[41] Tellingly, the Green Party nominee won almost 5 percent of the statewide vote and performed particularly well in liberal strongholds like Tompkins County (the home of Ithaca). With progressives angry at him, Cuomo would have trouble making a credible run for the presidency.

Unlike Cuomo, Ohio Republican Governor John Kasich's 2014 win strengthened his position as a possible dark horse establishment contender in the 2016 Republican field. Kasich decisively defeated Democratic Cuyahoga County Executive Ed FitzGerald by nearly 31 points, even winning FitzGerald's home county, a Democratic stronghold. After struggling to fundraise, FitzGerald's entire campaign fell apart in August 2014, precipitated by a bizarre report that in 2012 he was found in a parked car with a woman who wasn't his wife, followed by another strange revelation that he didn't have a driver's license. It's little wonder his top aides quit on him.[42] Like in Nevada, the lack of a top gubernatorial candidate led to poor Democratic turnout, dooming the party's other candidates down the ballot.

Speaking of odd developments, Democratic Governor John Kitzhaber always looked likely to win a fourth nonconsecutive term in Oregon, but events conspired to make the race more interesting. First, and more relevant to policy, the state's health care exchange as a part of Obamacare, Cover Oregon, proved to be an even worse debacle than the one in Maryland. Unlike Maryland, Oregon decided not to salvage it after the state found it would be far cheaper to move into the federal exchange than to fix the state-run portal. The failed exchange provided campaign fodder for Kitzhaber's opponent, Republican state Representative Dennis Richardson.[43] Then revelations about Kitzhaber's fiancée, Cylvia Hayes, took the race in a bizarre direction. It came to light that Hayes had at one time planned a marijuana farm and had once accepted payment to marry an Ethiopian to get the immigrant a green card. On top of this, ethics questions arose over whether Hayes had used her "First Lady" title for personal benefit in her consulting business.[44] Hayes's past may not have impacted the election a great deal—Kitzhaber won about the same percentage of the vote (49.8 percent) as he did in 2010 (49.3 percent)—but it surely earned the otherwise sleepy race plenty of attention.

Texas grabbed the spotlight in June 2013 when state Senator Wendy Davis, a Democrat, led a thirteen-hour-long filibuster of an anti-abortion bill in the state senate. The bill would later pass, but Davis became the new Democratic darling in the media and the party.[45] She parlayed this new-found fame into her party's nomination against Republican state Attorney General Greg Abbott in the race to succeed retiring Republican Governor Rick Perry, leading to breathless speculation that Democrats might make a play in the conservative Lone Star State. But Abbott, wheelchair-bound following a freak accident in the 1980s, built a campaign on his strong conservative credentials—he once defended Texas's right to keep a monument to the Ten Commandments on state grounds in front of the U.S. Supreme Court—to easily defeat Davis by 20 points. On top of Abbott's strengths, which has led some observers to see him as a future national candidate, Davis's campaign struggled with inconsistent messaging and stirred controversy when it ran an ad attacking Abbott on tort reform that used the image of an empty wheelchair.[46] The loss for Democrats surely hindered the progress of Battleground Texas, an organization working to make Texas more competitive for Democrats in future elections.[47]

Lastly, the Vermont election proved to be much closer than anyone fore-saw. Governor Peter Shumlin, the head of the Democratic Governors Association, found himself up by only 1.3 points on unheralded Republican businessman Scott Milne, and short of a majority of the vote. In Vermont, if no candidate wins a majority, the legislature elects the winner. Shumlin was saved by the Democratic majority in the Green Mountain State legislature, which duly reelected him in January 2015. But he certainly suffered a close call for the second time—Shumlin was originally elected in 2010 via the legislature as well.

OTHER GUBERNATORIAL ELECTIONS

Table 5.5 lays out the election data in the remaining twelve gubernatorial contests that have not been covered. In each of the dozen races, the view that the incumbent party would remain in power (whether the seat was open or not) was never really in doubt. On the Republican side, the incumbent winners were Governors Robert Bentley of Alabama, Terry Branstad of Iowa, Susana Martinez of New Mexico, Mary Fallin of Oklahoma, Nikki Haley of South Carolina, Dennis Daugaard of South Dakota, Bill Haslam of Tennessee, and Matt Mead of Wyoming. Branstad's victory means he will begin a sixth term in office; should he serve at least a year of it, he will become the long-serving governor in U.S. history.[48] Victories by Martinez and Haley will likely keep them in the picture as possible GOP vice presidential candidates in 2016. Meanwhile, newly elected Republican Governors Doug Ducey of Arizona and Pete Ricketts of Nebraska easily won open-seat contests in their states after advancing from competitive primaries. On the Democratic side, California Governor Jerry Brown won a fourth nonconsecutive term by 20 points, setting him up to lead the state until he's eighty years old, and Governor Mark Dayton of Minnesota turned back Republican Jeff Johnson by a little less than six points in a race that was never going to be a blowout but lacked suspense.

2014 STATE LEGISLATIVE ELECTIONS SUMMARY

At the start of 2014, Republicans effectively controlled fifty-nine of the country's ninety-eight partisan legislative chambers (Nebraska has a unicameral and nonpartisan body), with the GOP holding two chambers via coalitions with independent Democrats in the New York and Washington state senates. As in most electoral categories, the November 4 results only improved the GOP's standing in the state legislatures: Republicans added nine chambers to their total and took outright control of the New York and Washington state senates, increasing their total edge to sixty-eight chambers compared to the Democrats' thirty. The GOP also claimed control of both chambers in thirty legislatures, matching their previous high following the 1920 election. For all their success, Republicans will have unified control (both legislatures and the governorship) of the same number of state governments (twenty-three) as they did prior to the election, as many of their gubernatorial and legislative takeovers created divided governments in states such as Massachusetts and Minnesota. In fact, the number of divided governments increased from thirteen to nineteen. Adding to Democrats'

Table 5.5. Election Results in Other Gubernatorial Elections

State	Winner	Votes	%	Main Opponent	Votes	%	Margin
AL	Robert Bentley (R)*	750,231	63.6	Parker Griffith (D)	427,787	36.2	27.3
AZ	Doug Ducey (R)	805,062	53.4	Fred DuVal (D)	626,921	41.5	11.8
CA	Jerry Brown (D)*	4,388,368	60.0	Neel Kashkari (R)	2,929,213	40.0	19.9
IA	Terry Branstad (R)*	666,023	59.0	Jack Hatch (D)	420,778	37.3	21.7
MN	Mark Dayton (D)*	989,113	50.1	Jeff Johnson (R)	879,257	44.5	5.6
NE	Pete Ricketts (R)	308,751	57.2	Chuck Hassebrook (D)	211,905	39.2	17.9
NM	Susana Martinez (R)*	293,443	57.2	Gary King (D)	219,362	42.8	14.4
OK	Mary Fallin (R)*	460,298	55.8	Joe Dorman (D)	338,239	41.0	14.8
SC	Nikki Haley (R)*	696,645	55.9	Vincent Sheheen (D)	516,166	41.4	14.5
SD	Dennis Daugaard (R)*	195,477	70.5	Susan Wismer (D)	70,549	25.4	45.0
TN	Bill Haslam (R)*	951,796	70.3	Charlie Brown (D)	309,237	22.8	47.5
WY	Matt Mead (R)*	99,700	59.4	Pete Gosar (D)	45,752	27.3	32.1

Notes: *Signifies an incumbent.
Sources: Official state election results.

woes, states where they will hold unified control fell from thirteen to only seven.[49] Republican gains in state legislatures, in conjunction with their additional governorships and the gridlock in Washington, will have major policy implications across the country. This is particularly true in states where the GOP now has unified control, such as Nevada, and in states where Republicans markedly improved their standing by gaining one or both legislative chambers, such as West Virginia. In the Mountain State, Republicans gained full control of the legislature for the first time in eight decades.[50]

2015–2016 OUTLOOK

Just eleven states will choose governors in 2016 versus thirty-six in 2014, with New Hampshire and Vermont appearing in both, while three states will pick a new executive in 2015. The state of play moving forward finds the GOP positioned to add further governorships during the 2015–2016 cycle in part because three red states (Kentucky, Missouri, and West Virginia) have Democratic incumbents who are term limited, producing open-seat races in states where the GOP may have a natural advantage, particularly in the Age of Obama.

The 2015 trio features states that are reliably Republican in many respects, and Louisiana and Mississippi are likely to remain in GOP hands. Kentucky will probably feature a competitive contest, but after eight years of Democratic rule in the Bluegrass State, Republicans may benefit from a "time for change" feeling among the electorate, though Democrats did surprisingly well in the 2014 Kentucky legislative elections and remain strong on the state level despite the state's federal Republican leanings.

With Democratic Governor Earl Ray Tomblin term limited, Republicans in West Virginia may be able to position themselves to capture the governorship in 2016, potentially the cherry on top of their 2014 legislative gains. Much will depend on Democratic Senator Joe Manchin: Despite West Virginia's Republican turn, he has remained a force, easily winning his 2012 Senate race. Now in the minority in the Senate, Manchin is considering another run for governor.[51] If he runs, Manchin may be tough to beat; if he doesn't, the GOP will have better odds at winning back the governorship for the first time since former Republican Governor Cecil Underwood lost reelection in 2000.

In recent years, Missouri has become more Republican outside of the metropolitan areas of Kansas City and St. Louis, and after eight years of term-limited Democratic Governor Jay Nixon ruling the roost, Republicans may be natural favorites in what has become something of a center-right state. On the GOP side, former state House Speaker Catherine Hanaway has announced her candidacy, but given the state's rightward shift, many other Republicans are also eyeing the open-seat race. After some speculation, Democratic Senator Claire McCaskill announced in mid-January 2015 that she wouldn't seek the Show Me State governorship, leaving state Attorney General Chris Koster as probably the strongest potential Democratic recruit.

In Big Sky Country, Democratic Governor Steve Bullock will start his reelection run as a slight favorite, though Montana's conservative leanings won't make it easy for him. In New Hampshire, Democratic Governor Maggie Hassan could run for governor again or challenge Republican Senator Kelly Ayotte in the state's 2016 Senate contest. An open-seat gubernatorial race in the Granite State would almost certainly start as a toss-up, but Hassan will be at least a small favorite if she runs again. Next door, in Vermont, it's plausible that Republicans could make a play for the Green Mountain State governorship. Shumlin, should he run again, or another Democrat would benefit from the 2016 presidential race in deep blue Vermont, but Milne nearly pulled off a shocking upset in 2014 and might want to take another shot. Lieutenant Governor Phil Scott, the only elected statewide Republican, easily won reelection in 2014 and could also be a strong choice.

Republican Indiana Governor Mike Pence would be a safe bet to win reelection, but whether or not he will decide to stay in Indianapolis remains up in the air. Pence might seek the presidency, and he could be a strong player in the GOP field if he does. Should Pence run for the White House, an open-seat race in Indiana would probably be competitive, just as it was in 2012 when Pence defeated Democratic former state House Speaker John Gregg by only three percentage points. Gregg may run again, especially if Pence isn't in the way.

Democrats may only be on the offensive in North Carolina, where Republican Governor Pat McCrory's controversial first term leaves his future somewhat in doubt. State Attorney General Roy Cooper appears to be the likely Democratic nominee, and he's been gearing up to take on McCrory since 2013.[52] With the Tar Heel State's slight Republican lean and his incumbency, McCrory starts as a narrow favorite. Nonetheless, North Carolina will be a battleground state in 2016, and this contest may wind up being the most hard-fought and costly gubernatorial race of the cycle.

As for the unmentioned races, Democrats will start as strong favorites in Delaware and Washington, while Republicans will be good bets to hold onto North Dakota and Utah.

Should Republicans win the Kentucky race in 2015, they will tie their post–World War II high for total governorships controlled (thirty-two).

With the Missouri and West Virginia seats to target in 2016, it's very possible that the GOP will soon set a new high-water mark for total governorships held since 1946. Having suffered gubernatorial struggles throughout Obama's presidency, Democrats may be despondent to find themselves on the defensive yet again. Given the historical success of the out-of-White-House party in gaining governorships, the only cure for what ails Democrats may be a Republican presidency.

NOTES

1. "Maryland Governor Marvin Mandel," *National Governors Association,* accessed December 9, 2014, http://nga.org/cms/sites/NGA/home/governors/past -governors-bios/page_maryland/col2-content/main-content-list/title_mandel_mar vin.html.

2. John Wagner and Peyton Craighill, "As O'Malley's Approval Rating Falls, Md. Voters Not Confident in His Presidential Bid," *Washington Post,* October 11, 2014, accessed December 9, 2014, http://www.washingtonpost.com/local/md-politics/as -omalleys-approval-rating-falls-md-voters-not-confident-in-his-presidential-bid/ 2014/10/11/e48aebd2-5096-11e4-8c24-487e92bc997b_story.html; John Wagner, "Anthony Brown's Loss Will Complicate Gov. Martin O'Malley's Presidential Hopes," *Washington Post,* November 10, 2014 accessed, December 9, 2014, http:// www.washingtonpost.com/local/md-politics/anthony-browns-loss-will-complicate -gov-martin-omalleys-presidential-hopes/2014/11/10/1a753e16-6823-11e4-b053 -65cea7903f2e_story.html; "Maryland Officials Were Warned for a Year Of Problems with Online Health-Insurance Site," *Washington Post,* January 11, 2014, accessed December 9, 2014, http://www.washingtonpost.com/local/maryland-news /maryland-officials-were-warned-for-a-year-of-problems-with-online-health-insu rance-site/2014/01/11/f094ad94-6a98-11e3-8b5b-a77187b716a3_story.html.

3. "Maryland Governor—Hogan vs. Brown," *RealClearPolitics,* accessed December 9, 2014, http://www.realclearpolitics.com/epolls/2014/governor/md/maryland _governor_hogan_vs_brown-5098.html.

4. Nora Caplan-Bricker, "The Rehabilitation of Martha Coakley," *National Journal,* July 19, 2014, accessed December 9, 2014, http://www.nationaljournal.com/ magazine/the-rehabilitation-of-martha-coakley-20140718.

5. Kyle Cheney, "2014 Primary Election: Martha Coakley Survives Massachusetts Democratic Primary," *Politico,* September 9, 2014, accessed December 9, 2014, http://www.politico.com/story/2014/09/2014-primary-election-martha-coakley -massachusetts-110793.html.

6. Scot Lehigh, "Assessing Martha Coakley's Failed Campaign," *Boston Globe,* November 5, 2014, accessed December 9, 2014, http://www.bostonglobe.com/ opinion/2014/11/05/assessing-martha-coakley-failed-campaign/J0vBhufAf97wce MOJzWVXP/story.html.

7. Paul McMorrow, "GOP Super PAC Money Swamps Governor's Race," *CommonWealth Magazine*, November 3, 2014, accessed December 9, 2014, http://www .commonwealthmagazine.org/News-and-Features/Online-exclusives/2014/Fall/02 0-GOP-super-PAC-money-swamps-governors-race.aspx.

8. Rick Pearson, "Quinn Captures Lead, Not Hearts, Poll Finds," *Chicago Tribune*, September 13, 2014, accessed December 9, 2014, http://www.chicagotribune .com/news/ct-illinois-governor-race-met-0914-20140913-story.html.

9. Aamer Madhani, "Ill. Governor Quinn Finally Concedes Race to Rauner," *USA Today*, November 5, 2014, accessed December 9, 2014, http://www.usatoday .com/story/news/politics/2014/11/05/illinois-quinn-concedes-rauner-governor/ 18551491/.

10. Amy Sherman, "In Ad to Promote Rick Scott, Rothstein Investor Says He Was 'Swindled' by Charlie Crist," *PolitiFact Florida*, September 22, 2014, accessed December 9, 2014, http://www.politifact.com/florida/statements/2014/sep/22/ rick-scott/ad-promote-rick-scott-rothstein-investor-says-he-w/; Amy Sherman, "Charlie Crist Attacks Rick Scott's Rape Crisis Center Veto," *PolitiFact Florida*, October 28, 2014, accessed December 9, 2014, http://www.politifact.com/florida/state ments/2014/oct/28/charlie-crist/charlie-crist-attacks-rick-scotts-rape-crisis-cent/.

11. "Crist 42%, Scott 41% in Florida Gov Race, Quinnipiac University Poll Finds; Wyllie's 7% and 9% Undecided Are Keys to Outcome," Quinnipiac University Poll, November 3, 2014, accessed December 9, 2014, http://www.quinnipiac.edu/news -and-events/quinnipiac-university-poll/florida/release-detail?ReleaseID=2109.

12. "$150M Florida Governor's Race Smashes Records," *Tampa Bay Business Journal*, November 3, 2014, accessed December 9, 2014, http://www.bizjournals.com/ tampabay/blog/morning-edition/2014/11/150m-florida-governor-s-race-smashes -records.html.

13. "2014 Florida Governor: Scott vs. Crist," *Huff Post* Pollster, accessed December 9, 2014, http://elections.huffingtonpost.com/pollster/2014-florida-governor -scott-vs-crist; "Florida Governor—Scott vs. Crist vs. Wyllie," *RealClearPolitics*, accessed December 9, 2014, http://www.realclearpolitics.com/epolls/2014/gover nor/fl/florida_governor_scott_vs_crist_vs_wyllie-5147.html.

14. "Georgia Gov. Nathan Deal Takes Blame for Poor Storm Preparations," *Huffington Post (AP)*, January 30, 2014, accessed December 9, 2014, http:// www.huffingtonpost.com/2014/01/30/georgia-gov-nathan-deal-snow-storm_n_46 97537.html.

15. Larry Copeland, "New Ethics Memo Surfaces, Roiling Ga. Governor's Race," *USA Today*, July 16, 2014, accessed December 9, 2014, http://www.usatoday.com/ story/news/nation/2014/07/16/new-ethics-allegations-in-ga-govs-race/12738699/; "Jury Awards $700K to Ex Ethics Chief," *Atlanta Journal-Constitution*, April 4, 2014, accessed December 9, 2014, http://www.myajc.com/news/news/state-regional-govt -politics/state-ethics-commission-trial-in-hands-of-jury/nfR2g/#344d1c18.257099 .735429.

16. Dan Balz, "Will Conservative Kansas Vote Out Its Conservative Governor, Sam Brownback?" *Washington Post*, October 27, 2014, accessed December 9, 2014, http://www.washingtonpost.com/politics/will-conservative-kansas-vote-out-its-con

servative-governor-sam-brownback-/2014/10/27/c738247c-5dfd-11e4-9f3a-7e287 99e0549_story.html.

17. "2014 Kansas Governor: Brownback vs. Davis," *Huff Post* Pollster, accessed December 9, 2014, http://elections.huffingtonpost.com/pollster/2014-kansas-gov ernor-brownback-vs-davis; "Kansas Governor—Brownback vs. Davis," *RealClear-Politics*, accessed December 9, 2014, http://www.realclearpolitics.com/epolls/2014/ governor/ks/kansas_governor_brownback_vs_davis-4146.html.

18. Steve Mistler, "LePage Calls IRS the 'New Gestapo,'" *Portland Press Herald*, July 7, 2012, accessed December 9, 2014, http://www.pressherald.com/2012/07/ 07/governor-says-irs-new-gestapo-in-radio-address/.

19. Colin Woodard, "How Did America's Craziest Governor Get Reelected?" *Politico Magazine*, November 5, 2014, accessed December 9, 2014, http://www.poli tico.com/magazine/story/2014/11/paul-lepage-craziest-governor-reelection-112583 .html.

20. Mario Moretto, "Cutler Says Victory Is 'Long Shot,' Tells Supporters to Vote Accordingly," *Bangor Daily News*, October 29, 2014, accessed December 9, 2014, https://bangordailynews.com/2014/10/29/politics/cutler-to-make-election-announ cement-at-impromptu-news-conference-wednesday-morning/.

21. Amanda Terkel, "Rick Snyder: Right to Work Bills Signed into Law in Michi-gan," *Huffington Post*, December 11, 2012, accessed December 9, 2014, http:// www.huffingtonpost.com/2012/12/11/rick-snyder-right-to-work_n_2280050.html.

22. Timothy Noah, "Walker Victory Humiliates Labor," *Politico*, November 5, 2014, accessed December 9, 2014, http://www.politico.com/story/2014/11/walker -victory-humiliates-labor-112562.html.

23. "Michigan Governor—Snyder vs. Schauer," *RealClearPolitics*, accessed De-cember 9, 2014, http://www.realclearpolitics.com/epolls/2014/governor/mi/mi chigan_governor_snyder_vs_schauer-3506.html; Molly Ball, "From 'One Tough Nerd' to Embattled Governor," *The Atlantic*, October 17, 2014, accessed December 9, 2014, http://www.theatlantic.com/politics/archive/2014/10/from-one-tough -nerd-to-embattled-governor/381453/.

24. "Wisconsin Governor—Walker vs. Burke," *RealClearPolitics*, accessed Decem-ber 9, 2014, http://www.realclearpolitics.com/epolls/2014/governor/wi/wisconsin _governor_walker_vs_burke-4099.html.

25. "'Unity Ticket Forms in Alaska Gubernatorial Race," *Washington Times*, Sep-tember 2, 2014, accessed December 10, 2014, http://www.washingtontimes.com/ news/2014/sep/2/unity-ticket-forms-in-alaska-gubernatorial-race/.

26. Alex DeMarban, "Alaska's Governor's Race: Parnell Trailed Walker All Night," *Alaska Dispatch News*, November 4, 2014, accessed December 10, 2014, http:// www.adn.com/article/20141104/alaska-governors-race-parnell-trailed-walker-all -night.

27. Kurtis Lee, "Poll: Coloradans Support Death Penalty, Disapprove of Legisla-ture," *Denver Post*, June 6, 2013, accessed December 9, 2014, http://www.denver post.com/ci_23450964/poll-coloradans-back-death-penalty-disapprove-dunlap-re prieve.

28. David Freedlander, "Why Is Colorado's Governor Now Bashing His Own Gun-Control Laws?" *The Daily Beast*, June 20, 2014, accessed December 9, 2014,

http://www.thedailybeast.com/articles/2014/06/20/why-is-colorado-s-governor
-now-bashing-his-own-gun-control-laws.html.

29. Joseph de Avila, "Possible Connecticut Race a Dead Heat, New Poll Shows," *Wall Street Journal*, March 5, 2014, accessed December 9, 2014, http://www.wsj
.com/articles/SB10001424052702304815004579419111173348896.

30. David Freedlander, "Connecticut Governor Dan Malloy to Democrats: Grow a Pair," *The Daily Beast*, November 19, 2014, accessed December 9, 2014, http://
www.thedailybeast.com/articles/2014/11/19/connecticut-governor-dan-malloy-to
-democrats-grow-a-pair.html.

31. Sarah Schweitzer, "Defeated after 1 Term, N.H. Governor Fades Out," *Boston Globe*, November 4, 2004, accessed December 9, 2014, http://www.boston.com/
news/politics/governors/articles/2004/11/04/defeated_after_1_term_nh_governor
_fades_out/.

32. Katharine Seelye, "Defying Unions, Democrat Gina M. Raimondo Vies to Become Rhode Island's First Female Governor," *New York Times*, September 14, 2014, accessed December 10, 2014, http://www.nytimes.com/2014/09/15/us/defy
ing-unions-democrat-gina-m-raimondo-vies-to-become-rhode-islands-first-female
-governor.html.

33. Ted Nesi, "RI GOP Got Outspent More Than 12-to-1 in Fall Campaign," WPRI, December 3, 2014, accessed December 10, 2014, http://wpri.com/2014/12/
03/ri-gop-outspent-by-more-than-1m-in-fall-campaign/.

34. Ted Nesi, "Analysis: 18 Takeaways from the 2014 Election in RI," WPRI, November 6, 2014, accessed December 10, 2014, http://wpri.com/2014/11/05/18
-key-takeaways-from-the-2014-election-in-ri/.

35. "Arkansas Governor—Hutchinson vs. Ross," *RealClearPolitics*, accessed December 10, 2014, http://www.realclearpolitics.com/epolls/2014/governor/ar/arkan
sas _governor_hutchinson_vs_ross-3726.html.

36. "Why Is Pennsylvania's Governor So Incredibly Unpopular?" *The Wire*, November 26, 2013, accessed December 10, 2014, http://www.thewire.com/poli
tics/2013/11/why-pennsylvania-hates-its-governor/355550/; "Penn State Alumni Resentment Hangs Over Corbett," *Philadelphia Inquirer*, June 26, 2014, accessed December 10, 2014, http://articles.philly.com/2014-06-26/news/50859015_1_tom
-corbett-kathleen-kane-jerry-sandusky.

37. *CQ Guide to U.S. Elections*, vol. ii, 6th ed. (Washington: CQ Press, 2010), 1588.

38. Geoffrey Skelley, "Abercrombie Makes History the Wrong Way," *Sabato's Crystal Ball*, August 12, 2014, http://www.centerforpolitics.org/crystalball/articles/
abercrombie-makes-history-the-wrong-way/.

39. Tim Murphy, "The Idaho GOP Gubernatorial Debate Was Total Chaos," *Mother Jones*, May 15, 2014, accessed December 9, 2014, http://www.motherjones
.com/mojo/2014/05/idaho-gubernatorial-debate-otter-fulcher-brown-bayes.

40. Jon Ralston, "Poll: Two Most Popular Things in Nevada Are Margin Tax and Gov. Sunny," *Ralston Reports*, October 8, 2013, accessed December 10, 2014, https://
www.ralstonreports.com/blog/poll-two-most-popular-things-nevada-are-margin
-tax-and-gov-sunny.

41. Blake Zeff, "Another Cuomo Noninterference Story Falls Apart," *Capital*, September 2, 2014, accessed December 10, 2014, http://www.capitalnewyork.com/arti

cle/albany/2014/09/8551681/another-cuomo-noninterference-story-falls-apart; Liz Benjamin, "Why Is Andrew Cuomo Making a Women's Party?" *Capital*, Jul. 21, 2014, accessed December 10, 2014, http://www.capitalnewyork.com/article/al bany/2014/07/8549294/why-andrew-cuomo-making-womens-party.

42. Aaron Blake, "The Remarkable Implosion of Ed FitzGerald," *Washington Post*, August 26, 2014, accessed December 10, 2014, http://www.washingtonpost.com/blogs/the-fix/wp/2014/08/26/the-remarkable-implosion-of-ed-fitzgerald/.

43. Gosia Wozniacka, "Gov. Kitzhaber Recommends Dissolving Cover Oregon," *KGW (AP)*, September 5, 2014, accessed December 10, 2014, http://www.kgw.com/story/news/local/2014/09/05/kitzhaber-recommends-dissolving-cover-oregon/151 63795/.

44. Les Zaitz, "Cylvia Hayes' Astounding Month: Key Events as Her Past Unraveled," *The Oregonian*, October 29, 2014, accessed December 10, 2014, http://www.oregonlive.com/politics/index.ssf/2014/10/post_160.html.

45. Karen Tumulty and Morgan Smith, "Texas State Senator Wendy Davis Filibusters Her Way to Democratic Stardom," *Washington Post*, June 26, 2013, accessed December 10, 2014, http://www.washingtonpost.com/politics/texas-state-senator-wendy-davis-filibusters-her-way-to-democratic-stardom/2013/06/26/aace267c-de8 5-11e2-b2d4-ea6d8f477a01_story.html.

46. Reid Wilson, "The Likely Next Governor of Texas Is Full of Lone Star Swagger. Don't Be Surprised If He Runs for President," *Washington Post*, November 6, 2014, accessed December 10, 2014, http://www.washingtonpost.com/blogs/govbeat/wp/2014/10/30/the-likely-next-governor-of-texas-is-full-of-lone-star-swagger-dont-be-surprised-if-he-runs-for-president/; Jay Root, "Wendy Davis Lost Badly. Here's How It Happened." *Washington Post*, November 6, 2014, accessed December 10, 2014, http://www.washingtonpost.com/blogs/the-fix/wp/2014/11/06/wendy-davis-lost-really-badly-heres-how-it-happened/.

47. Amanda Marcotte, "What Happened to Wendy Davis?" *Slate*, November 6, 2014, accessed December 10, 2014, http://www.slate.com/blogs/xx_factor/2014/11/06/wendy_davis_lost_big_and_took_texas_democrats_with_her.html.

48. Jason Noble, "Terry Branstad Re-Elected to Historic Sixth Term," *Des Moines Register*, November 5, 2014, accessed December 10, 2014, http://www.desmoines register.com/story/news/elections/2014/11/04/iowa-governor-terry-branstad-reele cted-historic-win/18490693/.

49. "StateVote 2014: Pre-Election Analysis," *National Conference of State Legislatures*, November 6, 2014, accessed December 10, 2014, http://www.ncsl.org/re search/elections-and-campaigns/statevote-2014-elections.aspx; Tim Storey, "State-Vote 2014: Election Results," *National Conference of State Legislatures*, November 19, 2014, accessed December 10, 2014, http://www.ncsl.org/research/elections-and-campaigns/statevote-2014-post-election-analysis635508614.aspx; Tim Storey, "2014 State Legislative Election Wrap," *Sabato's Crystal Ball*, November 6, 2014, accessed December 10, 2014, http://www.centerforpolitics.org/crystalball/articles/2014-state-legislative-election-wrap/.

50. Jared Hunt, "Republicans Will Control Both Chambers of State Legislature," *Charleston Daily Mail*, November 5, 2014, accessed December 10, 2014, http://www.charlestondailymail.com/article/20141105/DM05/141109591/1276.

51. "Manchin May Consider Running for Governor in 2016," *The Register-Herald*, November 9, 2014, accessed December 10, 2014, http://www.register-herald.com/news/manchin-may-consider-running-for-governor-in/article_eb5b1936-dd24-560a-b865-f917dd23629d.html.

52. "Cooper Revs up NC Democrats for Gubernatorial Run," *WITN (AP)*, October 5, 2013, accessed December 10, 2014, http://www.witn.com/home/headlines/Cooper-Revs-Up-NC-Democrats-For-Gubernatorial-Run-226599171.html.

6

The Money Game

Emerging Campaign Finance Trends and Their Impact on 2014 and Beyond

Michael E. Toner and Karen E. Trainer

Continuing a consistent trend during the last decade of ever more expensive election cycles, the 2014 election was the costliest midterm election in history, with approximately $4 billion raised and spent overall in connection with federal elections nationwide.[1] To put that aggregate total in perspective, only $2.2 billion was spent overall on the 2002 midterm election, and only $2.8 billion was expended during the 2006 midterm election cycle.[2] The historic spending tally during the 2014 election cycle was fueled primarily by record-breaking fundraising by Super PACs and other outside groups, which played significant roles in federal races across the country. It was also aided by a favorable regulatory landscape and an important Supreme Court ruling that allows high net-worth individuals to contribute more funds in connection with federal elections than ever before.

Although unprecedented amounts of funds were raised and spent on the 2014 midterm election overall, it is important to note that not all sectors of the campaign finance system shared equally in the bounty. While Super PACs and outside groups spent record sums of money, total candidate fundraising actually declined in 2014 as compared with the 2012 and 2010 election cycles. Similarly, aggregate national political party fundraising was stagnant during the 2014 election cycle compared with the 2010 cycle, and national party receipts have actually declined in real dollars during the last decade when fundraising figures are adjusted for inflation. Increasingly, we are seeing a tale of two fundraising stories—one story for Super PACs and outside groups, which can accept unlimited contributions and which are thriving, and a very different story for candidates and parties, which labor under strict contribution limits and prohibitions. This growing imbalance in the campaign finance system will need to be watched very closely in the years ahead and could become even more pronounced in future election cycles.

AGGREGATE CONGRESSIONAL CANDIDATE FUNDRAISING DECLINED BY APPROXIMATELY $200 MILLION IN 2014 COMPARED WITH THE 2012 AND 2010 ELECTION CYCLES

U.S. House and U.S. Senate campaign committees collectively raised $1.63 billion in connection with the 2014 elections.[3] This aggregate total is 11 percent less than the $1.81 billion raised collectively by House and Senate campaigns in the 2012 elections, and 12.3 percent less than the $1.83 billion raised by House and Senate campaigns in the 2010 elections. Republican House and Senate candidates as a whole raised more than their Democratic opponents.

Table 6.1 compares House and Senate campaign fundraising totals in the 2014 election cycle with fundraising figures for the 2012 and 2010 election cycles.

Based upon spending only by campaign committees, the Kentucky Senate race involving Senator Mitch McConnell was the most expensive federal election in 2014, with $53.5 million spent by the various campaigns. Senate races in Georgia, Minnesota, Louisiana, and North Carolina were close behind with campaign spending totals in the $30 million to 45 million range.[4] These totals are well below the $77 million spent by campaigns on the 2012 Massachusetts Senate race, which holds the record for the most expensive Senate race in American history based solely on candidate committee spending.[5]

As Table 6.1 indicates, Republican Senate candidates as a whole outraised their Democratic opponents by 9.9 percent during the 2014 election cycle, and Republican House candidates collectively outraised their Democratic opponents by 29.6 percent. Although Republican House candidates as a whole outraised their Democratic counterparts, Democratic House candidates had a significant advantage in small-dollar fundraising. In September, a *National Journal* analysis showed that Democrats in competitive House races had raised $100,000 more in small-dollar contributions on average than their GOP opponents; overall, Democratic candidates had raised a total of $8.6 million in small-dollar donations as of that time, compared with only $4 million for Republican candidates.[6]

Table 6.1. Comparison of House and Senate Campaign Committee Fundraising[1]

2014			
Republican House Campaign Committees	$581 Million	Democratic House Campaign Committees	$448 Million
Republican Senate Campaign Committees	$310 Million	Democratic Senate Campaign Committees	$282 Million
Republican Campaign Total	$890 Million	Democratic Campaign Total	$730 Million
2014 Total Campaign Fundraising: $1.63 Billion			
2012			
Republican House Campaign Committees	$616 Million	Democratic House Campaign Committees	$486 Million
Republican Senate Campaign Committees	$377 Million	Democratic Senate Campaign Committees	$304 Million
Republican Campaign Total	$993 Million	Democratic Campaign Total	$789 Million
2012 Total Campaign Fundraising (Not Including Presidential Campaigns): $1.81 Billion			
2010			
Republican House Campaign Committees	$568 Million	Democratic House Campaign Committees	$516 Million
Republican Senate Campaign Committees	$414 Million	Democratic Senate Campaign Committees	$310 Million
Republican Campaign Total	$982 Million	Democratic Campaign Total	$826 Million
2010 Total Campaign Fundraising: $1.83 Billion			

Source: Center for Responsive Politics 2014 Election Overview (http://www.opensecrets.org/overview/index .php), 2012 Price of Admission (http://www.opensecrets.org/bigpicture/stats.php?display=T&type=A& cycle=2012), 2010 Price of Admission (http://www.opensecrets.org/bigpicture/stats.php?display=T&type =A&cycle=2010)

1. 2014 election cycle totals include fundraising data reported to the FEC through 11/24/14. Election cycle totals for 2012 and 2010 include fundraising data reported to the FEC through December 31 of the election year. Campaign fundraising totals for the cycle may not add up exactly because of additional fundraising by third-party candidates and because of rounding.

SUPER PACS AND OTHER OUTSIDE GROUPS
RAISED AND SPENT RECORD SUMS OF
MONEY FOR A MIDTERM ELECTION IN 2014

Passage of the McCain-Feingold campaign finance law, combined with recent court decisions permitting unlimited corporate, union, and individual contributions to finance independent expenditures sponsored by outside organizations such as Super PACs and 501(c) organizations, have led to a rapid proliferation of outside groups that are having a growing impact on federal elections. These outside groups, which have flourished on both the right and the left in recent years, are increasingly engaged in political activities that were once the province of political parties, such as voter registration drives, absentee ballot programs, GOTV, voter identification, and political advertising and issue advocacy efforts.

The McCain-Feingold law, which took effect during the 2004 presidential election cycle, prohibits the Republican National Committee ("RNC"), Democratic National Committee ("DNC"), and the other national political party committees from raising or spending soft-money funds for any purpose. "Soft money" is defined as funds raised outside of the prohibitions and limitations of federal law, including corporate and labor union general treasury funds and individual contributions in excess of federal limits. Funds raised in accordance with federal law come from individuals and from federally registered PACs and are harder to raise; hence, these funds are commonly referred to as "hard money." Prior to McCain-Feingold, the national political parties were legally permitted to accept unlimited corporate, union, and individual soft-money contributions and could use these funds to help underwrite a wide variety of political and electoral activities, including voter registration efforts, absentee ballot drives, GOTV activities, slate cards, and similar ticket-wide political activities. The national political parties prior to McCain-Feingold were also able to use soft-money contributions to help finance issue advertisements supporting and opposing federal candidates. "Issue advertisements" are public communications that frequently attack or promote federal candidates and their records, but which refrain from expressly advocating the election or defeat of any candidate (which is referred to as "express advocacy").

In *Citizens United v. FEC*, the U.S. Supreme Court in 2010 struck down the long-standing prohibition on corporate independent expenditures in connection with federal elections. In *SpeechNow v. FEC*, a federal appeals court invalidated limits on contributions from individuals to political committees that fund only independent expenditures for or against federal candidates. In advisory opinions issued after the *SpeechNow* decision, the FEC concluded that political committees formed strictly to make independent expenditures supporting or opposing federal candidates could accept unlimited contributions from individuals, corporations, and labor organizations.[7] These new political committees, which are prohibited from making contributions to federal candidates and to other federal political committees, are commonly referred to as "Super PACs."

501(c) organizations are entities that are organized and operate under Section 501(c) of the Internal Revenue Code, including social welfare organizations established under Section 501(c)(4) and trade associations and business leagues organized under Section 501(c)(6). 501(c)(4) and 501(c)(6) entities are permitted to accept unlimited corporate, union, and individual contributions and may engage in partisan political activities, provided such political activities do not become their primary purpose. By contrast, Super PACs, as political committees registered with the FEC, are by definition partisan entities and may spend all of their funds on partisan political activities. Super PACs are required to publicly disclose their donors; 501(c) organizations are generally not required to disclose their donors to the public.

Driven and made possible by these recent changes to the legal landscape, Super PAC and other outside group spending reached record levels during the 2014 election cycle. Reports published just before Election Day indicated that spending by outside groups in connection with the 2014 election totaled $480 million, which was 55 percent more than the $309 million spent by outside groups in connection with the last midterm election in 2010.[8] Table 6.2 identifies the top outside group spenders during the 2014 election cycle.

Analysis shows that Democratic-leaning Super PACs significantly outraised and outspent their Republican counterparts. For example, almost 69

Table 6.2. Largest Non-Political Party Outside Spenders (2013–2014 Election Cycle)

Name	2013–2014 Disclosed Spending	Entity Type
*American Crossroads/Crossroads GPS	$48 Million	Super PAC/501(c)
Senate Majority PAC	$47 Million	Super PAC
*U.S. Chamber of Commerce	$35 Million	501(c)
*House Majority PAC	$29 Million	Super PAC
Ending Spending	$29 Million	Super PAC/501(c)
National Rifle Association	$27 Million	501(c)
Freedom Partners Action Fund	$24 Million	Super PAC
NextGen Climate Action	$21 Million	Super PAC
League of Conservation Voters	$17 Million	Super PAC/501(c)
National Association of Realtors	$12 Million	Super PAC/501(c)

Source: http://www.opensecrets.org/outsidespending/summ.php?cycle=2014&chrt=V&disp =O&type=P
* These entities were also among the ten largest non-political party outside spenders for the 2011–2012 election cycle.

percent of spending by the six largest Super PACs supported Democratic candidates or opposed Republican candidates. However, published reports indicate that Republican-leaning 501(c) entities made up for the difference. In fact, of the six 501(c) organizations that spent the most funds in connection with the 2014 election, 81 percent of the groups' collective expenditures reportedly supported Republican candidates.[9]

In 2014, many Senate and House candidates were also supported by single-candidate Super PACs that spent all of their funds on a single federal race. Although 2012 was the first election cycle in which presidential candidate Super PACs became a necessity, 2014 was the first year in which single-candidate Super PACs became prevalent in down-ballot U.S. House and U.S. Senate races. As of July 2014, single-candidate Super PACs were reported to be active in 61 percent of 2014 Senate races.[10] In several cases, these Super PACs were funded by family members of the candidate.[11] Also as of July 2014, at least sixty-four Super PACs had reportedly spent $21 million on House races.[12] By the end of November 2014, ninety-four single-candidate Super PACs had raised $66 million and had spent $52 million in connection with the 2014 election.[13] Other types of organizations, including 501(c)(4) entities, also focused on particular races. For example, Oklahomans for a Conservative Future spent almost $1.3 million on the GOP primary for Oklahoma's 2014 special Senate election.[14]

The 2014 North Carolina Senate race was reportedly the most expensive Senate race in history, with a total of $113.3 million spent collectively on the race by candidates, Super PACs, and other organizations.[15] Of that amount, 71 percent was reportedly spent by outside groups.[16] By contrast, the 2012 Massachusetts Senate race was previously the most expensive Senate race in history with a total of at $84.4 million of expenditures, with outside group spending constituting only 9 percent of the total amount spent.[17]

So much money was spent on political advertising in the final weeks of the 2014 election that some studies found that political advertising constituted up to 20 percent of overall advertising revenue nationwide in certain months.[18] In late October 2014, published reports indicated that TV stations were unable to keep up with demand for political advertising time. One article noted that a station in Iowa started an additional news program in order to increase revenue from political advertising spots. The new program allowed the station to avoid paying syndication fees and ensured that political advertising would reach viewers interested in politics and the news.[19] Another study released in October 2014 found that advertising spending in connection with 2014 federal and gubernatorial elections had topped $1 billion and encompassed the airing of 2.2 million advertising spots.[20]

Because Super PACs and 501(c) organizations may not make contributions to federal campaign committees, traditional PACs—which can only accept contributions subject to federal contribution limits and source prohibitions—remain an important vehicle for supporting federal candidates.[21] Table 6.3 lists the ten largest PACs based upon the total amounts contributed to candidates during the 2014 election cycle. Each of these PACs are "connected" PACs associated with corporations, trade associations, labor organizations, and membership organizations. A number of connected PACs disseminated advertisements supporting or opposing federal candidates in addition to making direct contributions to candidates.

Table 6.3.   Largest PACs by Total Contributions (2014 Election Cycle)

PAC Name	2013–2014 Total Contributions
National Association of Realtors PAC	$3,583,955
National Beer Wholesalers Association PAC	$3,017,000
National Auto Dealers Association PAC	$2,729,350
Honeywell International PAC	$2,705,373
Lockheed Martin PAC	$2,625,750
American Bankers Association PAC	$2,410,875
Intl Brotherhood of Electrical Workers PAC	$2,385,314
AT&T Inc. PAC	$2,381,750
Credit Union National Association PAC	$2,359,500
Northrup Grumman PAC	$2,347,250

Source: https://www.opensecrets.org/pacs/toppacs.php

NATIONAL POLITICAL PARTY FUNDRAISING WAS FLAT IN 2014 COMPARED WITH RECENT MIDTERM ELECTION CYCLES

There are growing indications that national political party committees are becoming less relevant in federal elections as spending increasingly shifts to Super PACs and other outside groups that are not subject to the hard-dollar fundraising requirements that apply to the national party committees.[22] As Figures 6.1 and 6.2 demonstrate, total spending by national party committees during the 2014 election cycle made up a noticeably smaller proportion of overall outside spending than was the case during the 2010 midterm election cycle. In 2010, spending by parties constituted 38 percent of total outside spending; in 2014, this percentage dropped to 29 percent.

Because outside groups do not labor under the hard-dollar fundraising restrictions that apply to the national political parties, outside groups can raise large amounts of money from a small group of donors in a very short

Michael E. Toner and Karen E. Trainer

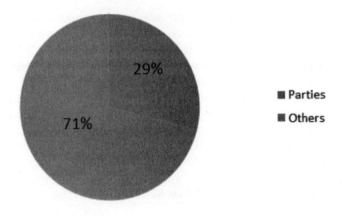

Figures 6.1 and 6.2   2010 and 2014 Outside Spending by Entity Type Data, retrieved from Center for Responsive Politics https://www.opensecrets.org/outsidespending/ cycle_tots.php?cycle = 2012&view = A&chart = N#viewpt. Figures created by Michael E. Toner and Karen E. Trainer.

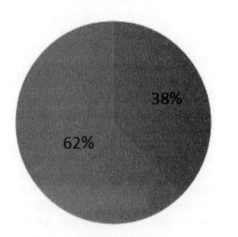

period of time. In addition, Super PACs, 501(c) organizations, and other types of outside groups are now spending more on independent expenditures and other election-related communications than are political party committees. Published reports indicate that the national political parties are outsourcing or relying on outside groups to conduct activities that were once part of the national parties' primary functions, including donor and voter list management, voter registration and GOTV activities, and opposition research.[23]

In addition, some analysts have pointed to passage of the McCain-Feingold law as a key factor in the decline of political party activity in recent years. Between the 2002 election cycle, which was the last election cycle prior to McCain-Feingold, and the 2010 election cycle, national political party fundraising declined by 17 percent.[24] Given that the Supreme Court's *Citizens United* ruling was not issued until 2010, the decline of political parties appears to be attributable to other factors, almost certainly including the McCain-Feingold law.[25] Tables 6.4 and 6.5 and Figure 6.3 outline national party fundraising figures for the 2014 election cycle as compared with the 2010 and 2006 election cycles.

Political party committee fundraising continued to be aided by extensive use of joint fundraising activities. Under FEC regulations, candidates and

Table 6.4. 2013–2014 National Political Party Committee Receipts

DNC	$161,085,028	RNC	$188,793,761
DSCC	$166,651,438	NRSC	$125,748,553
DCCC	$202,646,082	NRCC	$151,287,282
Total Democratic	$530,382,548	Total Republican	$465,829,596

Source: Federal Election Commission Data.

Table 6.5. Comparison of National Political Party Fundraising

Year	Party	Nominal Dollars	Constant Dollars
2014	Democratic Party Committees	$530.3 Million	$530.3 Million
2014	Republican Party Committees	$465.8 Million	$465.8 Million
2010	Democratic Party Committees	$518.3 Million	$564.4 Million
2010	Republican Party Committees	$444.7 Million	$484.2 Million
2006	Democratic Party Committees	$392.1 Million	$461.8 Million
2006	Republican Party Committees	$657.1 Million	$773.9 Million

Source: Campaign Finance Institute, "Democrats Were Up at the Half-Way Point and Republicans Down, Especially with Small Contributions," http://www.cfinst.org/pdf/federal/parties/2014/Parties14_12M_Table3 .pdf, and Federal Election Commission Data.

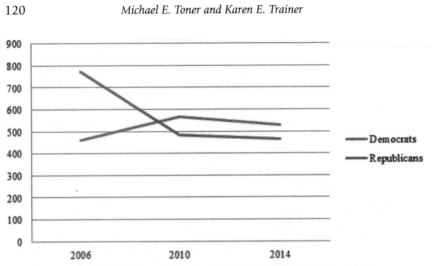

Figure 6.3   National Party Committee Fundraising in Constant Dollars (Millions)
Campaign Finance Institute, "Democrats Were Up at the Half-Way Point and
Republicans Down, Especially with Small Contributions," http://www.cfinst.org/pdf/
federal/parties/2014/Parties14_12M_Table3.pdf, and Federal Election Commission
Data. Figure created by Michael E. Toner and Karen E. Trainer.

political parties may simultaneously raise hard-dollar funds through joint
fundraising committees ("JFCs"), which permit candidates and parties to
combine the per-recipient contribution limits and solicit greater amounts
of money from donors at any one time.[26] During the 2014 election cycle, a
record-setting 599 JFCs registered with the FEC,[27] which represented a 57
percent increase over the number of JFCs registered in the 2010 election
cycle.[28] In addition, 2014 cycle JFCs raised more than twice what JFCs collected during the 2010 election cycle.[29]

One interesting element of national party fundraising in 2014 was the
fundraising advantage that the Democratic Congressional Campaign Committee enjoyed over the National Republican Congressional Committee. As
was noted in Table 6.4, the DCCC raised $202,646,082 for the 2014 elec-
tion, which was 34 percent more than the NRCC's $151,287,282. The
DCCC's fundraising advantage in 2014 was highly unusual given that the
Democrats were in the minority in the House, were not expected to regain
the majority, and lost more than ten House seats in the election. Analysis
of DCCC and NRCC FEC reports reveals that the DCCC's fundraising
advantage derived primarily from stronger small-dollar fundraising. Based
on 2014 fundraising data available as of June 2014, more than 40 percent
of the DCCC's contributions came from individuals whose contributions
aggregated $200 or less during the year. By contrast, only 20 percent of the

NRCC's contributions came from individuals below this monetary threshold.[30] By the end of November 2014, the DCCC's low-dollar fundraising percentage was approximately 40 percent, and the NRCC's was approximately 15 percent.[31]

The DCCC has achieved this small-dollar fundraising edge over the NRCC only during the last two election cycles. For many years Republican party committees significantly outraised the Democratic party committees in hard dollars—sometimes by a margin as high as two-to-one—and the GOP edge was driven largely by great success in low-dollar direct-mail fundraising.[32] Some analysts argue that the Democrats' recent low-dollar fundraising advantage stems from investments in online fundraising and technological advances, such as the ability to accept credit card contributions online.[33] Whatever the cause for the disparity, the NRCC will undoubtedly seek to close the gap with the DCCC among low-dollar donors in the upcoming election cycle.

THE SUPREME COURT'S DECISION IN *McCUTCHEON V. FEC* ALLOWED WEALTHY INDIVIDUALS TO CONTRIBUTE MORE FUNDS IN CONNECTION WITH THE 2014 ELECTION

In April 2014, the Supreme Court in *McCutcheon v. FEC* invalidated the individual biennial aggregate limit on federal campaign contributions as unconstitutional under the First Amendment. Since the 1970s, federal law had capped the total amount of money that individuals could contribute to federal candidates and other federal political committees collectively during each two-year election cycle. Before the biennial aggregate contribution limit was struck down, individuals were prohibited from contributing more than $123,200 to all federal candidates and political committees combined during the 2014 election cycle. The aggregate contribution limit existed in addition to the per-recipient "base limit" that applies to particular campaign committees, political party committees, and other federal political committees.[34] With the aggregate contribution limit gone, individual donors now need to adhere only to the base contribution limits and are free to contribute to an unlimited number of candidate committees and other political committees.

The Center for Responsive Politics published a study finding that as of June 30, 2014, 310 donors had exceeded the $123,200 aggregate contribution limit that was in place prior to the *McCutcheon* ruling.[35] The study further found that these 310 individuals contributed $49.8 million in total, which was $11.6 million more than they could have contributed under the aggregate contribution limits that were in place prior to *McCutcheon*.[36] By the day after the 2014 election, the number of donors that exceeded the biennial limit had increased to 498.[37] The Center for Responsive Politics study also determined that more than two-thirds of contributions from these donors were made to Republican candidates and committees, while only one-third went to Democrats. Of the amount contributed by these donors, the RNC reportedly received the most funds.[38] A separate study determined that the contributions from top individual donors to Republican candidates benefited more moderate candidates, rather than more conservative candidates such as Tea Party candidates.[39]

The Supreme Court's *McCutcheon* decision also had a notable impact on joint fundraising activities in 2014. As was noted above, under FEC regulations, candidates and political parties may simultaneously raise hard-money funds through JFCs, which permit the fundraising participants to combine the per-recipient contribution limits and solicit greater amounts of money from donors at any one time. In the wake of *McCutcheon*, campaigns, political parties, and other political committees have been able to form JFCs with a larger number of participants without having to worry about donors exceeding the old aggregate contribution limit. In 2014, such "Super JFCs" included Targeted State Victory, which raised $2.3 million in the third quarter of 2014 alone and included 14 party committee participants, as well as Grassroots Victory Project 2014, which raised $1.3 million in the third quarter of 2014 and included twenty-six different fundraising participants.[40]

Some analysts believe that massive Super JFCs may be formed for the 2016 presidential election. A Super JFC that included a presidential campaign, all fifty state party committees, and the national party committees could accept contributions of nearly $1.2 million per contributor per election cycle. If such Super JFCs come into existence, they may help facilitate increased candidate and party committee fundraising for the 2016 presidential election.

LOOKING AHEAD TO 2016

No sooner had the ballots been counted on election night in 2014 than active planning began for the 2016 presidential race, which will almost certainly be the most expensive presidential election in American history.

The 2012 presidential election was the first race since 1972 in which neither major-party nominee accepted public funds for either the primary or general election phase of the campaign, as both President Obama and Mitt Romney financed their campaigns entirely with private contributions.[41] Obama raised approximately $740 million for his 2012 campaign—including nearly $300 million for the general election alone—

and Romney raised approximately $475 million for the 2012 race, including over $250 million during the course of winning a protracted Republican primary over multiple GOP rivals.[42] To put those fundraising tallies in historical perspective, George W. Bush, who was a prolific campaign fundraiser, raised only $100 million for the primaries in 2000 and $270 million for the primaries in 2004, which were record-breaking fundraising totals at the time.[43] Given the extraordinary growth in presidential campaign fundraising during the last decade, it is certain that both the Democratic and Republican nominees—whomever they are—will reject public funds for both the primary and general election and will finance their entire campaigns with private contributions.

As of this writing, Hillary Rodham Clinton is a prohibitive frontrunner in the nascent 2016 Democratic presidential field.[44] Given Clinton's dominant political standing, her near-universal name ID, and her and her husband's deep and broad fundraising network, Clinton would likely smash all presidential campaign fundraising records should she seek and win the Democratic nomination in 2016. In fact, Clinton could potentially raise $1 billion or even more for her presidential campaign alone, which would make hers the first billion-dollar campaign committee. Vice President Joseph Biden and Senator Elizabeth Warren would also likely have significant fundraising strength should they enter the Democratic primary field.

The bench of potential Republican presidential candidates for 2016 is deep and strong, which includes, among others, former Florida Governor Jeb Bush, New Jersey Governor Chris Christie, Kentucky Senator Rand Paul, and Florida Senator Marco Rubio. If Jeb Bush opted to run, his deep and established fundraising network might allow him to keep pace with Clinton's extraordinary fundraising prowess. The other Republican candidates would likely be outraised by Clinton, but they could be expected to rely on the RNC, Super PACs and other outside groups to help bridge the fundraising divide.

With Super PACs and other outside groups able to raise and spend unlimited sums of money, the need for presidential campaigns in 2016 to raise record sums of money will never be greater. An open seat for president, strong top-tier candidates in both parties, a highly polarized electorate, and a deregulatory legal terrain all conspire to set the stage for the 2016 presidential race to be the most expensive in American history.

The authors would like to thank Rachel Shelbourne for her outstanding research assistance in preparing this chapter.

NOTES

1. Rebecca Ballhous, "At $4 Billion, 2014 Is Most Expensive Midterm Ever," *Wall Street Journal*, October 23, 2014. *See also* "Overall Spending Inches Up in 2014:

Megadonors Equip Outside Groups to Capture a Bigger Share of the Pie," Center for Responsive Politics, accessed December 15, 2014, http://www.opensecrets.org/news/2014/10/overall-spending-inches-up-in-2014-megadonors-equip-outside-groups-to-capture-a-bigger-share-of-the-pie/.

2. Ballhous, "At $4 Billion, 2014 Is Most Expensive Midterm Ever." Approximately $3.6 billion was spent in connection with the 2010 midterm election.

3. Individuals can contribute up to $2,600 per election to Congressional campaigns (the primary and general elections are considered separate elections) and federal multicandidate political action committees (PACs) may contribute up to $5,000 per election. Congressional campaigns are barred from accepting contributions from corporations or labor unions.

4. "Most Expensive Races," Center for Responsive Politics, accessed December 15, 2014, https://www.opensecrets.org/overview/topraces.php.

5. "Most Expensive Races (2012)," Center for Responsive Politics, accessed December 15, 2014, http://www.opensecrets.org/bigpicture/topraces.php?cycle=2012&display=currcands.

6. Shane Goldmacher, "Democratic House Candidates Are Walloping Republicans in the Small-Money Game," *National Journal*, September 28, 2014.

7. FEC Advisory Opinions 2010–2009 and 2010–2011.

8. "Overall Spending Inches Up in 2014: Megadonors Equip Outside Groups to Capture a Bigger Share of the Pie," Center for Responsive Politics, accessed December 15, 2014, http://www.opensecrets.org/news/2014/10/overall-spending-inches-up-in-2014-megadonors-equip-outside-groups-to-capture-a-bigger-share-of-the-pie/

9. Kenneth P. Vogel, "Democrats Win PACs, Lose Money War," *Politico*, December 6, 2014, accessed December 15, 2014, http://www.politico.com/story/2014/12/democrats-gop-super-pacs-fundraising-113362.html.

10. Paul Blumenthal, "A Personal Super PAC Is the Latest Weapon for This Year's Senate Candidate," *Huffington Post*, July 19, 2014, accessed December 15, 2014, http://www.huffingtonpost.com/2014/07/19/super-pacs-2014_n_5599999.html.

11. *Ibid.*

12. Matea Gold and Tom Hamburger, "Must-Have Accessory for House Candidates in 2014: The Personalized Super PAC," *Washington Post*, July 18, 2014, accessed December 15, 2014, http://www.washingtonpost.com/politics/one-candidate-super-pac-now-a-must-have-to-count-especially-in-lesser-house-races/2014/07/17/aaa2fcd6-0dcd-11e4-8c9a-923ecc0c7d23_story.html.

13. "2014 Outside Spending, by Single-Candidate Super PAC," Center for Responsive Politics, accessed December 15, 2014, https://www.opensecrets.org/outsidespending/summ.php?chrt=V&type=C.

14. Robert Maguire, "Dark Money Hits $100 Million with Help from Single-Candidate Groups," Center for Responsive Politics, October 9, 2014, accessed December 15, 2014, http://www.opensecrets.org/news/2014/10/dark-money-hits-100-million-with-help-from-single-candidate-groups/.

15. Russ Choma, "Money Won on Tuesday, but Rules of the Game Changed," Center for Responsive Politics, November 5, 2014, accessed December 15, 2014, http://www.opensecrets.org/news/2014/11/money-won-on-tuesday-but-rules-of-the-game-changed/.

16. *Ibid.*

17. *Ibid.*

18. Jonathan Sims, "Local Cable Political Ad Spending Accelerating," *Viamedia*, October 7, 2014, accessed December 15, 2014, http://www.viamediatv.com/blog/local-cable-political-ad-spending-accelerating.

19. Cecelia Kang and Matea Gold, "With Political Ads Expected to Hit a Record, News Stations Can Hardly Keep Up," *Washington Post*, October 31, 2014, accessed December 15, 2014, http://www.washingtonpost.com/business/technology/with-political-ads-expected-to-hit-a-record-news-stations-can-hardly-keep-up/2014/10/31/84a9e4b4-5ebc-11e4-9f3a-7e28799e0549_story.html.

20. "Ad Spending Tops $1 Billion," Wesleyan Media Project, October 29, 2014, accessed December 15, 2014, http://mediaproject.wesleyan.edu/releases/ad-spending-tops-1-billion/.

21. Traditional PACs, unlike Super PACs, may make contributions to federal candidates and other federal political committees. Traditional PACs are prohibited from accepting corporate and labor union contributions and may accept contributions from individuals up to $5,000 per calendar year. Traditional PACs are referred to herein as "PACs."

22. The Republican national party committees are the Republican National Committee ("RNC"), the National Republican Senatorial Committee ("NRSC"), and the National Republican Congressional Committee ("NRCC"). The Democratic national party committees are the Democratic National Committee ("DNC"), the Democratic Senatorial Campaign Committee ("DSCC"), and the Democratic Congressional Campaign Committee ("DCCC"). National political party committees are prohibited from accepting corporate and labor union contributions and may accept contributions from individuals of up to $32,400 per calendar year. The national political parties may also receive contributions from individuals of up to $32,400 per year to defray the cost of election recounts and election contests.

23. Robert Kelner and Raymond La Raja, "McCain-Feingold's Devastating Legacy," *Washington Post*, April 11, 2014.

24. *Ibid.*

25. *Ibid.*

26. For example, if a JFC included a Senate campaign, a national political party committee, and two state political party committees, individual donors could contribute up to $57,600 to the JFC—up to $5,200 to the Senate campaign ($2,600 for the primary and $2,600 for the general election), $32,400 to the national political party, and $10,000 each to the two state political parties. Any prior contributions that individual donors made to any of the entities participating in the JFC would count against what could be contributed to the JFC.

27. https://www.opensecrets.org/jfc/

28. *Ibid.*

29. *Ibid.*

30. Aaron Blake, "Democrats Aren't Winning Back the House. So How Are They Raising So Much Money?" *Washington Post*, June 9, 2014, accessed December 15, 2014, http://www.washingtonpost.com/blogs/the-fix/wp/2014/06/09/democrats-arent-winning-back-the-house-so-how-are-they-raising-so-much-money/.

31. Federal Election Commission data.

32. Thomas B. Edsall, "Milking the Money Machine," *New York Times*, July 22, 2014, accessed December 15, 2014, http://www.nytimes.com/2014/07/23/opin ion/thomas-b-edsall-milking-the-money-machine.html.

33. Aaron Blake, "Democrats Aren't Winning Back the House. So How Are They Raising So Much Money?" *Washington Post*, June 9, 2014.

34. These "base limits" include a $2,600 per election limit on individual contributions to federal campaign committees and a $5,000 annual limit on individual contributions to federal PACs.

35. Russ Choma, Lalita Clozel, and Viveca Novak, "Cracking the Contribution Cap: One in a Million Americans," Center for Responsive Politics, September 2, 2014, accessed December 15, 2014, http://www.opensecrets.org/news/2014/09/cracking-the-contribution-cap-one-in-a-million-americans/.

36. *Ibid.* This amount does not include contributions to nonfederal candidates and committees, contributions to Super PACs, contributions to recount funds, or contributions to other entities that are not required to register with the FEC as political committees.

37. Russ Choma, "Money Won on Tuesday, but Rules of the Game Changed," Center for Responsive Politics, November 5, 2014.

38. Russ Choma, Lalita Clozel, and Viveca Novak, "Cracking the Contribution Cap: One in a Million Americans," Center for Responsive Politics, September 2, 2014.

39. Adam Bonica and Jenny Shen, "How Wealthy Campaign Donors May Reduce Political Polarization and Weaken the Tea Party," *Washington Post*, April 24, 2014, accessed December 15, http://www.washingtonpost.com/blogs/monkey-cage/wp/2014/04/24/how-wealthy-campaign-donors-may-reduce-political-polarization-and -weaken-the-tea-party/.

40. Russ Choma, "Super JFC Donors Emerge in Third Quarter," Center for Responsive Politics, October 15, 2014, accessed December 15, 2014, http://www .opensecrets.org/news/2014/10/super-jfc-donors-emerge-in-third-quarter/.

41. Under the presidential public financing system, candidates can receive matching public funds for the primaries and a public grant for the general election to finance their campaigns if they meet certain criteria and adhere to campaign spending limits. In 2012, each presidential candidate could receive a maximum of $22 million in matching public funds for the primaries, and the two major-party nominees were eligible to receive a grant of $95 million for the general election phase of the campaign. See Federal Election Commission Brochure, "Presidential Spending Limits for 2012," http://www.fec.gov/pages/brochures/pubfund_limits _2012.shtml#ssearch=presidential%20spending%20limits%20for%202012, and Press Release, http://www.fec.gov/press/press2012/20120828/_SteinMatchFund .shtml.

Candidates who decline to accept matching funds for the primaries and turn down the public grant for the general election are free to raise and spend as much money as they want subject to the contribution limits. Because the major-party nominees and other top-tier candidates have been able to raise vastly more funds in recent years outside of the presidential public financing system than they could raise and spend within the system, increasingly only second- and third-tier presidential candidates have accepted public funds during the last ten years.

42. Michael E. Toner and Karen E. Trainer, "The Six-Billion Dollar Election: The Impact of Federal Election Laws," *Barack Obama and the New America: The Changing Face of Politics*, ed. Larry J. Sabato (Lanham, MD: Rowman & Littlefield, 2013).

43. *Ibid.* George W. Bush accepted public funds for the general election in 2000 and 2004. Bush raised $100 million for the 2000 race under the pre-McCain-Feingold $1,000-per-person contribution limit. The McCain-Feingold law doubled the individual contribution limit to $2,000 per election for the 2004 election and indexed the contribution limit for inflation going forward. The individual contribution limit was $2,500 per election for the 2012 presidential race and likely will be $2,700 for the 2016 race.

44. Interest in a potential Clinton candidacy was so strong among Democrats that the pro-Clinton "Ready for Hillary" Super PAC raised in excess of $12 million in 2013 and 2014, well before Clinton even decided whether to enter the presidential race (Federal Election Commission Data).

7

The State of the Polling Industry

Mark Blumenthal and Ariel Edwards-Levy

Democrats lost big in the 2014 elections, but in the aftermath, polling also took a hit for largely understating the size of Republicans' win. While most polls and poll-based models correctly forecast that Republicans would win a Senate majority, they often suggested closer contests and generally understated GOP margins.

"The results were another black eye for pollsters, in what are already some tough times," *Politico*'s Steven Shepard wrote immediately after the election. "As Americans become even harder to reach by phone—and emerging methodologies, such as Internet polling, remain unproven—the poor performance of pollsters this year casts serious doubt on the reliability of surveys during the 2016 presidential race."[1]

How wrong were the polls, really?

At first glance, the final polling averages on 2014 Senate contests appeared to show more error than they had in recent midterm elections in estimating the margins separating the candidates. "The polls really were worse than usual," Kyle Kondik and Geoffrey Skelley of *Sabato's Crystal Ball* at the University of Virginia Center for Politics concluded in examining the average misses by two polling aggregators—the polling averages of *RealClearPolitics* and our own estimates at *HuffPost* Pollster. Their chart (Figure 7.1) showed the average misses in competitive Senate races higher in 2014 than in the elections held from 2006 to 2012.[2] As Kondik and Skelley noted, these differences were driven in part by some unusually large misses in individual races, including double-digit underestimates of Republican margins in the Arkansas and Virginia Senate races, and misses nearly as high in Kansas and Kentucky.

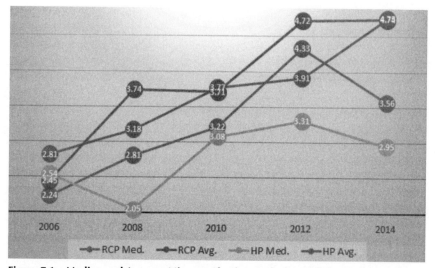

Figure 7.1   Median and Average Miss per Election Cycle for *RealClearPolitics* and *HuffPost* Pollster Poll Averages, 2006–2014

The analyses of the National Council on Public Polls provide another, broader benchmark, based on statewide contests for Senate and governor. Between 2002 and 2010, their computation of "candidate error"—a measure of the average error for the top two candidates on individual polls conducted in the last week of the race—has ranged between 2.0 and 2.3 percentage points in the midterm elections.[3] In 2014, our computation of the NCPP statistics finds a rate of error in final week polls (2.2 percentage points) slightly higher than in 2006 or 2010, but slightly lower than 2002 (see Figure 7.2).

The polling misfires of 2014 have greater precedent if we broaden the comparison to include different measures and elections held in the 1990s and earlier. For example, Nate Silver's initial assessment of average bias—whether polls collectively favored one party or the other—in 2014 found an average four percentage point understatement of Republican Senate margins. However, this calculation also revealed an equally large bias against the Republicans (+ 4.0) in 2002 and an even bigger bias against the Democrats (+ 4.9) in 1998.[4]

A somewhat different assessment, from Eric McGhee, finds that the greater volume of polling in elections since 2004 has made poll-based *forecasts* (based on aggregating all polls) more accurate. McGhee used a statistical measure called the Brier Score that evaluates how often and how

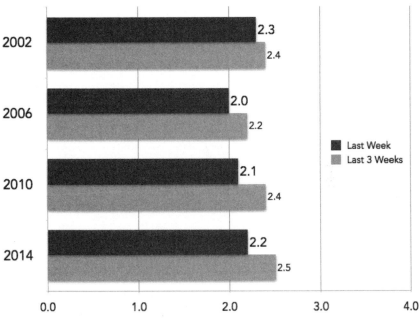

Poll Error Rate in 2014 Similar to 2002-2010

Figure 7.2 Average NCPP Candidate Error for Polls on Races for Governor and U.S. Senate Conducted in Final Week and Final Three Weeks of Campaign

confidently a forecast predicts the correct winner (regardless of the margin of victory predicted). When applied to forecasts produced by the probabilistic model he created for the *Washington Post*'s Election Lab, McGhee found that the average miss (see Figure 7.3) has declined since the volume of polling increased substantially, roughly ten years ago. While the average miss in 2014 "was a little higher (worse) this year than in some other recent years," according to McGhee, "we are still clearly in a world of better accuracy" in his models as compared to 2002 and earlier.[5]

While polling averages in Senate races appeared to miss by more than usual, broader measures of polling error were roughly in line with previous midterm elections, and the 2014 Senate polls collectively predicted the correct winners in all but one race. However, these findings may not settle the nerves of a profession already roiling from changes in technology and communications habits that threaten to reshape it significantly in the future.

Three decades ago, the state of the polling industry was very different. Well over 90 percent of Americans, and an even greater portion of voters,

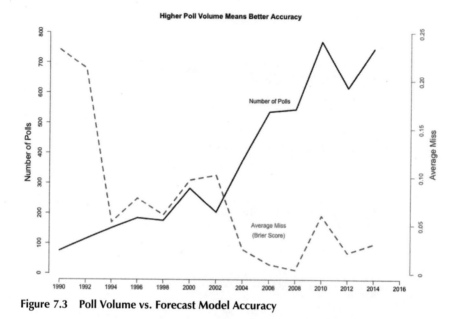

Figure 7.3   Poll Volume vs. Forecast Model Accuracy

had landline phone service at home. Although "answering machines" were proliferating, nearly everyone answered their telephone when it rang. Caller ID service was in its infancy. Telephone polls from anonymous commercial polling firms could easily attain cooperation from a majority of their contacts, and polls conducted by academic institutions or media outlets could (and did) do far better.

As a result, by the mid-1980s, most of the media outlets and political campaigns that conducted polls had moved away from expensive, cumbersome in-person surveys—the dominant survey methodology from the 1950s to the 1970s—to less expensive, faster telephone polls. Pollsters could contact a true random sample of U.S. households by generating telephone numbers at random, a technique that reached all working phones whether listed in public directories or not. Since nearly every household had a landline phone, the probability of reaching any given individual by telephone was easily calculated.

Now, thirty years later, the rapid advance of technology has revolutionized the way Americans communicate and fundamentally disrupted the nature of telephone surveys. In 2009, media pollster Jay Leve described the changed reality:

> [Today] you don't have a home phone; your number can ring anywhere in the world; you're not waiting for your phone to ring; nobody calls you on the

phone anyway they text you or IM you; when your phone rings you don't answer it—your time is precious, you have competing interests, you resent calls from strangers, you're on one or more do-not-call lists, and 20 minutes [the length of many pollsters' interviews] is an eternity.[6]

A series of technical advances that made it cheaper and easier to conduct legitimate surveys by telephone—including computer-assisted telephone interviewing, auto dialing, and more easily accessible digital databases— also led to an explosion of telemarketing, including automated recorded- voice sales pitches and solicitations under the guise of surveys. The deluge of incoming calls made Americans seek out barriers to calls from strangers.

Caller ID, which was first introduced in the late 1980s, was being used by a majority of Americans by as early as 2003, the same year the Federal Trade Commission introduced a Do Not Call registry. Four years later, 72 percent of Americans had signed up for the registry. Pollsters are exempt from the registry's prohibitions, but Americans who believe they have opted out of all unwanted interruptions may be that much harder to poll.[7]

THE CHALLENGES OF POLLING TODAY AND
HOW POLLSTERS ARE COPING

Americans today are less likely both to answer the phone when pollsters call and to complete the survey even if they pick up. A 2012 Pew Research report found that response rates to their surveys had dropped by twenty- seven points in fifteen years, from 36 percent in 1997 to just 9 percent in 2012. "These declines result from the increasing difficulty in making con- tact with someone in a household, as well as in gaining cooperation once contact is made," the authors of the Pew report noted. "The standard survey made contact with 62 percent of households, down from 72 percent of households in 2009, 79 percent in 2003 and 90 percent in 1997."

Despite the decline, the Pew Research study found, "telephone surveys that include landlines and cell phones and are weighted to match the demographic composition of the population continue to provide accurate data on most political, social and economic measures." Nevertheless, they also found that telephone surveys tend to overstate civic engagement: "Peo- ple who volunteer are more likely to agree to take part in surveys than those who do not do these things."[8]

The biggest disruption by far has come from the nearly universal adop- tion of mobile telephones and—more to the point—from the rapidly increasing portion of American households that have discontinued land- line telephone service or simply stopped answering their landline phones. Over the last decade, the percentage of "cell phone only" adults, those with a cell phone but no landline, has increased from 3 percent in 2003 to 39 percent in the latter half of 2013, according to in-person surveys conducted by the Centers for Disease Control. Another 18 percent of adults now say that although they have both landline and mobile service, they receive "all or almost all" of their calls on their mobile phones.[9]

This shift has great consequence for pollsters, since the demographics of the cell-phone-only households are very different from those with land-lines. Cell-only Americans are more likely to be low-income, minority, and, especially, younger. All of these groups have been more supportive of the Democrats. More than half of Americans between eighteen and thirty-four rely on cell phones, as do a majority of Latinos, those living in poverty, and those who rent their home or live with roommates.[10]

The rapid decline in landline telephone usage over the past half-dozen years left media pollsters with little choice. Of those who use live interviewers, virtually all at the national level, and most who do statewide surveys, have shifted to calling respondents on both landline and cell phones.

The transition, however, has been costly. A study by the American Association for Public Opinion Research (AAPOR) found that it typically costs twice as much per completed interview to conduct a survey via cell phone rather than landline, when sampling randomly generated telephone numbers, with costs increasing three- or four-fold in some situations. The higher costs owe to several factors, including the need for dual overlapping samples and for interviewers to hand dial calls placed to mobile phones, because federal law prohibits the use of automatic dialers to call mobile phones.[11]

The use of dual samples of landline and cell phones also makes the underlying methodology increasingly complex. Pollsters now need to determine how much overlap to allow for Americans who use both landline and cell phones, and the weighting schemes used to combine these samples are far more complicated. Pollsters approached this issue in different ways, but as the AAPOR report highlighted, "there is as yet no consensus on whether one of the approaches is always preferable."[12]

In the midst of this rapid evolution in telephone communications, another technical advance led to the proliferation of a different type of survey. Automated surveys, typically known to pollsters by the acronym IVR for "interactive voice response," use a recorded voice to ask questions that respondents answer by pressing the touch-tone keys on their phones. IVR polls were initially shunned by research professionals due to lower response rates and because most make no effort to choose a random individual within each sampled household (selecting instead the person who happens to answer the call). As live interviewer response rates plummeted, however, and their costs increased, the IVR polls were at less of a disadvantage. The Internet enabled firms like Rasmussen Reports and Public Policy

Polling, who promoted their businesses by disseminating results via blogs and news websites. In elections between 2002 to 2008, the automated polls did as well or better at predicting election outcomes as those produced by conventional live-interviewer methods.[13]

As Americans started abandoning landline phones in significant numbers over the past six years, however, the IVR pollsters faced an existential crisis. Since the federal prohibition on the use of "autodialers" excludes their method from cell phone interviewing, IVR surveys are missing an ever-increasing chunk of the electorate, with their ability to reach young voters, minorities, and other Democratic-leaning blocs growing increasingly compromised. In the 2010 elections and 2012 elections, several prominent automated polling firms significantly understated the performance of Democratic candidates.[14]

During the 2014 election cycle, many of the most prolific automated pollsters, including Rasmussen Reports, SurveyUSA, and the Democratic firm Public Policy Polling, which together made up just over half of the statewide public polling released in 2014, attempted to compensate. While some tried to combine live calls to cell phones with automated calls to landlines, most found that combination too costly. The vast majority attempted to supplement their calls to landline phones with online interviews selected from non-random panels of respondents who had volunteered to complete surveys on the Internet. So far, the sources and methods used for these supplemental interviews have been poorly disclosed.[15]

While public polls, particularly at the national level, have shifted to the use of dual samples of landline and mobile telephone numbers, the pollsters who conduct "internal" surveys of political campaigns have moved in a different direction. Virtually all now draw their samples from lists of registered voters compiled by state voting officials (a method known to pollsters as "registration-based sampling," or RBS).

Media pollsters have often shied away from such "voter file" samples, partly due to a concern over voters that cannot be reached due to missing phone numbers. List vendors attempt to match the names and addresses in official voter lists to public telephone directories with widely varying results, and the sometimes low "match rates" leads to a coverage problem analogous to the cell-phone-only problem now facing random digit samples: Voters without listed telephone numbers are often different than those easily matched.

Campaign pollsters have grown more willing to accept the trade-off because of the additional data available on the voter files. With random digits, pollsters have only a crude sense of the geographic location of the sampled household (an association growing increasingly less accurate as younger Americans move, taking mobile cell numbers obtained in one state to new residences in another). With voter files, the pollster usually has available the exact address, age, gender, partisan registration status (in many states), and previous voting history of each sampled voter.

Campaigns have used this data to create modeled scores of partisanship and turnout propensity for all voters, and pollsters have these scores available for all sampled voters, not just those they are able to contact and interview. Thus, pollsters can base their "likely voter" models on actual vote history, and if low coverage or response rates introduce a bias in partisanship—or Democrats are more willing to be interviewed than Republicans, or vice versa—the pollsters can correct it with weighting.

"Given the other new challenges that are occurring with doing accurate polling in terms of compliance rates and the difficulty of finding people on cell phones," Democratic pollster Geoff Garin explained to us in 2013, "it really is at this stage hard to imagine accurate polling without us having the benefit of that information in drawing the sample and analyzing the data."[16]

In 2014, the Democracy Corps project, run by Democratic Party consultants Stanley Greenberg and James Carville, shifted to the use of voter file samples for their publicly released national polling.[17] Bill McInturff, senior partner at the powerhouse Republican polling firm Public Opinion Strategies, long a champion of random-digit sampling, announced that his firm "has entirely moved to registration-based samples" for its political campaign work.[18]

Many nonpartisan polls have also begun using voter file sampling with success, including the Field Poll in California, MassINC/WBUR in Massachusetts, and the Monmouth University polls in New Jersey and other states.

Perhaps the most dramatic and controversial change in the polling world involves the use of so-called "non-probability" methods to conduct surveys on the Internet. Nearly nine out of ten Americans (87 percent) reported using the Internet in 2014, according to surveys conducted by the Pew Research Internet Project. While that level of coverage approaches the penetration of landline telephone service in the early 1970s, when pollsters began to move from in-person surveys to telephone methodologies, the Internet has a unique set of challenges.

While telephone polls typically begin with true probability samples of either working telephone numbers of voters drawn from official lists, the Internet allows no way to randomly select a sample of all email addresses or to randomly intercept all who are online. Instead, most Internet research companies recruit large "panels" of respondents, usually via web advertising, who agree to participate in online surveys.

Several media outlets entered into new partnerships with such companies during the 2014 election cycle.

The Associated Press, for example, began fielding all of their national surveys online in late 2013 in partnership with the survey research firm GfK. Their effort makes use of GfK's "Knowledge Panel," which uses random sampling to recruit Americans to join their panel.[19]

Both the *Huffington Post* and the *New York Times*/CBS News partnership joined with the research company YouGov to conduct surveys of Americans during the 2014 election cycle. The *Times*/CBS project was more ambitious, involving more than 100,000 respondents nationwide and individual estimates of voter preferences in all of the races for governor, U.S. Senate, and U.S. House of Representatives. YouGov begins with a non-representative panel of adults, recruited largely from Internet advertising. It uses weighting and a technique called sample matching to bring demographic and other characteristics in line with those of the adult U.S. population.

The CBS/*Times*/YouGov partnership was a "big deal in the polling world," as Scott Keeter, Pew Research's director of survey research, put it, because of the willingness of two venerable news organizations to embrace "non-probability methods."[20] The move set off a debate between pollsters who fretted over the lack of "grounding in theory" of the new methods and those who worried that too much traditionalism, in the form of "rigid faith in technology and theories or 'standards' determined in the 1930s" would handicap the survey industry in a period of rapid change.[21]

The 2014 cycle also brought announcements of another set of partnerships involving "non-probability" polls. SurveyMonkey, which offers do-it-yourself surveys for companies, schools, and other organizations, announced both a new partnership with NBC News and a collaboration with the Pew Research Center and Westat.[22] Both projects aimed to evaluate their methods with an eye toward developing better survey measures. In 2014, SurveyMonkey ran cursory tests whose results were shared with us at the *Huffington Post* before the election (but not published until after) that outperformed other public polls.[23]

CONCLUSION

The confluence of rapid changes in the polling industry has left pollsters, regardless of their preferred methodology, in a state of flux: grappling for the best way to deal with increased costs, the rising prevalence of cell phones, and falling response rates.

Many are satisfied that conventional telephone surveys that sample both landline and cell phones remain the best option and fear that alternatives amount to an abandonment of quality methods. Others see the days of the telephone polls as numbered and are more enthusiastic about exploring new methods.[24]

"It's not hard to imagine a future for polling that looks very different from the past," wrote the *New York Times'* David Leonhardt, imagining surveys delivered on television or via text message. "Each of these new methods would bring some challenges, chief among them the question of how surveyors would ensure their respondents were a true cross-section of the population. But given what's happening to telephone usage, the same goes for traditional polling."[25]

NOTES

1. Steven Shepard, "Who Else Had a Bad Night? Pollsters," *Politico*, November 5, 2014, accessed December 16, 2014, http://www.politico.com/story/2014/11/2014-midterms-polls-112593.html.

2. Kyle Kondik and Geoffrey Skelley, "14 From '14: Quick Takes on the Midterm," *Sabato's Crystal Ball*. November 13, 2014, accessed December 16, 2014, http://www.centerforpolitics.org/crystalball/articles/14-from-14-quick-takes-on-the-midterm/.

3. "National Council on Public Polls Analysis of Final 2012 Pre-Election Polls," National Council on Public Polls, Jan. 1, 2013, accessed December 16, 2014, http://ncpp.org/files/NCPP%20Election%20Poll%20Analysis%202012%20-%20FINAL%20012413.pdf. Computations for 2002, 2010, and 2006 (final week only) are from the National Council on Public Polls report. Computations for 2014 and for the final three weeks in 2006 are by the authors.

4. Nate Silver, "The Polls Were Skewed Toward Democrats," *FiveThirtyEight*, November 5, 2014, accessed December 16, 2014, http://fivethirtyeight.com/features/the-polls-were-skewed-toward-democrats/.

5. Eric McGhee, "The 2014 Polls Were Still Really Good at Predicting Winners," *Washington Post*, December 12, 2014, accessed December 16, 2014, http://www.washingtonpost.com/blogs/monkey-cage/wp/2014/12/12/the-2014-polls-were-still-really-good-at-predicting-winners/.

6. Mark Blumenthal, "Is Polling as We Know It Doomed?" *National Journal*, August 10, 2009, accessed December 16, 2014, http://www.nationaljournal.com/njonline/is-polling-as-we-know-it-doomed-20090810.

7. Mario Callegaro, Allan L. McCutcheon, and Jack Ludwig, "Who's Calling? The Impact of Caller ID on Telephone Survey Response," *Field Methods* 22, no. 2 (2010): 176, doi: 10.1177/1525822X09356046; Executive Office of the President and Council of Economic Advisers, *Economic Report of the President (2009)* (Washington, DC: U.S. Government Printing Office, 2009), 244; Marjorie Connelly, "Why Do-Not-Call Lists Don't Work Against Pollsters," *New York Times*, May 8, 2014, accessed December 16, 2014, http://www.nytimes.com/2014/05/09/upshot/why-do-not-call-lists-dont-work-against-pollsters.html.

8. "Assessing the Representativeness of Public Opinion Surveys," Pew Research Center for the People and the Press, May 15, 2012, accessed December 16, 2014, http://www.people-press.org/2012/05/15/assessing-the-representativeness-of-public-opinion-surveys/.

9. Stephen J. Blumberg and Julian V. Luke, "Wireless Substitution: Early Release of Estimates From the National Health Interview Survey, July–December 2013," Centers for Disease Control and Prevention, July 2014, accessed December 16, 2014, http://www.cdc.gov/nchs/data/nhis/earlyrelease/wireless201407.pdf.

10. Drew DeSilver, "For Most Wireless-Only Households, Look South and West," Pew Research Center, December 23, 2013, accessed December 16, 2014, http://www.pewresearch.org/fact-tank/2013/12/23/for-most-wireless-only-households-look-south-and-west/.

11. "New Considerations for Survey Researchers When Planning and Conducting RDD Telephone Surveys in the U.S. with Respondents Reached via Cell Phone Numbers," American Association for Public Opinion Research Cell Phone Task Force, 2010, 77–78, 95–108, https://www.aapor.org/AAPORKentico/AAPOR_Main/media/MainSiteFiles/2010AAPORCellPhoneTFReport.pdf.

12. *Ibid.*, 27.

13. Mark Blumenthal, "The Case For Robo-Pollsters," *National Journal*, September 14, 2009, accessed December 16, 2014, http://www.nationaljournal.com/njonline/the-case-for-robo-pollsters-20090914.

14. Nate Silver, "Rasmussen Polls Were Biased and Inaccurate; Quinnipiac, SurveyUSA Performed Strongly," *FiveThirtyEight* (*New York Times*), November 4, 2010, accessed December 16, 2014, http://fivethirtyeight.blogs.nytimes.com/2010/11/04/rasmussen-polls-were-biased-and-inaccurate-quinnipiac-surveyusa-performed-strongly/; Nate Silver, "Which Polls Fared Best (and Worst) in the 2012 Presidential Race," *FiveThirtyEight* (*New York Times*), November 10, 2012, accessed December 16, 2014, http://fivethirtyeight.blogs.nytimes.com/2012/11/10/which-polls-fared-best-and-worst-in-the-2012-presidential-race/.

15. Mark Mellman, "Mark Mellman: Exclude the Excluders," *The Hill*, July 15, 2014, accessed December 16, 2014, http://thehill.com/opinion/mark-mellman/212371-exclude-the-excluders; Mark Blumenthal and Ariel Edwards-Levy, "HUFFPOLLSTER: Do Robopolls Get It Wrong?" *Huffington Post*, July 16, 2014, accessed December 16, 2014, http://www.huffingtonpost.com/2014/07/16/robopolls_n_5593149.html.

16. Mark Blumenthal and Ariel Edwards-Levy, "HUFFPOLLSTER: What Happened with the Polling in Virginia?" *Huffington Post*, November 6, 2013, accessed December 16, 2014, http://www.huffingtonpost.com/2013/11/06/huffpollster-what-happene_n_4228712.html.

17. Mark Blumenthal and Ariel Edwards-Levy, "HUFFPOLLSTER: How Much Will Voter Disaffection Help the GOP?" *Huffington Post*, October 28, 2014, accessed December 16, 2014, http://www.huffingtonpost.com/2014/10/28/gop-polls_n_6060470.html.

18. Transcribed from McInturff's comments at "2014 Election Polling: A Post-Mortem and Look to the Future" (Roper Center and Washington-Baltimore Chapter of the AAPOR event, Washington, DC, November 13, 2014), http://www.ropercenter.uconn.edu/elections/2014-election-post-mortem.html.

19. Mark Blumenthal and Ariel Edwards-Levy, "HUFFPOLLSTER: Dysfunctional Government Now America's Biggest Worry," *Huffington Post*, October 9, 2013, accessed December 16, 2014, http://www.huffingtonpost.com/2013/10/09/dysfunctional-government-_n_4073451.html.

20. Drew DeSilver, "Q/A: What the New York Times' Polling Decision Means," Pew Research Center, July 28, 2014, accessed December 16, 2014, http://www .pewresearch.org/fact-tank/2014/07/28/qa-what-the-new-york-times-polling-deci sion-means/.

21. David Rothschild and Andrew Gelman, "Modern Polling Requires Both Sampling and Adjustment," *Huffington Post*, August 4, 2014, accessed December 16, 2014, http://www.huffingtonpost.com/david-rothschild/modern-polling-requires -b_b_5646174.html; Michael Link, "The Critical Role of Transparency & Standards in Today's World of Polling and Opinion Research," American Association for Public Opinion Research release, August 1, 2014.

22. "Westat Collaborates with the Pew Research Center and SurveyMonkey," Westat, December 5, 2014, accessed December 16, 2014, https://www.westat.com/ news/westat-collaborates-pew-research-center-and-surveymonkey.

23. Mark Blumenthal and Ariel Edwards-Levy, "HUFFPOLLSTER: Experimental 2014 Polls Show Promise," *Huffington Post*, December 4, 2014, accessed December 16, 2014, http://www.huffingtonpost.com/2014/12/04/polls-2014_n_6268604 .html.

24. Kathleen Caulderwood, "Midterm Elections 2014: Why Everything You've Heard About Inaccurate Poll Data Is Wrong," *International Business Times*, November 4, 2014, accessed December 16, 2014, http://www.ibtimes.com/midterm-elections -2014-why-everything-youve-heard-about-inaccurate-poll-data-wrong-1718168; Drew DeSilver, "Q/A: What the New York Times' Polling Decision Means," Pew Research Center, July 28, 2014, accessed December 16, 2014, http://www.pew research.org/fact-tank/2014/07/28/qa-what-the-new-york-times-polling-decision -means/.

25. David Leonhardt, "Polling's Past, Present and Future," *New York Times*, October 3, 2014, accessed December 16, 2014, http://www.nytimes.com/2014/10/04/ upshot/letter-from-the-editor-pollings-past-present-and-future.html.

8

Obama's Last Chance to Come Through in a Crunch

Jill Lawrence

Barack Obama has shown throughout his political life that he is never more energized or determined than when his back is to the wall. The last two years of his presidency promise a stiff test of that resilience as he fights for his ideas, his party, and his place in history.

If Republicans were expecting a chastened president after Democrats' crushing midterm losses, or someone preoccupied with his post-presidential life and library, those hopes were quickly dashed. Far from waving a white flag, Obama emerged more assertive than ever after a 2014 campaign fought on hostile political turf. "The president was held back in a lot of ways from being an advocate for his agenda," a senior White House aide said in a post-midterm interview. No longer constrained by "worrying about how things we say or do affect senators in very red states," he's back to arguing for his policies and doing what he can to advance them.

A two-year roller coaster of intense clashes and selective deal-making lies ahead as Obama and Republicans vie to dominate the national debate. Some in the GOP are itching for a sustained state of siege against Obama. Others, including House Speaker John Boehner and Senate Majority Leader Mitch McConnell, argue that in addition to defining its agenda, the party must demonstrate governing capacity to prepare for a post-Obama future. As for the president, he intends to be "very aggressive," according to the White House aide, "but we do not view aggressive executive action and legislative cooperation as mutually exclusive."

The rapidly improving economy, though it did not help Democrats in the midterms, will put a sheen on Obama's final years and could generate money for wish lists in both parties. That in turn could ease some negotiations on Capitol Hill. Still, there are myriad complications ahead for Obama, and many will be out of his control.

The Supreme Court could gut the Affordable Care Act, a pillar of his legacy, by summer 2015. The shrunken Democratic presence on Capitol Hill will hobble progress on most liberal priorities. The Middle East continues to roil, along with arguments over Obama's policies to fight the Islamic State and contain Vladimir Putin. There is another congressional report on the 2012 Benghazi attacks in the works, and newly empowered Senate Republicans will join their House counterparts in launching oversight and investigative hearings across the executive branch. Republican lawsuits challenging Obama's use of executive power will be working their way through the courts. National reckonings on race and police behavior will pose a continuing challenge for the administration. So will the GOP's numerous 2016 presidential hopefuls, who are competing hard for the title of most anti-Obama.

There's discontent on the president's team as well. Obama heads a party that has eroded at every level during his tenure, and some Democrats blame him for the decline. In his 2015 State of the Union address, Obama laid out a "middle-class economics" agenda with broad appeal, but it won't paper over all Democratic differences. In a sign of the difficulties ahead, and of the divergent interests of the president and his party, scores of liberals led by Nancy Pelosi and Elizabeth Warren broke publicly with Obama at the end of 2014. They risked a government shutdown to oppose the massive "cromnibus" spending bill for 2015, chiefly because it loosened regulations on big banks.

The rap on two-term presidencies in general is that they are incubators for final-quarter scandals, quagmires, inertia, and fatigue. There is evidence of that (the Bill Clinton impeachment trial and the Iraq war are good examples), and yet right from the start these periods have also yielded notable achievements. George Washington signed a treaty with Spain that gave America free access to the Mississippi River—a boon for settlement of the Ohio River Valley and trade with Europe via New Orleans.[1] James Madison cemented the need for and existence of a central bank.[2] James Monroe established that the federal government had a constitutional role to play in national transportation systems. He also declared the Americas closed to colonization by European nations—a dramatic pronouncement now known as the Monroe Doctrine.[3] More recently, Ronald Reagan negotiated a treaty with Soviet leader Mikhail Gorbachev to eliminate intermediate-range ballistic and cruise missiles, and George W. Bush convinced Congress to pass a massive bank bailout that headed off the collapse of Wall Street.

Obama started his post-midterm lame-duck period as if he'd been shot out of a cannon. He announced an agreement with China to limit carbon emissions that contribute to climate change. His Environmental Protection

Agency issued regulations to limit ozone emissions that can aggravate asthma and other conditions and raise the risk of premature death from heart or lung disease. He issued three veto threats in one day against bills the administration said would compromise the environment and scientific freedom.

Eight days later, through spokeswoman Jennifer Friedman, Obama threatened to veto an emerging bipartisan tax deal because "it would provide permanent tax breaks to help well-connected corporations while neglecting working families."[4] Diving into controversy, Obama urged federal regulators to protect net neutrality with "the strongest possible rules." He also took a series of aggressive steps to resolve problems and conflicts that have simmered for decades. He announced that he would reopen diplomatic relations with Cuba and designate most of the Arctic National Wildlife Refuge as wilderness—a status that would prohibit oil drilling and road construction. And he issued a sweeping immigration order that is expected to shield more than four million people from deportation.

White House officials said that after two years of House inaction on immigration, including its refusal to consider a bipartisan Senate bill, there was no point in waiting any longer. "The idea that now that we have a more conservative Congress, that this would be right around the corner, seems a bit far-fetched to me," senior adviser Dan Pfeiffer said shortly after the midterms. "And every day the president waits is another day that these families would be living under the threat of deportation."[5]

Angry Republicans said the immigration move would make it impossible for them to work with Obama on other issues. The threat amused Charles Brain, the White House liaison with Congress during Clinton's last two years. Even after the House had found Clinton "worthy of being removed from office for high crimes and misdemeanors," Brain said at an American University forum in December, "they found a way to work with us."[6]

Cooler heads were beginning to prevail even before Obama told the Business Roundtable in December that "one of the habits that this town has to break is this notion that if you disagree on one thing, then suddenly everybody takes their ball home and they don't play." Boehner defused an incipient movement to block Obama's State of the Union address in the House chamber with a crack that preserved both the invitation and his own credibility with the GOP's scorched-earth anti-Obama wing: "The more the president talks about his ideas, the more unpopular he becomes. Why would I want to deprive him of that opportunity?"

A KNOTTY CAPITOL HILL PARTNERSHIP

Coming out of the midterms, a CNN/ORC poll found that the parties were at rough parity in terms of favorability. In the poll, a snapshot of the nation's post-election mood, 68 percent of adults said Republicans weren't cooperating enough with Obama (57 percent said the same of Obama) and half would blame the GOP for a shutdown (33 percent would blame Obama). Perhaps most relevant for Boehner-McConnell planning purposes, while 74 percent called the midterm results a rejection for Democrats, only 16 percent said they were a mandate for Republicans.[7]

Not surprisingly, GOP leaders want brinksmanship and government shutdown threats off the table. Their playbook is to project sober responsibility, pursue a serious agenda, and hope less temperate members at some point accept that, electoral triumphs aside, there's still a Democrat in the White House. Filing lawsuits, blocking some nominations, and selectively withholding government funds remain tools the Republican Congress can use to thwart Obama when he makes them unhappy, as he did with his broad immigration order. At the same time, they are tools that won't cripple the government or push it to the verge of default.

The cathartic but symbolic "Preventing Executive Overreach on Immigration Act of 2014," a bill passed by House Republicans during the 2014 lame-duck session to roll back Obama's order in immigration, hinted of the two years ahead. "There will be things Republicans work through with the president in terms of trying to get something signed," pollster David Winston, a strategic adviser to House and Senate Republicans, said in an interview. But he said there will also be "moments when you want to define a choice"—that is, bills that Republicans know Obama won't sign, but are valuable as messages to their party and the country. Obama can expect to receive "message" bills that, among other things, repeal the Affordable Care Act, approve the Keystone XL pipeline, and halt EPA plans to limit carbon emissions at existing coal plants.

Obama's power to veto bills and merely threaten vetoes gives him considerable leverage to preserve his achievements, shape legislation, and block laws. By year's end Obama was already stepping up contacts with fellow Democrats on the Hill, according to the *Washington Post*, to solidify relations and ensure that his prospective vetoes stick (Republicans would need two-thirds majorities in both chambers to override them, and they are far short of that in the House and the Senate).[8]

Some turbulence is inevitable on nominations. That goes quadruple if a Supreme Court seat opens up, and passions will spike to exponential levels if the vacancy is one that could shift the current ideological balance of five conservatives and four liberals. That is not out of the question. Conservatives Antonin Scalia and Anthony Kennedy, both born in 1936, are two of the three oldest justices on the court. The most senior, liberal Ruth Bader Ginsburg, is a cancer survivor who had heart surgery in November 2014 at age eighty-one.

Contentious debate over Obama's foreign and defense policies is also a certainty, given Obama's dramatic moves on Cuba, his controversial nuclear talks with Iran, deteriorating conditions in Syria, a resurgent Taliban in Afghanistan, and the prospect of a congressional vote on authorizing use of military force against the Islamic State. The administration is well into a campaign of air strikes on IS targets in Iraq and Syria, and it has already sent 3,000 troops to Iraq to train Iraqi forces. Obama does not believe he needs congressional authority for the military campaign, but the White House says congressional buy-in would strengthen his hand and is working toward that.

What Obama may need most from a Republican Congress could be the hardest thing for him to get—namely, a minor but momentous technical fix to the Affordable Care Act. The Supreme Court will decide in 2015 whether one errant phrase in the extensive law means people who buy insurance through the federal healthcare.gov marketplace are ineligible for subsidies to offset the cost of coverage. Such a ruling would cripple the law, since more than 80 percent who buy policies receive subsidies and thirty-four states rely on federal rather than state-run shopping sites.[9]

Republican Trent Lott, the former Senate majority leader, says Congress should fix the problematic phrase and perhaps combine that with repeal of a medical devices tax sought by Republicans and a few Democrats. "I would think they should work at that," Lott said in December. "One of the things I'm looking for, who would be the leader in the House or the Senate, Republicans or even Democrats, that would try to find a way to do some improvements without demolishing the bill."[10] However, Obama is not inclined to reward the medical device industry for having the best lobbyists by repealing the tax (which helps pay for the law), and is firm about keeping a requirement that large employers offer health coverage (a top item on the GOP and business make-it-disappear list). The hypothetical Republican path to a deal is even steeper. Almost all Republicans ran in 2014 on pledges to repeal the entire law, and McConnell was explicit about his hope that the Supreme Court would "take it down" in 2015, setting the stage for "a major do-over."[11]

In other areas, the general midterm message of "fix this!" could bring results. "Getting some things done, moving things forward, will probably be helpful to both parties," said Winston, the GOP strategist, and there are some opportunities for that. Obama would like to sign sentencing reforms and a revamped surveillance law, both of which have bipartisan support. Other possibilities track an agenda shared by Obama and the business community—patent reform, immigration reform, tax reform, trade agreements, and new spending on public works. Obama told the Roundtable leaders that tax reform should be first up because "you need a pretty long runway for that," probably six to nine months, for an agreement to solidify.

Lott says he's hopeful because the new chairmen of the tax-writing committees, Representative Paul Ryan and Senator Orrin Hatch, are "both known to be a little independent sometimes" and "might get out of control of their leadership" if they see their way to a deal.[12] But complications already loom, from the GOP hard line against raising taxes to Obama's warning that tax reform can't just be a gift to corporations. "It's going to have to be balanced. We're not going to leave EITC [earned income tax credit] or the child tax credit behind and just do a corporate piece on its own," he told the business leaders. Opening up another front for debate, Obama sees corporate tax reform as a vehicle for "a one-time big push on infrastructure." Aides suggest the new tax structure could yield up to $150 billion from a one-time fee on repatriated corporate earnings and believe some Republicans are privately receptive to the idea. As for a stand-alone infrastructure bill, Obama said it's unlikely because Republicans are "very sensitive . . . to anything that might be construed as a tax. Of course, it's hard to pay for things if you don't have some sort of revenue stream."

New spending on roads, bridges, and other public works would be a crowd-pleaser across the political spectrum. But Democrats are divided over another Obama priority: closing huge trade deals with Asian-Pacific nations and the European Union. Obama says he will urge Democrats and unions not to "fight the last war" by opposing the two agreements. He argues that the Asia pact would raise wages, labor standards, and environmental standards in some countries. "Those who oppose these trade deals ironically are accepting a status quo that is more damaging to American workers," he said in the Business Roundtable session, an apparent reference to the competitive advantage of overseas companies that don't have to meet such standards. He may not convince many Democrats, but he may not need many of them, given relatively strong GOP support.

By contrast, liberals would be thrilled if Obama could finally get Congress to help him close the U.S. prison for terrorist suspects at Guantanamo Bay, Cuba. The importance of the 2008 campaign promise was underscored as Obama did some year-end shopping at Politics and Prose, an independent bookstore in a liberal Washington neighborhood. "Hope you can close Guantanamo," a customer told him. "We're working on it," Obama replied. "Any other issues?" he asked jokingly, but no one raised any. The main obstacle to shutting down Guantanamo is a congressional ban on moving its inmates to U.S. prisons. The White House continues to transfer remaining inmates to other countries and intends to keep working to end the ban on sending some to U.S. prisons.

In the end, the principal unfulfilled pledge of 2008 could be statutory immigration reform that offers most undocumented immigrants a path to citizenship, or at least permanent legal residency. As the 2016 election approaches and the GOP need for Latino support rises, there is a chance that Congress could supersede Obama's immigration order by sending him a reform bill. That's the solution he habitually offers—"pass a bill"—when Republicans sound off about his immigration "overreach." But it's not at all clear that a Republican Congress could produce a bill or a package he'd be willing to sign.

Another likely casualty is a "grand bargain" to reduce the federal debt by raising taxes and curbing the growth of spending on Medicare and Social Security. Failed efforts by Obama to reach an agreement with Boehner during his first term left a legacy of mutual mistrust. As the final stage of Obama's presidency dawned, his administration celebrated a sharp drop in the federal deficit to 2.8 percent of the overall economy, down from 10.1 percent in 2009. But Republicans fastened on a different milestone, bemoaning the rise of the accumulated national debt above $18 trillion.[13] Everybody was right.

THE EXPANSIVE EXECUTIVE OPTION

Republicans often accuse Obama of acting like a king or emperor in his use of executive powers, a charge hardly any president has escaped. In Obama's case, he has stepped into a vacuum left by Congress. The 112th Congress of 2011–2012 set a record for low productivity with a total of 283 laws enacted, according to federal records. The 113th Congress managed to beat that (albeit barely) by passing 296 new laws.[14]

"Republicans used their majority foothold in the House to guarantee that Congress would be the graveyard of serious policymaking," congressional scholar Thomas E. Mann wrote in November on the FixGov blog at the Brookings Institution. "The cost of such unrelenting opposition and gridlock is that policymaking initiative and power inevitably will flow elsewhere—to the executive and the courts."[15]

Obama's avalanche of executive-branch activity right after the midterms was partly due to timing (for instance, he went to China and came home with the bilateral climate agreement) but mostly because Obama sat on his to-do list to help red-state Democratic senators pursuing reelection. After they lost, months of pent-up policies spilled out of the White House. It's a pattern that presages Obama's final two years. The all-Republican 114th Congress is almost certain to surpass the divided 113th Congress when it comes to passing bills and even making deals with Obama. But Democratic priorities will be up to the president, and he plans to continue tending to them.

Discussing what he called a "tough election" with ABC's George Stephanopoulos, Obama said he told his Cabinet and staff that "Even if Congress doesn't do another thing, even if you don't get a dime's more money or no new program is set up, you can figure out over these next two years how to make this thing work just a little bit better" for people who need jobs, can't afford college or are in danger of losing their home.[16]

Much of what Obama does administratively will be vulnerable to reversal by the next Republican president. But some of his policies could endure if future chief executives, perhaps operating in a different environment, decide they are acceptable or it would be politically risky to upset the status quo.

Perhaps the most important item on the executive agenda—and perhaps the most important issue for the planet's future—is how to slow down carbon emissions, which are a key contributor to climate change. Obama has moved on his own in the face of strong congressional resistance. The steps he has taken—including regulations to limit emissions at new and existing coal plants and a commitment from automakers to increase vehicle efficiency—go a long way toward meeting the requirements of the agreement he signed with China. A future president who prefers a different path would have to factor in the potentially far-reaching consequences of breaking that deal.

Pushed in part by the U.S.-China accord, more than 190 nations pledged in December 2014 to draw up plans to limit greenhouse gas emissions to prepare for talks on a global treaty a year later at a United Nations conference in Paris. There's practically zero chance Obama could win the two-thirds Senate vote needed to ratify an international climate treaty. A more practical outcome may be bilateral and multilateral agreements that require only Obama's signature. But of course, like the China pact, they would be subject to the desires of future presidents.

Obama has already done much of what is unilaterally possible in the area of income inequality, including requiring federal contractors to pay a minimum wage of $10.10. There is at least one income booster still to come. In March 2014, Obama asked the Labor Department to update overtime regulations to apply to more workers. There have been only two inflation adjustments in forty years to the minimum salary to qualify for overtime, the administration said. It has slipped to $23,660 a year, making overtime mandatory for only 12 percent of salaried workers, down from 65 percent in 1975. New regulations to cover more people are expected in 2015.[17]

Several important aspects of Obama's final two years are being handled by the Justice Department, which will be led by Loretta Lynch if the new GOP Congress confirms her to succeed departing Attorney General Eric Holder. The department is reviewing thousands of clemency applications as part of an initiative to free non-violent offenders who would be out of prison by now under current sentencing requirements. And it is involved in closely watched legal challenges to restrictive voter laws in North Carolina, Ohio, and Wisconsin, cases that depending on the outcome could help or hurt Obama's quest for a Democratic successor in 2016.

The Justice Department is also Obama's chief avenue for dealing with anger and frustration over the failure of grand juries to indict white police officers for killing black men in Ferguson, Missouri, and Staten Island, New York. Federal authorities are conducting civil rights investigations into the two deaths and into the Ferguson department overall, and a national task force is studying issues such as police militarization and body cameras.

Those looking for fire and emotion from the first black president to command the bully pulpit likely won't find it. Obama has called the tragedies "an American problem" and responded with typical restraint. To those who are furious and mistrustful, he advises patient, persistent work for change. "When you're dealing with something as deeply rooted as racism or bias, in any society, you gotta have vigilance," he said in an interview with Black Entertainment Television, "but you have to recognize that it's going to take some time and you just have to be steady."[18]

POLITICS AS HELP AND HINDRANCE

If there's hope for less gridlock in Obama's final two years, it stems from political imperatives for Republicans in 2016 that did not exist in 2013–2014. The party's presidential ticket, all of its House members, and many GOP senators and governors will be facing the larger, less conservative, more Democratic electorate that turns out in presidential elections. Those in swing states and districts will need to appeal to moderates and independents, not just hard-core conservatives.

There are several freshmen senators who rode in on an earlier GOP wave in states that Obama won twice: Marco Rubio of Florida, Mark Kirk of Illinois, Kelly Ayotte of New Hampshire, Rob Portman of Ohio, Pat Toomey of Pennsylvania, and Ron Johnson of Wisconsin. Richard Burr of North Carolina could also be vulnerable. If they run for reelection, as opposed to retiring or running for president, they may be open to bipartisan projects that position them as problem-solvers who are practical rather than doctrinaire.

A similar dynamic could develop on the House side among an enlarged group that *Politico*'s Alex Isenstadt has christened "the Obama Republicans": twenty-six members from districts that Obama won in 2012, nine more than in the previous Congress. That may give Boehner a bit more running room in his quest to maintain stability and pass some bills Obama can sign.[19]

There are countervailing forces in play, however, embodied by three senators who are likely GOP presidential candidates: Rubio, Ted Cruz, and Rand Paul. Cruz is already an agitator trying to push the House as well as the Senate to the right, and the others may feel called to compete for the mantle. The pressure will be on all three to impress markedly conservative primary voters in the leadoff states of Iowa and South Carolina. Once there is a GOP nominee, the pressure will move in a different direction, toward the broadest possible appeal. Depending on who tops the ticket that could be a window for congressional action—maybe even on immigration.

Democratic presidential candidates, likely led by Hillary Clinton, will have a different set of problems. The White House maintains it is not anticipating criticism of Obama in the Democratic primaries. The president's post-midterm approval rating among Democrats was nearly 87 percent in the *RealClearPolitics* polling average.[20] "Distancing yourself from Obama is not a path to the Democratic nomination," the White House aide said.

That doesn't mean it won't happen. There was a brief furor when Clinton, Obama's former secretary of state, told *The Atlantic* that "don't do stupid stuff" (reportedly an Obama team mantra) is not an organizing principle for foreign policy and said failed administration policy in Syria had led to the rise of the Islamic State.[21] For his part, Obama unhelpfully said on ABC that voters in 2016 will want a candidate with "that new car smell"—someone who doesn't have "as much mileage as me."[22] At sixty-seven, with a resume that includes former first lady of Arkansas, former first lady of the United States, and New York senator as well as secretary of state, Clinton arguably has even more mileage than Obama. But the two former 2008 rivals appear to take each other's missteps and strategic decisions in stride. They continue to talk regularly, including occasional chats at the White House. Obama calls Clinton a friend who was an "outstanding" secretary of state and would make a "terrific" president.

Potential candidates less prominent than Clinton, including Vermont Senator Bernie Sanders, former Virginia Senator Jim Webb, and former Maryland governor Martin O'Malley, are already talking about what they'd do differently from Obama on immigration, national security, and the economy. It's a foreshadowing of the 2016 general election campaign. Obama's approval rating among all adults was in the low to mid-40s throughout 2014.[23] Unless it soars in the next two years, the eventual Democratic nominee will be trying to simultaneously embrace and separate from Obama.

The president has produced a mixed political legacy reflected in his own standing with different slices of the electorate. His approval rating among working-class, non-college white voters plummeted from 48 percent in 2009 to 27 percent in 2014, with overall white approval at 32 percent.[24] To rebuild party support among this group, the 2016 nominee will have to clearly convey that this will not be a third Obama term. At the same time, he or she will need to energize the minority voters who elected Obama twice and continue to hold him in high esteem. His 2014 approval rating among blacks was 84 percent. It was in the two-thirds range for Asians, and after his immigration order, it jumped to 68 percent among Hispanics.[25] That's a lot of people you don't want to alienate.

In order to achieve what matters most to him, Obama stands ready to help the Democratic nominee as either a cheerleader or, reprising his 2014 role, taking what he calls "dings" as a scapegoat. "I am very interested in making sure that I've got a Democratic successor," Obama told Stephanopoulos.[26] Considering the chasm between the parties and the extent to which he has relied on executive action, much of his legacy depends on it.

NOTES

1. George Washington "Foreign Policy" essay, Miller Center, University of Virginia, accessed December 6, 2014, http://millercenter.org/president/washington/essays/biography/5.

2. James Madison "Domestic Affairs" essay, Miller Center, University of Virginia, accessed December 6, 2014, http://millercenter.org/president/madison/essays/biography/4.

3. James Monroe essays, Miller Center, University of Virginia, accessed December 6, 2014, http://millercenter.org/president/monroe.

4. Brian Faler, "White House Threatens to Veto Tax Deal," *Politico*, November 25, 2014, accessed December 6, 2014, http://www.politico.com/story/2014/11/tax-breaks-corporations-draft-113169.html.

5. "*Christian Science Monitor* Breakfast with Dan Pfeiffer," C-SPAN, November 21, 2014, accessed December 6, 2014, http://www.c-span.org/video/?322876-1/christian-science-monitor-breakfast-senior-white-house-adviser-dan-pfeiffer.

6. Transcribed from Brain's comments at "White House Congressional Relations: Strategic Options for the President and the Congress" (American University's Center for Congressional and Presidential Studies event, Washington, DC, December 11, 2014), http://www.american.edu/spa/ccps/2014_events.cfm.

7. CNN/ORC Poll, November 21–23, 2014, accessed December 6, 2014, http://i2.cdn.turner.com/cnn/2014/images/12/01/cnnorcpoll12012014.pdf.

8. Juliet Eilperin, "Obama, Looking to Mend Fences with Congress, Is Reaching Out. To Democrats," *Washington Post*, December 3, 2014, accessed December 6, 2014, http://www.washingtonpost.com/politics/obama-looking-to-mend-fences-with-congress-is-reaching-out-to-democrats/2014/12/03/3fdf9078-7a40-11e4-9a27-6fdbc612bff8_story.html.

9. Larry Levitt, Gary Claxton and Anthony Damico, "How Much Financial Assistance Are People Receiving Under the Affordable Care Act?" Kaiser Family Foundation, March 27, 2014, accessed December 6, 2014, http://kff.org/health-reform/issue-brief/how-much-financial-assistance-are-people-receiving-under-the-affordable-care-act/.

10. "*Christian Science Monitor Breakfast* with Tom Daschle and Trent Lott," C-SPAN, December 4, 2014, accessed December 7, 2014, http://www.c-span.org/video/?323069-1/christian-science-monitor-breakfast-tom-daschle-trent-lott.

11. Greg Sargent, "Mitch McConnell: We Can't Repeal Obamacare, But Supreme Court May 'Take It Down' Instead," *Washington Post*, December 2, 2014, accessed December 7, 2014, http://www.washingtonpost.com/blogs/plum-line/wp/2014/12/02/mitch-mcconnell-we-cant-repeal-obamacare-but-supreme-court-may-take-it-down-instead /.

12. "*Christian Science Monitor Breakfast* with Tom Daschle and Trent Lott," C-SPAN, December 4, 2014.

13. Christopher Condon, "U.S. Deficit Decline to 2.8% of GDP Is Unprecedented Turn," *Bloomberg*, November 4, 2014, accessed December 7, 2014, http://www.bloomberg.com/news/2014-11-04/u-s-deficit-decline-to-2-8-of-gdp-is-unprecedented-turn.html.

14. "Browse Public Laws, 113th Congress," Library of Congress, accessed January 23, 2015, http://thomas.loc.gov/home/LegislativeData.php?&n = PublicLaws &c = 113.

15. Thomas E. Mann, "Obama's Immigration Order Isn't a Power Grab," Brookings Institution, November 20, 2014, accessed December 7, 2014, http://www .brookings.edu/blogs/fixgov/posts/2014/11/20-obama-executive-order-immigration -speech-mann.

16. George Stephanopoulos, "Full Interview Transcript: President Obama on 'This Week'," *ABC News*, November 23, 2014, accessed December 7, 2014, http:// abcnews.go.com/blogs/politics/2014/11/full-interview-transcript-president-obama -on-this-week/.

17. "FACT SHEET: Opportunity for All: Rewarding Hard Work by Strengthening Overtime Protections," The White House, March 13, 2014, accessed December 7, 2014, whitehouse.gov, http://www.whitehouse.gov/the-press-office/2014/03/13/ fact-sheet-opportunity-all-rewarding-hard-work-strengthening-overtime-pr.

18. Jeff Johnson, "Exclusive: President Barack Obama Sits Down with BET," Black Entertainment Television, December 7, 2014, accessed December 7, 2014, http://www.bet.com/shows/106-and-park/news/2014/12/president-barack-obama -sits-down-with-bet-networks-for-an-interview-at-the-white-house-to-discuss-recent -unrest-in-america.html.

19. Alex Isenstadt, "The Obama Republicans?" *Politico*, November 30, 2014, accessed December 7, 2014, http://www.politico.com/story/2014/11/the-obama -republicans-113221.html#ixzz3KgQUGhr3.

20. "President Obama Job Approval Among Democrats," *RealClearPolitics*, accessed December 7, 2014, http://www.realclearpolitics.com/epolls/other/pres ident_obama_job_approval_among_democrats-1046.html.

21. Jeffrey Goldberg, " 'Failure' to Help Syrian Rebels Led to the Rise of ISIS," *The Atlantic*, August 10, 2014, accessed December 7, 2014, http://www.theatlantic.com/ international/archive/2014/08/hillary-clinton-failure-to-help-syrian-rebels-led-to -the-rise-of-isis/375832/.

22. George Stephanopoulos, "Full Interview Transcript: President Obama on 'This Week,'" *ABC News*, November 23, 2014.

23. "Presidential Approval Ratings—Barack Obama," Gallup, accessed December 7, 2014, http://www.gallup.com/poll/116479/barack-obama-presidential-job-ap proval.aspx.

24. Frank Newport, "Presidential Approval Drops Among Working-Class Whites," Gallup, November 25, 2014, accessed December 7, 2014, http://www.gal lup.com/poll/179753/obama-approval-drops-among-working-class-whites.aspx.

25. Philip Bump, "Hispanic Approval of President Obama Surges Following Immigration Announcement," *Washington Post*, December 1, 2014, accessed December 7, 2014, http://www.washingtonpost.com/blogs/the-fix/wp/2014/12/ 01/hispanic-approval-of-president-obama-surges-following-immigration-announce ment/.

26. George Stephanopoulos, "Full Interview Transcript: President Obama on 'This Week,'" *ABC News*, November 23, 2014.

9

Barack Obama and the Democrats' 2016 Dilemma

Jamelle Bouie

George W. Bush began 2007 with abysmal approval ratings.[1] His party had lost its grip on both chambers of Congress, and the country was barreling toward a recession that would give Democrats both the presidency and their largest majorities in a generation.

Compared to this, the Barack Obama of 2015 looks *okay*. Yes, his party faced its second midterm wave and lost the Senate—ceding control to the GOP—but as of late January 2015 the president is actually slightly more popular than he was at the beginning of 2014, which is to say, modestly unpopular with an average approval rating of approximately 45 percent (versus about 43 percent in January 2014).[2] And while his legislative agenda has long since stalled, he's made ample use of executive authority to protect his core accomplishment—the Affordable Care Act—and advance priorities in immigration, climate change, and civil rights.

But none of that will stand if the Democratic Party can't hold the White House in 2016. And while President Obama and the Democrats in 2015 aren't as bad off as Bush and the Republicans were in 2007, they're not in a good place either. At 32 percent, according to a November survey from the Pew Research Center, Democratic Party identification is at its lowest point since 2008 (although Republican Party identification remains in the high 20s).[3]

Likewise, pluralities of Americans don't trust Democrats to handle core issues like the economy and foreign policy. In an October *USA Today* poll,[4] 41 percent of respondents said they thought Republicans in Congress

153

would do a "better job" of handling foreign affairs and the economy. And in a November *Wall Street Journal* survey—taken just before the midterm elections—39 percent of respondents said the Republican Party would do a better job of "dealing with the economy," versus 30 percent for Democrats.[5]

There's an argument—a strong one—that the Democratic Party holds a natural advantage in presidential elections. From the get-go, when you tally the electoral votes of reliably "blue" states in the Northeast, the Rust Belt, and the West Coast, Democrats start with a thirty-seven electoral vote advantage over Republicans, 190 to 153. If you add lean Democratic and lean Republican states to the mix—places where a party consistently wins with margins between five and ten percentage points—Democrats start the 2016 presidential election with *257 electoral votes* out of the 270 they need to win. Add Virginia to the total—which has gone blue in four out of its last five statewide elections—and Democrats have the presidency.[6]

But this model is deceptive in that it assumes static conditions: a growing economy, relative peace, and either a popular Democratic incumbent (2012) or an unpopular Republican president (2008). If present projections are accurate, we'll have a growing economy in 2016.[7] And barring a new war, we'll have relative peace. But we may also have an unpopular Democratic president and a public that—after eight years—will likely want a change of pace. In that environment, anything can happen. Democrats could capture the presidency, or their national strength could collapse as the country makes another swing to the Republican Party.

To this, add the unusual intraparty circumstances of 2016. Like 2000, Democrats will have to run with the burden of a presidential legacy. But unlike then—when Al Gore was the clear choice to succeed Bill Clinton —no one in the administration stands as an obvious successor. Vice President Joe Biden has the credentials of a nominee, but he is surprisingly marginal for his position, with little support among Democratic voters and a modest position with the thousands of activists, donors, officials, and politicians that drive party decision making.[8] Instead, the presidential field looks more like the one in 2008: an open space, with room for any number of candidates to stake a claim for the party.

It doesn't help that Democrats are in slight disarray. Despite his political success and powerful legacy—the first Democrat since Franklin Roosevelt to command a majority of the popular vote in two elections *and* the first black president *and* the namesake to the largest social safety net expansion since Lyndon Johnson's Great Society—Barack Obama presides over a divided party. One wing, personified by Massachusetts Senator Elizabeth Warren, is furious with Obama's relationship to Wall Street, his penchant for compromise, and his willingness to always take a half loaf—to never take a stand against his ideological opponents in the conservative movement.

They wanted a president who would speak to their concerns, who would reverse the Bush years and usher in a new progressive era. They have had scathing criticism for Obama's economic and foreign policies, and they want to preserve the best of his tenure—such that it is—while making a definitive break with the style and conduct of his administration. "Enough is enough with Wall Street insiders getting key position after key position and the kind of cronyism that we have seen in the executive branch," said Warren in a fiery December 2014 speech on the Senate floor. "Enough is enough with Citigroup passing eleventh-hour deregulatory provisions that nobody takes ownership over but everybody will come to regret. Enough is enough."[9]

The other wing is the mainstream of the Democratic Party. It's content with the progress of the Obama administration and more interested in protecting their gains from a radical-minded Republican Party than expanding the possible of liberal politics. You can see some of this instinct for self-preservation in the reactions of the midterm wipeout, as some senior Democrats—like New York Senator Chuck Schumer—searched for something that could have saved their majority from the GOP. "Unfortunately, Democrats lost the opportunity the American people gave them. We took their mandate and put all of our focus on the wrong problem—health care reform," said Schumer in a November speech at the National Press Club in Washington.[10]

Ideologically, this wing hasn't tried to grapple with the shifting winds of Democratic politics. The most glaring example of this was the December funding fight, where the White House and its allies sacrificed parts of Dodd-Frank financial reform in order to fund the government for the next fiscal year. The political logic was sound: Cutting a deal with a Democratic Senate and a Republican House in a lame duck session is much preferable to cutting a deal with GOP majorities in both chambers. But the attack on financial reform—led by Democrats and Republicans—enraged liberals, who—led by Senator Warren—tried to scuttle the bill and shut down the government. The White House eventually prevailed, but not without harming itself further with anti-Wall Street liberals.[11]

All of this is to say that if presidential primaries are places where parties define themselves, then 2016 has all the makings of a war, where Democrats fight to chart a direction for the next decade. Or it would, if not for one figure.

WHAT HILLARY CLINTON MEANS FOR
THE DEMOCRATIC PARTY

At the risk of cliché, Hillary Rodham Clinton stands as one of the most unique figures in modern American politics.

A former first lady turned U.S. senator and then secretary of state, she came close to making history as the first woman to win a major party's nomination for the presidency. And when President Obama finishes his term in two years, she will stand as his most obvious successor.

To start, she's one of the most popular political figures in the country. As of this writing, *HuffPost* Pollster's average gives her a 46 percent favorable and 45 percent unfavorable rating.[12] As an isolated number, that sounds just okay. But consider this: President Obama, the sitting president, has a 44 percent favorable rating and a 50 percent unfavorable rating.[13] Vice President Joe Biden has a 41 percent favorable rating and 46 percent unfavorable rating, and Senate Minority Leader Harry Reid—albeit less well known than the president and vice president—has a 23 percent favorable rating and a 49 percent unfavorable rating.[14] Even Elizabeth Warren—crusader of the Democratic left—has just a 31 percent favorable rating (and a 33 percent unfavorable rating as well).[15]

Among Democrats, there's no competition. In the most recent average, Clinton takes 61.4 percent of the primary vote. Her next two competitors—Warren and Biden—take 12.3 percent and 9.0 percent, respectively.[16] This is a huge contrast to 2006 and 2007, when she was at most a modest favorite for the nomination.[17]

The answer for *why* Clinton is so popular (among Democrats, at least) is easy: Not only is she strongly associated with one of the most well-liked presidents in recent memory—her husband, Bill Clinton—but she also retains considerable goodwill from her first presidential campaign and her service in Obama's State Department.

As an aside, this is why—if Clinton is the 2016 Democratic nominee—it would be wrong to call her triumph a "coronation." We have a template for "coronations" in American politics: The 2000 Republican primary, when party leaders all but cleared the field for Texas Governor George W. Bush, who owed his political career to his deep roots in GOP politics by way of his father. If Clinton has the overwhelming support of the Democratic Party network—from donors and establishment figures to activists and ordinary voters—it's because she *earned it*, the dividends paid after a remarkable 2008 campaign and loyal service in her opponent's administration.

And as for Clinton versus Republicans? Among her hypothetical opponents, such as Jeb Bush (33 percent favorable, 46 percent unfavorable), New Jersey Governor Chris Christie (33 percent favorable, 45 percent unfavorable), Florida Senator Marco Rubio (31 percent favorable, 35 percent unfavorable), or Wisconsin Governor Scott Walker (26 percent favorable, 31 percent unfavorable), none have comparable ratings.[18] Indeed, there's no one of Hillary Clinton's visibility and prominence who is as popular as she is. And it shows up in other polling. As of late January 2015, in hypothetical match-ups against Bush, Christie, Rubio, Texas Senator Ted Cruz, Kentucky Senator Rand Paul, and Wisconsin Representative Paul Ryan, Clinton wins with 50-plus percent of the vote.[19] And in a December 2014 poll from NBC News, 50 percent of Americans say they could support Clinton for president, dwarfing everyone else, even as 40 percent say they want a Republican in the White House.[20]

But Hillary Clinton's popularity isn't just a fun observation. It's the defining fact of the present Democratic Party. Clinton's strength—her influence across the breadth of the Democratic Party—is a unifying force. The polls make it clear that almost every constituency in the party, from liberals and Blue Dogs to black Americans and working-class whites, is ready for her candidacy. The ideological divide in the Democratic coalition—the fight between Wall Street–friendly Democrats in the center and populist Democrats on the left—is dampened by her presence, not because of any sudden love or affection, but because the various factions see Clinton as the key to keeping the White House and saving the gains of the Obama administration from a hard right—and come 2016, restless—Republican Party. It's no surprise that the bulk of the Democratic Party machinery has fallen behind Clinton.[21] Given the stakes, no one wants open warfare.

But, we should be clear, it's not as if she isn't on a side. Hillary Clinton is tightly tied to the centrist mainstream of the Democratic Party. Not only was she part of the "Third Way" of pro-market reform Democrats in the 1990s, but she was also a New York senator who voted for the wars in Iraq and Afghanistan. And in the years since, she's maintained her hawkishness (as revealed in her 2014 book, *Hard Choices*) and her ties to Wall Street.[22] In a sense, the fact of her strength is a sign that anti-Wall Street Democrats are *weak*, that they can't actually contest leadership of the party.

Then again, there's no evidence that's the goal, at least right now.

WHAT ABOUT WARREN?

For the last year, Elizabeth Warren has fielded one, relentless question from the Washington press corps: *Are you running for president?* In December 2013, after writer Noam Scheiber suggested it in a story for *The New Republic*, she denied the thought.[23] "I am not running for president," Warren said. "I am working as hard as I can to be the best possible senator that I can be and to fight for the things that I promised during my campaign to fight for."[24] During the tour for her book, *A Fighting Chance*, she was asked and she answered. "I'm not running for president," said Warren to an audience of enthusiastic supporters.[25] And after her recent crusade against a spending bill that weakened Dodd-Frank—yielding a viral speech in which she slammed "cronyism" in the "executive branch"—Warren told NPR host Steve Inskeep that she wasn't running. Four times.[26]

Despite her support for a Clinton candidacy—she signed a letter endorsing Hillary last year—and her willingness to forgive Clinton for supporting pro–Wall Street legislation, the assumption is that Warren *must* have a challenge in mind. After all, the most vocal Republican senators—Rubio, Paul, and Cruz—are all angling for the nomination, and Warren—with her unabashed ideology and strident attacks on opponents—has more in common with them than she does quieter, less media-savvy senators.

But there's another possibility: Warren isn't running for president, she's trying to build influence. Elizabeth Warren, to borrow an argument from the *Washington Post*'s Dana Milbank, is the Democrat's Jim DeMint, an ideological leader for a "left-wing analogue to the tea party." Warren, Milbank notes, has rallied liberals to oppose White House deals and White House nominees, like investment banker Antonio Weiss, Obama's pick for the number-three position at the Treasury Department. DeMint "cared about policy and took a long view of politics," and Warren seems to be following suit.[27]

In which case, what she wants is to set the agenda for the party and the nominee, to ensure that any Democrat who runs for president is also committed to a set of core issues. Which is just another way to say that Warren doesn't want to beat Clinton as much as she wants to pull her to the left. As a candidate, Warren can't do this—Clinton is just too strong. But as someone who can claim allegiance from other candidates (more on that later) and give a seal of approval, she might succeed.

And what would all of this mean in practice? Potentially, it means a Hillary Clinton who is less solicitous of Wall Street, less interested in small, incremental solutions, and unafraid of conservative attacks on core liberal priorities. It's a Hillary Clinton who might push bold proposals for expanded Social Security and a "public option" for the Affordable Care Act.

It's a long shot, but it's potentially the only chance liberal Democrats have to reorient the party for the next ten years. If Hillary Clinton is too powerful to beat outright, then the next best option is to do as much as possible to co-opt her platform. We'll see how Warren fares.

ALTERNATIVE FUTURES

But what if Hillary Clinton doesn't run? What if—after nearly monopolizing the infrastructure of the Democratic Party—Clinton decides to step away from presidential politics to spend time with other pursuits?

Then the Democrats have a problem. Well, two problems. First, as previously mentioned, the ideological fights in the party will spill out into the open. The unity created by Clinton will fall apart, as centrist Democrats fight to retain their influence and liberal Democrats fight to displace it. In this world, you might see a Warren candidacy, and you'd certainly see efforts from the handful of Democratic politicians with ambitions in 2016.

That means former Maryland Governor Martin O'Malley and former Virginia Senator Jim Webb—who have both taken the earliest and most unambiguous steps toward declaring a candidacy—as well as Vermont Senator Bernie Sanders, an "independent socialist," and, potentially, Minnesota Senator Amy Klobuchar, who has made moves in the direction of a candidacy.[28]

You'll notice that these are obscure names. One of the real problems of the Democratic Party, both for 2016 and looking forward, is the extent to which it lacks a bench of nationally viable leaders. It's not just that, if Hillary Clinton doesn't run, Democrats will have to choose from a group of unknown and unfamiliar faces. It's also that—across all offices—the party has a shocking lack of new talent.

"Today," wrote Amy Walter of the *Cook Political Report* after the 2014 elections, "about 55 percent of all state legislative seats in the country are held by Republicans. That's the largest share of GOP state legislators since the 1920s." What's more, "just 11 states have an all Democratic-controlled legislature," and Democrats hold single-party control in just seven states. By contrast, "Republicans have a legislative majority in 30 states, including the battleground states of Florida, Ohio, Pennsylvania, and North Carolina," and single-party control in most of the South.[29]

Not only do Republicans stand to control the redistricting process in 2020—solidifying their majority in the House of Representatives—but they also have a huge farm team of new candidates. To that point, two of the brightest stars of the GOP's 2014 class—Senators Joni Ernst of Iowa and Thom Tillis of North Carolina—came from state legislatures. Democrats are less lucky. Their losses mean only a few places stand as incubators for progressive ideas, strategies, and candidates. Indeed, liberal counterparts to Republican governors like Christie, Wisconsin's Scott Walker, Indiana's Mike Pence, and Ohio's John Kasich—ideologically motivated leaders with national profiles—don't exist.

The simple fact is that even if everything goes well for Democrats in 2016, even if they hold the presidency and pick up the Senate as well, their long-term prospects are dire. After eight years in the White House, the party has atrophied, and given the partisan and demographic trends that are driving American politics—in particular, the demographic divergence in midterm and presidential elections—it's not clear what Democrats can do to fix the problem.[30]

Here's where we are: Far more than its competitor, the Democratic Party in 2015—and soon, 2016—is at a crossroads. At the moment, it's being held together by its president and his potential successor, Hillary Clinton. But this obscures intraparty conflict and the extent to which the party is in desperate need of rebuilding for the second and third decades of the twenty-first century.

This, of course, is normal. After an eight-year term with the White House, incumbent parties are often exhausted. But with likely vacancies on an ideologically split Supreme Court—to say nothing of the programs of the Obama administration—the stakes for the next election are high. Winning the White House is vital for Democrats, and even with Clinton at the helm, it's very unclear if Democrats can succeed.

NOTES

1. Thirty-seven percent, according to Gallup. "Presidential Job Approval Center," Gallup, accessed December 18, 2014, http://www.gallup.com/poll/124922/presidential-approval-center.aspx.

2. "Obama Job Approval," *HuffPost* Pollster, accessed January 26, 2015, http://elections.huffingtonpost.com/pollster/obama-job-approval.

3. "November 2014 Post-Election Survey Final Topline," Pew Research Center, November 12, 2014, accessed December 18, 2014, http://www.people-press.org/files/2014/11/11-12-14-Post-election-topline-for-release.pdf.

4. Susan Page, "Poll: High Anxiety, Low Expectations as Election Nears," *USA Today*, October 30, 2014, accessed December 18, 2014, http://www.usatoday.com/story/news/politics/elections/2014/10/30/usa-today-poll-high-anxiety-low-expectations/18118403/.

5. NBC News/*Wall Street Journal* Survey (October 30–November 1, 2014), November 2, 2014, accessed December 18, 2014, http://online.wsj.com/public/resources/documents/WSJNBCpoll11022014.pdf.

6. See Alan Abramowitz's chapter in this volume for further discussion.

7. Danny Vinik, "The Economic Forecast for 2016 Favors Hillary Clinton," *New Republic*, December 1, 2014, accessed December 18, 2014, http://www.newrepublic.com/article/120449/hillary-clinton-can-adopt-obamas-economic-agenda-if-economy-improves.

8. "2016 National Democratic Primary," *HuffPost* Pollster, accessed December 19, 2014, http://elections.huffingtonpost.com/pollster/2016-national-democratic-primary.

9. "'Enough Is Enough': Elizabeth Warren Launches Fiery Attack after Congress Weakens Wall Street Regs," *Washington Post*, December 12, 2014, accessed December 18, 2014, http://www.washingtonpost.com/blogs/wonkblog/wp/2014/12/12/enough-is-enough-elizabeth-warrens-fiery-attack-comes-after-congress-weakens-wall-st reet-regulations/.

10. Sahil Kapur, "Schumer: Democrats Screwed Up by Passing Obamacare in 2010," *Talking Points Memo*, November 25, 2014, accessed December 18, 2014, http://talkingpointsmemo.com/livewire/schumer-obamacare-the-wrong-problem.

11. Ashley Park and Robert Pear, "House Narrowly Passes Bill to Avoid Shutdown; $1.1 Trillion in Spending," *New York Times*, December 11, 2014, accessed December 18, 2014, http://www.nytimes.com/2014/12/12/us/congress-spending -bill.html; Peter Schroeder and Kevin Cirilli, "Warren, Left Fume Over Deal," *The Hill*, December 10, 2014, accessed December 18, 2014, http://thehill.com/regula tion/finance/226638-democrats-balking-at-dodd-frank-changes-in-cromnibus.

12. "Hillary Clinton Favorable Rating," *HuffPost* Pollster, accessed January 26, 2015, http://elections.huffingtonpost.com/pollster/hillary-clinton-favorable-rating.

13. "Barack Obama Favorable Rating," *HuffPost* Pollster, accessed January 26, 2015, http://elections.huffingtonpost.com/pollster/obama-favorable-rating.

14. "Joe Biden Favorable Rating," *HuffPost* Pollster, accessed January 26, 2015, http://elections.huffingtonpost.com/pollster/joe-biden-favorable-rating; "Harry Reid Favorable Rating," *HuffPost* Pollster, accessed January 26, 2015, http://elections .huffingtonpost.com/pollster/harry-reid-favorable-rating.

15. "Elizabeth Warren Favorable Rating," *HuffPost* Pollster, accessed January 26, 2015, http://elections.huffingtonpost.com/pollster/elizabeth-warren-favorable -rating.

16. "2016 National Democratic Primary," *HuffPost* Pollster, accessed January 26, 2015, http://elections.huffingtonpost.com/pollster/2016-national-democratic -primary.

17. See "White House 2008: Democratic Nomination," PollingReport.com, http://www.pollingreport.com/wh08dem2.htm. Based on that data, in polls from late 2006 and early 2007 Clinton's average lead was around fifteen points.

18. "Jeb Bush Favorable Rating," *HuffPost* Pollster, accessed January 26, 2015, http://elections.huffingtonpost.com/pollster/jeb-bush-favorable-rating; "Chris Christie Favorable Rating," *HuffPost* Pollster, accessed January 26, 2015, http:// elections.huffingtonpost.com/pollster/chris-christie-favorable-rating; "Marc Rubio Favorable Rating," *HuffPost* Pollster, accessed January 26, 2015, http://elections .huffingtonpost.com/pollster/marco-rubio-favorable-rating; "Scott Walker Favorable Rating," *HuffPost* Pollster, accessed January 26, 2015, http://elections.huf fingtonpost.com/pollster/scott-walker-favorable-rating.

19. "2016 General Election: Bush vs. Clinton," *HuffPost* Pollster, accessed January 26, 2015, http://elections.huffingtonpost.com/pollster/2016-general-elec tion-bush-vs-clinton; "2016 General Election: Christie vs. Clinton," *HuffPost* Pollster, accessed January 26, 2015, http://elections.huffingtonpost.com/pollster/ 2016-general-election-christie-vs-clinton; "2016 General Election: Rubio vs. Clinton," *HuffPost* Pollster, accessed January 26, 2015, http://elections.huffington post.com/pollster/2016-general-election-rubio-vs-clinton; "2016 General Election: Cruz vs. Clinton," *HuffPost* Pollster, accessed January 26, 2015, http://elections .huffingtonpost.com/pollster/2016-general-election-cruz-vs-clinton; "2016 General Election: Paul vs. Clinton," *HuffPost* Pollster, accessed January 26, 2015, http://elec tions.huffingtonpost.com/pollster/2016-general-election-paul-vs-clinton; "2016 General Election: Ryan vs. Clinton," *HuffPost* Pollster, accessed January 26, 2015, http://elections.huffingtonpost.com/pollster/2016-general-election-ryan-vs-clinton.

20. Mark Murray, "Poll: Hillary Clinton the Early 2016 Frontrunner, But Barely," *NBC News*, December 17, 2014, accessed December 18, 2014, http://www.nbcnews

.com/politics/politics-news/poll-hillary-clinton-early-2016-frontrunner-barely-n26
9601.

21. "For Democrats, Hillary Clinton Just Has to Say 'Go.' For Voters, She'll Have
to Say Much More." *Washington Post*, November 22, 2014, accessed December 18,
2014, http://www.washingtonpost.com/politics/it-was-a-big-day-in-the-big-apple
-for-hillary-clinton/2014/11/22/3ef252f8-725d-11e4-a2c2-478179fd0489_story
.html.

22. A good description of Clinton's views—as articulated in her book—can be
found in Michiko Kakutani, "Hillary Clinton's Book 'Hard Choices' Portrays
a Tested Policy Wonk," *New York Times*, June 7, 2014, http://www.nytimes.com/
2014/06/08/books/hillary-clintons-book-hard-choices-portrays-a-tested-policy
-wonk.html.

23. Noam Scheiber, "Hillary's Nightmare? A Democratic Party That Realizes Its
Soul Lies with Elizabeth Warren," *New Republic*, November 10, 2013, accessed
December 18, 2014, http://www.newrepublic.com/article/115509/elizabeth-war
ren-hillary-clintons-nightmare.

24. Noah Bierman, "Elizabeth Warren Says She's Not Seeking Presidency," *Boston
Globe*, December 5, 2013, accessed December 18, 2014, http://www.bostonglobe
.com/news/nation/2013/12/04/elizabeth-warren-pushing-back-presidential-spec
ulation-pledges-fulfill-her-senate-term/gMaKvOvWYYVBSTnjlngRAI/story.html.

25. M.J. Lee, "Elizabeth Warren's Book Tour: 'Run, Liz, Run!' *Politico*, April 24,
2014, accessed December 18, 2014, http://www.politico.com/story/2014/04/eliza
beth-warren-book-tour-106017.html.

26. Steve Inskeep, "'Warning Shot': Sen. Warren on Fighting Banks, and Her
Political Future," NPR, December 15, 2014, accessed December 18, 2014, http://
www.npr.org/blogs/itsallpolitics/2014/12/15/370817279/-warning-shot-sen-eliz
abeth-warren-on-fighting-the-banks-and-her-political-futur.

27. Dana Milbank, "Elizabeth Warren Is Not the Left's Ted Cruz. She Is the Left's
Jim DeMint," *Washington Post*, December 16, 2014, accessed December 18, 2014,
http://www.washingtonpost.com/opinions/dana-milbank-elizabeth-warren-is-not
-the-lefts-ted-cruz-she-is-the-lefts-jim-demint/2014/12/16/8c370e88-8553-11e4
-b9b7-b8632ae73d25_story.html.

28. Ben Jacobs, "2016 Overachiever Martin O'Malley Now Has 11 Staffers Working in Iowa," *The Daily Beast*, September 12, 2014, accessed December 18, 2014,
http://www.thedailybeast.com/articles/2014/09/12/2016-overachiever-martin-o
-malley-now-has-11-staffers-working-in-iowa.html; Maggie Haberman, "Jim Webb
Launches 2016 Committee," November 20, 2014, accessed December 18, 2014,
http://www.politico.com/story/2014/11/jim-webb-2016-committee-113055.html;
David Weigel, "Klobucharmania: Catch It!" *Slate*, September 16, 2014, accessed
December 18, 2014, http://www.slate.com/blogs/weigel/2014/09/16/klobuchar
mania_catch_it.html.

29. Amy Walter, "Democrats' Downballot Troubles," *Cook Political Report*,
December 3, 2014, accessed December 18, 2014, http://cookpolitical.com/story/
8123.

30. I explore this in detail in "The Disunited States of America," *Slate*, November
6, 2014, http://www.slate.com/articles/news_and_politics/politics/2014/11/the
_disunited_states_of_america_why_demographics_republican_obstructionism.html.

10

A Brief Celebration

The Future of the Republican Party

Robert Costa

The Republican Party enters the 2016 campaign season elated by its victories in the 2014 midterm elections, where it won control of both congressional chambers and numerous statewide races. Most Republican leaders are pleased with the emerging field of White House hopefuls, which includes popular governors and charismatic senators.[1] And the rise of outside political groups and Super PACs has infused the party with new money and support.[2]

Yet beneath the surface and the assured posturing of GOP officials, the party is still struggling to find a path out of the wilderness following Mitt Romney's defeat in the 2012 presidential election. There are heated and unresolved debates on several policy fronts, no clear front-runner for the presidential nomination, and a conservative base that remains deeply suspicious of the leadership and intent on veering the party's agenda to the right.

Grappling with these issues and tensions in the run-up to the 2016 Republican national convention will be the party's chief challenge. Before wooing over voters in the general election, Republicans will first have to internally settle questions on what the party stands for, who will lead them, and whether they are going to remain steeped in conservatism and closely aligned with the once ascendant but now flagging Tea Party movement, as they have been during Barack Obama's presidency.[3]

This familial and likely painful experience, endured under an intense media glare, will make the Republicans' triumphant 2014 takeover of the Senate majority and its retention of the House majority a brief celebration. But it is a necessary process for Republicans, who are searching for a political strategy in the post-Obama years and attempting to expand the party's reach. After eight years of railing against a Democratic president and gaining from his missteps, they are about to lose their favorite foil.[4]

This analysis examines the three aforementioned areas of concern within the party. First, there will be a select look at the current policy scene, with a focus on foreign policy and an emphasis on the politics that will drive it during the swirling storm of the 2016 presidential primary. Second, there will be an overview of the presidential field and its various components, as seen in early 2015 as the jockeying for position begins. Third, there will be a review of the GOP base and of how conservatives are preparing to remain at the core of the party in the coming years, albeit with modified priorities and tactics, due to the shifting political winds.

FOREIGN POLICY

A renewed foreign policy debate within the Republican Party has been evident in recent years, with hawks and doves inside and outside of Congress clashing over U.S. military involvement in the Middle East and the scope of national security surveillance.[5] The 2016 presidential primary campaign will be a consequential battle between these blocs, testing whether Republicans will continue to support the muscular worldview that was championed by President Ronald Reagan and later by President George W. Bush.

At the fore of the camp that comprises the party's non-interventionists is freshman Senator Rand Paul, a Republican from Kentucky and son of former Texas Representative Ron Paul. For the past two decades, the elder Paul has been a prominent and often lonely GOP voice against war. He opposed the military campaigns in Iraq and Afghanistan, extensive U.S. foreign aid, and boosting the Pentagon's budget.[6] Now retired from politics, he has left to his son a sprawling and powerful network of like-minded conservative activists who are eager to see Ron Paul's passions embraced.

But unlike his father, who also mounted an unsuccessful bid for the presidency in 2008, Rand Paul is not preparing to run for the White House as a zealous advocate for a contrarian foreign policy.[7] Instead, spurred by polls that show he has more than an outsider's shot at winning the nomination, the senator spent much of 2014 making nuanced appeals to the donors and center-right officials his father ignored, shying away from his father's strident libertarianism, and recasting his own global outlook as "common-sense realism" in order to win over wary voters.

"We need a foreign policy that recognizes our limits and preserves our might, a common-sense realism of strength and action. We can't retreat from the world, but we can't remake it in our own image, either," Paul said in an October 2014 speech at the Center for the National Interest. He added, "Americans yearn for leadership and for strength, but they don't yearn for war."[8]

Paul's message wasn't hawkish, nor was it isolationist. Rather, Paul appears to be trying to straddle the two predominant foreign policy poles of the Republican Party, hoping to rise into contention with the backing of anti-war conservatives while remaining an acceptable candidate to a primary electorate that has for many years nominated less provocative candidates. According to his aides, his goal is to subtly prod GOP voters to reconsider their views without urging them to abandon those views.[9] Earlier in the year, to underscore his hybrid positioning, Paul brought on Richard Burt, a former Reagan ambassador, and Lorne Craner, a former State Department official in the George W. Bush administration, as advisers.[10]

How Paul balances the political capital he inherited from his father with his desire to win votes from more moderate Republican constituencies will likely be one of the defining questions of the 2016 presidential primary campaign and say much about the vibrancy of the GOP deliberations over the U.S. role in the world. "I'm talking about all or none," Paul said in December 2014 at a *Wall Street Journal* summit. "That's a caricature and I will have to fight that."[11] And if there is to be a foreign policy debate that features more than a flurry of competing platitudes, it will almost certainly have Paul at the center, instigating a more substantive discussion about the foreign policy principles in the party's ranks that have calcified. There are few others on the national stage with the depth of support among conservatives to build and then argue a convincing alternative case.[12]

But many Republicans do not appear ready to have such a heated back-and-forth on foreign policy and believe that the party, in spite of the popularity of Paul with elements of the GOP, remains a coalition that generally approves of U.S. military action abroad and of a ramped up surveillance system at home.[13] An example of this tendency, and of the hurdles facing those who contest it, came in the second half of 2014, when the Islamic State began to take over parts of northern Iraq. During the heart of the campaign ahead of the midterm elections, most Republican Senate candidates issued full-throated endorsements for the involvement of U.S. military forces.[14]

As talk of a U.S. response grew among Republicans, even Paul felt compelled to weigh in and adjust to the groundswell, saying that President Obama should "seek congressional authorization to destroy ISIS militarily."[15] It was a stark departure from the tone of an op-ed article Paul published two-months earlier in the *Wall Street Journal*, where he wrote that "many of those clamoring for military action now are the same people who made every false assumption" about previous military action in Iraq. Paul, as he pushes for a shift in GOP thinking, seemed to acknowledge with his former statement that he could only push so far against the party's foreign policy consensus, especially when Republican voters are rallying to take out terrorists.[16]

Politico reported that the muted response by Paul left the party without much dissent about how to move forward. "With [Senator Ted] Cruz [of Texas] and Paul largely on the sidelines during this debate—so far anyway—the party is still turning to [Senator John] McCain [of Arizona] and [Senator] Lindsey Graham [of South Carolina] on how to engage in Iraq and the argument that the U.S. should never have totally withdrawn."[17] Graham and McCain are prominent hawks in the GOP.

Paul's rivals for the 2016 nomination are counting on the above inclinations and instincts with rank-and-file Republicans to give them a lift and that GOP primary voters will ultimately settle with a candidate who has traditional and straightforward views on foreign policy. In meetings and strategy sessions, they have been looking to the party's recent nominees—Romney, McCain, and Bush—as their models as they develop their platforms, rather than looking to Ron Paul or trying to pitch a fresh approach that departs from the long-held GOP perspectives.[18] Harkening back to Reagan is a regular habit of many White House aspirants, as is endorsing more funding for the U.S. military and taking aggressive stances on Russian and Middle East policy.[19]

Nonetheless, as the 2016 candidates use hawkish rhetoric and bet on the churning debate moving in their direction, the foreign policy scuffles within the party continue with no sign of ending soon and more controversies on the horizon. Many congressional GOP lawmakers opposed President Obama's proposed airstrikes in Syria in September 2013, and in July 2013, libertarian Republicans in the House nearly convinced their colleagues to rein in the National Security Agency and limit its ability to collect telephone records, losing by a narrow, 217 to 205, vote.[20] Throughout 2015, Republicans expect to have more votes on authorizing the president to send U.S. forces and materials to combat the Islamic State, ensuring that foreign policy will be a top-tier item on the campaign trail and on Capitol Hill.[21]

The hawks, to be sure, are closely watching these movements, and some of them even fear the contentions eventually becoming more than side scuffles. Near the end of 2014, the looming prospect of Paul and his allies changing the party's view of foreign policy led two hawkish leaders, former United Nations Ambassador John Bolton and New York Representative Peter King, to consider longshot presidential bids to counter him specifically on foreign policy.[22] "I'm looking at this because I see people like Rand

Paul," King said in a CNN interview. He said he wants to ensure that the "realistic foreign policy wing" of the GOP reigns.[23] How hard Paul's watered-down "common-sense realism" runs against King's view remains an open question, as does the direction the party will take as the nomination contest unfolds.

THE PRESIDENTIAL FIELD

At first blush, the similarity between the 2016 Republican presidential primary field and the 2012 presidential pack begins with the number of candidates: by late 2014, more than a dozen Republicans were considering bids.[24] The main difference is that during 2012, when a colorful and crowded field of candidates clamored for the GOP nomination, from former pizza magnate Herman Cain to fiery Minnesota Representative Michele Bachmann, the frontrunner from the start was Mitt Romney. While Romney occasionally fumbled and found it hard to deflect his rivals, he was consistently seen as the most viable and favored candidate by the party's financial class and political elites.[25] This time around, there is no such leading contender at the outset, only a growing assembly jumping in, leaving the race unpredictable and dynamic.

Without a big-name standard-bearer, some new faces with ideologies that signal a departure from the party's past are quickly coming into view, with Paul and his previously mentioned foreign policy positioning a major part of that development. But Paul is far from the only addition to the national Republican arena that brings both promise and potential weakness to the presidential race. From the states to Capitol Hill, a new class of Republicans is ascending and beginning to attempt to shape the party in their image, with the hope of playing significant roles in 2016.[26] Many, but not all, of these Republicans have seen their politics and reputations forged during the Obama years, such as Governor Scott Walker of Wisconsin, who beat back a 2012 recall election after curbing collective bargaining for public employees, and Senator Ted Cruz of Texas, who was the leader of the conservative charge for a showdown over health care policy in 2013, a fight that led to a shutdown of the federal government.

As these often youthful and somewhat politically raw stars begin to stake out ground in the primary, they will encounter a playing field that has unique contours and power centers. At a foundational level are the political fault lines, the way the primary is unofficially structured and how candidates are slotted. While some candidates, like Paul, may hope to ultimately overlap blocs in the Republican Party and establish partnerships across the spectrum, the initial priority for most GOP presidential primary candidates is winning the support of one critical group of voters that will elevate them in the discussion and serve as a political base for their fledging campaigns.[27]

The most coveted group, since history shows winning its backing is one of the most surefire ways to win the nomination, is the amalgamation of money men, wealthy donors, consultants, and elected leaders that form the Republican establishment.[28] Former Florida Governor Jeb Bush, New Jersey Governor Chris Christie, and Romney are on that group's short list as the race begins, with Wisconsin Representative Paul Ryan and Senator Marco Rubio of Florida hovering near them in the establishment's second tier (though Romney and Ryan have said they won't run).[29] What defines this group isn't so much ideology, because they share many of the views of the Republican base and have moved to the right along with the rest party. The quality that defines their personas is temperament and an ability to connect with the high-dollar donors who manage Super PACs and serve as political bundlers.

Top GOP players see Bush, Ryan, Romney, and Rubio as the party's even-tempered conservatives who could play well in a general election. When it comes to battling the White House, these establishment-types are mentioned together as the leaders who don't push forcefully for GOP intransigence or politically fueled shutdowns.[30] Bush, for his support of comprehensive immigration reform and popularity in Florida, is touted as a Republican who could win over Hispanic voters. The same goes for Rubio. Ryan, the 2012 vice presidential nominee, has long been slotted as the fiscal policy wonk with a pleasant disposition; his former running mate, Romney, is the party's elder statesman.[31]

In past GOP primaries, the road to the nomination has frequently gone through the establishment. By either collecting a slew of early and influential endorsements, or making a strong showing in the New Hampshire primary, which places less emphasis on social politics, Republican candidates have seen rising fortunes. George W. Bush won early establishment backing and went on to win the nomination, as did then-Kansas Senator Bob Dole in 1996. McCain used his stature in the party and his victory in New Hampshire to surge ahead in 2008. Romney followed the same playbook in 2012.[32]

Christie, who has been dogged by a bridge-closing scandal in New Jersey since late 2013, will attempt to recover politically throughout 2015 and once again become an establishment darling. His center-right politics, coupled with his brash persona and middle-class background, have drawn notice and cheers from GOP brass and in spite of his troubles with the bridge and New Jersey's rocky economy, his advisers are confident that he can come back and compete first for this wing of the party and for the nomination.[33] His work as chairman of the Republican Governors Association in 2014, where he raised millions and helped the party pick up seats in blue states, was a step in that direction and earned him praise from senior party figures.[34]

Outside of the establishment, the lanes for Republican candidates are versions of conservative. Among them is the bloc of religious Republican voters who continue to play an outsized role in the Iowa Republican caucuses, the first nominating contest.[35] Former Arkansas Governor Mike Huckabee, a Baptist preacher who won the caucuses, is considering another run and would be formidable as that faction's advocate.[36] Walker, the son of a Baptist preacher, is expected to try to bridge his establishment bona fides, as a two-term purple-state governor, with his religious roots. Indiana Governor Mike Pence, Cruz, and neurosurgeon Ben Carson, who has become a Tea Party dignitary in recent years, could also compete for this group.[37] Riding an Iowa win or victory in the conservative-dominated South Carolina primary, any of them could find their way to the primary race's final lap. The hard part, of course, is sustaining conservative momentum and translating it into political success. From Pat Buchanan in 1992 to Huckabee in 2008, many conservatives have found it difficult to overcome the establishment pick's financial advantages and vast political network.[38]

Looming over the scene is former Secretary of State Hillary Rodham Clinton, the leading potential candidate for the Democratic presidential nomination. If Clinton continues to rise as her party's likely nominee, Republicans will be under pressure to keep her profile in mind when choosing their own nominee.[39] That thinking may include taking foreign policy, widely considered by Clinton's supporters to be her strongest selling point, into greater consideration and making sure that either the presidential nominee or the vice presidential nominee has gravitas and knowledge in that area. An example of how primary voters have strategized in such a way is the 2004 Democratic presidential primary, when Vietnam veteran and then-Senator John Kerry of Massachusetts was backed by voters who wanted a nominee that would be seen as a foreign policy equal to George W. Bush, a wartime president. For months prior to Kerry's nomination, liberal Vermont governor Howard Dean was gaining momentum, but Dean faded as the interest grew in having a Democrat who could be an effective counterweight to Bush.[40]

Regardless of who ends up running, the field will be large—and for understandable reasons beyond the appeal of being on the national Republican ticket. In the last few cycles, the political and financial benefits of running for president have expanded. Even if one falls behind in the scramble for the nomination, a losing effort could lead to opportunities in the private sector, book deals, and television contracts. Herman Cain has gone on to host a talk-radio program; Michele Bachmann plans to be active on the paid speaker circuit now that she is retired from Congress.[41] Former Pennsylvania Senator Rick Santorum, who finished second to Romney in

2012, went on to run a Christian movie studio and publish a book—and he is yet another Republican who is putting out feelers to donors about getting into the 2016 race.[42]

THE CONSERVATIVES

A third and important part of the picture ahead of 2016 is the base—the conservatives who have driven much of the Republican Party, in spirit and pitch, since they helped the party win the House majority in 2010. Foreign policy may animate Republicans and could be a party-defining issue in 2016, and the presidential field will have much say over the party's future, but it is the base and its precepts that still matter in nearly every Republican sector. The trend in this sphere in recent years has been two-fold. First, the Tea Party movement, once the white-hot center of the GOP, has seen its power and influence over Congress wane as others, from grassroots organizations to less conservative candidates, have risen. Second, many conservatives on the intellectual right have been reshaping their manifestos to offer new ideas and solutions ahead of 2016, but so far have had mixed results.

Polling released over the course of the 2014 campaign hints at the Tea Party's problems. According to a Gallup poll released that May, only 22 percent of American adults support the Tea Party. Among Republicans, support for the Tea Party dropped from 61 percent in Gallup's 2010 poll of GOP voters to 41 percent among that same group in the months before this year's midterms.[43]

The Tea Party's loosening grip on the Republican Party began early in the 2014 cycle. Learning from its experience in the 2010 and 2012 cycles, national Republican leaders began to recruit less volatile and less conservative candidates to run for Senate in key states, with the ambition of protecting nominees nationwide from having to answer for the mistakes or gaffes of Tea Party candidates who managed to win Senate nominations, such as Delaware's Christine O'Donnell in 2010 and Missouri's Todd Akin in 2012. The former was bizarrely drawn into a kerfuffle over whether she had dabbled in witchcraft; the latter has spoken of "legitimate rape." Those incidents led GOP officials to convince themselves that if only they had better candidates, they could have won a slew of seats.[44]

Come 2014, they were ready to have a political shootout with the Tea Party. In Mississippi, state Senator Chris McDaniel, a Tea Party favorite, nearly beat longtime Senator Thad Cochran in a June primary runoff. But thanks to heavy financial support from the U.S. Chamber of Commerce and a bevy of party luminaries, such as former Mississippi Governor Haley Barbour, McDaniel was defeated. In Kansas, Senator Pat Roberts fended off a Tea Party candidate. Senator Mitch McConnell also survived his primary in Kentucky. This was a stark change from the 2010 cycle, when insurgents toppled some Republicans, including Senator Robert Bennett of Utah, in primaries or conventions. Much of the rest of the GOP's 2014 Senate slate was full of businessmen and polished GOP lawmakers: former executive David Perdue in Georgia, plus House members Shelley Moore Capito in West Virginia, Bill Cassidy in Louisiana, Cory Gardner in Colorado, Tom Cotton in Arkansas, James Lankford in Oklahoma, and Steve Daines in Montana. All won.[45]

Also damaging the Tea Party's standing in the party was the sixteen-day government shutdown in October 2013. Cruz had rallied his colleagues to stand with him and make a statement by sending an ultimatum to President Obama: defund the Affordable Care Act or else risk a shutdown. When the government shut down, Republicans' poll numbers plummeted.[46] Ever since then, Tea Party members of Congress have had a harder time convincing their colleagues to mount standoffs against Democrats. One illustration is the fight over immigration policy following Obama's executive actions to protect some undocumented workers from deportation. Cruz and those in his camp spoke of holding up government funding until the president relented, but congressional Republicans discarded that advice and funded the government.[47]

There have been flashes of enduring influence. When then-House Majority Leader Eric Cantor was stunningly defeated in a 2014 primary against Tea Party candidate David Brat, it sent shockwaves through the party's establishment and served as a reminder that the movement was far from over. But that Brat victory became a rare monumental win for the movement in a cycle that was dominated by nominees who beat Tea Party foes.[48] And wide-reaching and well-heeled national organizations, such as American Crossroads, the National Republican Senatorial Committee, and the Chamber of Commerce, were in most races willing to take on the grassroots organizers that labored to get their Senate candidate to the general election. This constant frenzy of money and hardball tactics from party leaders has left the Tea Party, which lacks an official leader and party structure, reeling and unsure of how it will sustain itself long term. "The Tea Party does have an overarching agenda that extends beyond simple opposition to the president and his agenda."[49] "Fear and anxiety drives their desire to arrest change by any means necessary," wrote Christopher S. Parker in a 2014 Brookings Institution study. "For now, simply directing their representatives to say 'no' serves that end."[50]

Meanwhile, a constellation of conservative writers and thinkers who work for publications like *National Review* or *The Weekly Standard*, or who are employed by conservative think tanks such as the American Enterprise Institute and the Heritage Foundation, are revamping their intellectual framework ahead of 2016, with the intent of crafting an agenda for the party, particularly on domestic policy issues such as education and taxes, that could get a foothold in the debate and help revive the GOP as a party of ideas, rather than simply a political operation that sells the same product year after year.[51]

"Now the trumpet summons Republicans again—or so, at least, does a loose, informal confederation of conservative thinkers and legislators devoutly hope. These days, they speak of themselves as leading a 'conservative reform project' and often call themselves 'reform conservatives,'" wrote E.J. Dionne in a 2014 article for *Democracy*. "They are not exactly the Constructive Republicans of old—the absence of liberal Republicans means the intellectual compass of this group points farther right than did the lodestar of those Constructive Republicans two generations ago. But the Reformicons do have ambitions."[52]

Among the policies forwarded by these "reform conservatives" include a child tax credit, block granting Medicaid funds to the states, and reforming long-term federal spending programs, as well as offering a revived economic message that speaks to the gap between the rich and the poor.[53] In September 2014, taking cues from this group of reformers, Rubio and Senator Mike Lee of Utah, a Republican, unveiled their own tax-reform plan that would include a child-tax credit.[54] There has been resistance from the supply-side economics proponents in the GOP who do not support tweaking the tax code for families and some hardline conservatives have criticized the compassion-themed, "goo-goo" arguments used in their essays and scholarship.[55]

Those critiques have not stopped these conservative intellectuals and their project. "The Reagan-era catechism is insufficient to meet contemporary challenges, and where the Republican Party is currently offering a set of policies and slogans that simply aren't responsive to the anxieties of Americans who aren't already securely in the upper class," wrote Ross Douthat of the *New York Times*, a self-described "reform conservative," in May 2013.[56] How Republican presidential candidates pick and choose from these offerings will say much in 2016 about how the party is listening to its base. Heeding the party's conservative activists is but one gesture. Monitoring and considering the proposals of a new crop of conservative thinkers is another.

CONCLUSION

From foreign policy to the presidential field to the conservative movement, the Republican future is a complicated and roiling stew of lingering passions and new ambitions, past political headaches, and opportunities. After the 2014 elections, the party was able to see gains in Congress, but it was a brief celebration due to the obstacles ahead. Questions abound, and without a clear party leader or revived planks on some fundamental issues, as well as fissures in the base, the next few years will be more of a trial than exaltation. Although the GOP now controls both congressional chambers, it has lost the presidency for two straight presidential cycles. To get back to the White House, it will have to deftly navigate these three terrains, among others.

Broadly speaking, the Republican Party is entering a period of unknowns. The energy of the Tea Party has faded, but the movement remains central to Republican politics at large, shaping how lawmakers approach problems and who they listen to, be it conservative leaders or talk-radio hosts. At the same time, with a new governing mentality pervading much of the congressional leadership, the party is looking to reestablish itself as a governing majority with voters who have grown wary of the GOP and its tactics during the Obama era. Beyond Congress, an array of interests in the Republican ranks, from younger libertarians to social conservatives committed to having a place at the table, are competing and pushing the party in their respective directions, be it on domestic policy or on foreign policy.

The party's navigators, more than lawmakers, will be the candidates for president. Whether it's a reconfigured foreign policy of "common-sense realism," as recommended by Rand Paul, or a tax plan based on "reform conservatism" that has been advocated by a group of right-wing intellectuals, the adoption of new ideas and solutions into the Republican firmament will depend on how candidates espouse them and use them to bolster their campaigns. But it will likely take a full presidential primary campaign to get any definitive answers on where the party is going. After a bruising 2012 and momentary elation in 2014, 2016 will be a cycle of decisions, beginning with a scrum and possibly ending with some clarity on what lies ahead.

NOTES

1. Michael Barbaro and Jonathan Martin, "A Deep Republican Presidential Field Reflects Divisions in Age and Ideology," *New York Times*, November 23, 2014.

2. *Super PACs: The New Force in Federal Elections*, eds. Derrick D. Jamison and Gina Gore (Hauppauge, NY: Nova Science Publishers, 2012).

3. Robert Draper, *Do Not Ask What Good We Do: Inside the U.S. House of Representatives* (New York: Free Press, 2012).

4. David Corn, *Showdown: The Inside Story of How Obama Battled the GOP to Set Up the 2012 Election* (New York: William Morrow, 2012).

5. Sebastien Payne and Robert Costa, "Rise of Islamic State Tests GOP Anti-Interventionists," *Washington Post*, September 3, 2014.

6. Kedar Pavgi, "Ron Paul's Foreign Policy," *Foreign Policy*, November 17, 2011.

7. Ryan Lizza, "The Revenge of Rand Paul," *New Yorker*, October 6, 2014.

8. Rand Paul, "The Case for Conservative Realism," an address to the Center for the National Interest, October 23, 2014, accessed December 8, 2014, http://nationalinterest.org/feature/rand-paul-the-case-conservative-realism-11544.

9. Eliana Johnson, "Rand Paul's Non-Isolationism," *National Review*, October 23, 2014.

10. Philip Rucker and Robert Costa, "In the 'Credentials Caucus,' GOP's 2016 Hopefuls Study Policy and Seek Advisers," *Washington Post*, April 6, 2014.

11. Beth Reinhard, "Sen. Rand Paul Says Foreign Policy Stance Puts Him in Mainstream," *Wall Street Journal*, December 2, 2014.

12. Robert Costa, "Dick Cheney Advises House GOP on Foreign Policy, as Some Republicans Ignore Him," *Washington Post*, September 9, 2014.

13. Interview: Jonathan Chait and Robert Costa, "Chait vs. Costa: Is McCain Savvy or Unhinged?" *New Republic*, July 30, 2013.

14. Burgess Everett, "Return of the GOP Hawks," *Politico*, June 17, 2014, accessed December 8, 2014, http://www.politico.com/story/2014/06/iraq-crisis-john-mccain-lindsey-graham-marco-rubio-107973.html.

15. Sebastien Payne and Robert Costa, "Rise of Islamic State Tests GOP Anti-interventionists," *Washington Post*, September 3, 2014.

16. Rand Paul, "America Shouldn't Choose Sides in Iraq's Civil War," *Wall Street Journal*, June 19, 2014.

17. Burgess Everett, "Return of the GOP Hawks," *Politico*, June 17, 2014.

18. Philip Rucker and Robert Costa, "In the 'Credentials Caucus,' GOP's 2016 Hopefuls Study Policy and Seek Advisers," *Washington Post*, April 6, 2014.

19. Burgess Everett, "Return of the GOP Hawks," *Politico*, June 17, 2014.

20. Scott Clement, "Opposition to Syria Airstrikes Rises as Republicans Shift Sharply Against Action," *Washington Post*, September 9, 2013.

21. Jacqueline Klimas and Stephen Dinan, "Rand Paul Forces Iraq War Debate, but Boehner Says House Will Wait Until Next Year," *Washington Times*, December 4, 2014.

22. Robert Costa, "Bolton 2016?" *National Review*, August 22, 2013.

23. Peter King, from interview on CNN's *The Situation Room with Wolf Blitzer*, May 16, 2014, accessed January 30, 2015, http://edition.cnn.com/TRANSCRIPTS/1405/16/wolf.01.html.

24. Michael Barbaro and Jonathan Martin, "A Deep Republican Presidential Field Reflects Divisions in Age and Ideology," *New York Times*, November 23, 2014.

25. John McCormick, "Republican Review of 2012 Losses Calls for Many Changes," Bloomberg News, March 18, 2013, accessed December 8, 2014, http://www.bloomberg.com/news/2013-03-18/republican-review-of-election-loss-calls-for-dozens-of-changes.html.

26. Mike Allen, "20 Republican Wannabes to Watch," *Politico*, November 19, 2014, accessed December 8, 2014, http://www.politico.com/story/2014/11/2016-elections-republicans-to-watch-113014.html.

27. Larry J. Sabato, Kyle Kondik, and Geoffrey Skelley, "GOP Presidential Update: For Republicans, a Vacancy at the Top," *Sabato's Crystal Ball*, September 4, 2014, accessed December 9, 2014, http://www.centerforpolitics.org/crystalball/articles/2016-presidential-update-for-republicans-a-vacancy-at-the-top/.

28. Nicholas Confessore, "G.O.P. Donors Seek to Anoint a 2016 Nominee Early," *New York Times*, December 9, 2014.

29. Larry J. Sabato, Kyle Kondik, and Geoffrey Skelley, "GOP Presidential Update: For Republicans, a Vacancy at the Top," *Sabato's Crystal Ball*, September 4, 2014.

30. Robert Costa, background interviews with senior Republican officials and donors, as part of reporting for *Washington Post*, October-November 2014.

31. Philip Rucker and Robert Costa, "Can't Quit Mitt: Friends Say Romney Feels Nudge to Consider a 2016 Presidential Run," *Washington Post*, October 13, 2014.

32. Henry Olsen, "A GOP Dark Horse?" *National Affairs*, Summer 2011, vol. 8, accessed December 9, 2014, http://www.nationalaffairs.com/publications/detail/a -gop-dark-horse.

33. Mark Leibovich, "Chris Christie Is Back," *New York Times Magazine*, November 20, 2014.

34. Scott Conroy, "Christie's Fundraising Prowess Offers Comeback Path," *RealClearPolitics*, April 30, 2014, accessed December 9, 2014, http://www.realclearpoli tics.com/articles/2014/04/30/christies_fundraising_prowess_offers_comeback_ path_122464.html.

35. David Freedlander, "The Santorum Slot," *The Daily Beast*, August 9, 2013, accessed December 9, 2014, http://www.thedailybeast.com/articles/2013/08/09/ the-santorum-slot-desperately-seeking-social-conservatives.html.

36. Tom Hamburger and Robert Costa, "Huckabee Rebuilds Political Team with Eye on Another Presidential Run," *Washington Post*, November 12, 2014.

37. Philip Rucker, "GOP Presidential Hopefuls Start Jockeying for Position," *Washington Post*, November 9, 2014.

38. Henry Olsen, "A GOP Dark Horse?" *National Affairs*, Summer 2011, vol. 8.

39. Philip Rucker and Robert Costa, "In the 'Credentials Caucus,' GOP's 2016 Hopefuls Study Policy and Seek Advisers," *Washington Post*, April 6, 2014.

40. Meryl Gordon, "Memories of a Dean Administration," *New York Magazine*, July 12, 2004.

41. Brian Stelter, "Herman Cain to Host a National Radio Show," *New York Times*, June 4, 2012.

42. Kevin Lincoln, "Why Is Rick Santorum Running a Movie Studio?" *National Journal*, June 21, 2014.

43. Frank Newport, "Four Years in, GOP Support for Tea Party Down to 41%," Gallup, May 8, 2014, accessed December 9, 2014, http://www.gallup.com/poll/ 168917/four-years-gop-support-tea-party-down.aspx.

44. Philip Rucker and Robert Costa, "Battle for the Senate: How the GOP Did It," *Washington Post*, November 5, 2014.

45. *Ibid.*

46. Mark Murrary, "NBC/WSJ Poll: Shutdown Debate Damages GOP," *NBC News*, October 10, 2013, accessed December 9, 2014, http://www.nbcnews.com/ news/other/nbc-wsj-poll-shutdown-debate-damages-gop-f8C11374626.

47. Ashley Parker and Jeremy W. Peters, "House Republicans Ready Plan to Avoid a Government Shutdown," *New York Times*, December 2, 2014.

48. Jenna Portnoy and Robert Costa, "Eric Cantor's Tea Party Opponent in Virginia May Be Picking Up Momentum," *Washington Post*, May 13, 2014.

49. Philip Rucker and Robert Costa, "Battle for the Senate: How the GOP Did It," *Washington Post*, November 5, 2014.

50. Christopher S. Parker, "Wither the Tea Party? The Future of a Political Movement," *Issues in Governance Studies*, The Brookings Institution, June 2014, vol. 66.

51. Sam Tanenhaus, "Can the G.O.P. Be a Party of Ideas?" *New York Times Magazine*, July 2, 2014.

52. E.J. Dionne, "The Reformicons," *Democracy*, Summer 2014, vol. 33.

53. *Ibid.*

54. Mike Lee and Marco Rubio, "A Pro-Family, Pro-Growth Tax Reform," *Wall Street Journal*, September 22, 2014.

55. Andrew Sullivan, "The Challenge of Reform Conservatism," *The Dish*, July 8, 2014, accessed December 9, 2014, http://dish.andrewsullivan.com/2014/07/08/the-challenge-of-reform-conservatism/.

56. Ross Douthat, "What Is Reform Conservatism?" *New York Times*, May 30, 2013.

11

Fighting the Last Battle, Fighting the Same Battle

The 2016 Presidential Nomination Process

Joshua T. Putnam

As much as the 2012 presidential nomination process was about solidifying Mitt Romney as the Republican presidential nominee and renominating President Barack Obama on the Democratic side, it was also a study in how the rules—or perhaps more accurately, rule changes—that govern the process can affect the progress of the nomination cycle and the transition into the general election phase. In fact, in looking back at 2012 and ahead to 2016, it is clear that the national parties are constantly battling against the unintended consequences of and for the lessons learned from the immediately prior cycle. Increasingly though, as states have gotten more creative in their part in the process, this is less an issue dealt with in-house at the national party level than it is an inter-party problem collectively faced through some form of informal coordination. This chapter will explore both dynamics and how they have affected the crafting of the rules that will govern the 2016 presidential nomination processes in both parties. Additionally, the focus will turn toward a preliminary examination of what the rules changes in 2013–2014 will mean for the 2016 cycle.

TOWARD A THEORY OF DELEGATE SELECTION RULES CHANGES

At the 1968 Democratic National Convention in Chicago, the party, through the McGovern-Fraser Commission, set about to reshape the way in which, ultimately, the two major parties in the United States select nominees to vie for the presidency. The charge of the commission was to pull the nomination decision making out of smoke-filled rooms dominated by party elites and open it up to more rank-and-file members in the grassroots of the Democratic Party.[1] Often that is conceptualized as the national party decentralizing the decision-making process from party elites to voters in state-level primaries and caucuses. From a different angle, however, this can be thought of as a shifting of the coordination problem that is a presidential nomination process. Instead of it being a matter of bartering among the viable candidates and the various state delegations (with competing interests) at the national convention, it became a process in which national convention delegates were not only selected but *bound* to candidates through contests designed at the state level, albeit with some national party oversight of the rules governing those processes. This spread to the Republican process as well, but overall it also altered the group of players involved in the process and the incentives that drove them.

The rules by which national convention delegates are selected and allocated today for either the Democratic or Republican Party nominations are a patchwork of state-level rules created in reaction to guidelines crafted at the national party level. It is sequential within election cycles, then, but it is also an iterative process across cycles in that both the national parties and the states take into account lessons learned from the experiences of previous cycles. Sometimes that means a national party confronting the unintended consequences of a previous rules change. Other times that translates to states finding loopholes in the new rules and/or correcting non-compliant behavior in the nominations process from the immediately preceding cycle.

In terms of the sequence, the starting point of this presidential nomination coordination problem has traditionally differed across parties. The Republican Party has typically settled on delegate selection rules for the next cycle at the prior convention. In that tradition, as it has existed post-McGovern-Fraser reforms, the rules for 2016 would have been drafted at the 2012 convention. However, for the 2012 and 2016 cycles, the Republican National Committee shifted toward a model similar to what the Democrats have been using throughout the McGovern-Fraser era: reexamining the rules in a setting outside of the convention. Typically, the Democratic National Committee has empowered a commission to consider rules changes and set new rules during the midterm election year. The process was slightly different following the 2012 nomination cycle. Both the DNC and RNC opted to handle any rules tinkering for 2016 in-house in their existing rules-making committees rather than form smaller commissions.

Regardless, both national parties have provided themselves with the flexibility of creating a set of delegate selection rules outside of the national conventions. That not only creates additional time for the national parties to consider any rules changes, but also shrinks the time period in which states have to react to the guidelines the national parties hand down. That is the modern sequence: The national parties create the rules that will govern the next nomination process by the midterm election year and then the states spend the odd year between the midterm and the presidential election year setting the rules—within those national party guidelines—for their primaries or caucuses.[2] The rules are intricate, and thus there are numerous points of potential national party and state conflict, but there are two main areas where states have tended to run afoul of the national party rules: contest timing and method of delegate allocation.

Not only does the iterative give and take between the national parties and the states *across* election cycles emerge from the fact that some states opt to break the national party rules, but that exchange also highlights the incentive structure that drives the behavior of each player. A reactive decision on the state level to move a primary to an early date non-compliant with national party rules in one cycle can, for example, drive a change in the national party rules and penalties structure in the next cycle. That, in turn, potentially changes state-level behavior in the next cycle.

Underneath the sequence within presidential election cycles and the iteration across cycles are the incentives driving the players involved. The national parties often have to, in the words of former New Hampshire Governor John Sununu, tread the fine line between managing and controlling the overall presidential nomination process.[3] Controlling the process is elusive for the national parties while managing it within and across cycles is less so. That management requires a consistency in the rules, not a wholesale change in the delegate selection process from cycle to cycle. The goal from the national party perspective is to create an orderly and fair democratic process that produces a nominee who will be well positioned to win the White House in the general election.[4]

At the state level the goals are different. A consistent set of rules provides for a fairer application of the rules to and in the states over time. There is some certainty in that from the state perspective. Yet that certainty does allow the state-level actors to reexamine the states' positions within the process. States are not necessarily motivated to act in accordance with the national party rules, and thus, to play a role in creating an orderly and fair process. Part of that is structural. State-level reactions to the national party delegate selection rules are a function of the extent to which state parties and state governments are on the same page.[5] A state Republican Party may, for instance, reflect the Republican National Committee, but the governmental apparatus in that state may not be controlled or controlled fully by Republicans. In primary states that may mean that compliance with the national party rules on the date of the primary is not within control of

Republicans in that state. In other words, actors in the opposite party might be motivated to have an earlier or later primary; a point hypothetically inconsistent with, in this case, the Republican National Committee rules. This phenomenon only tends to affect primary states, where the state government not only decides on the date but funds and administers the primary election. In caucus states that is the domain of the individual state parties.

There can be, then, some divergence between what the national parties want and what the states want in and from the delegate selection process. Only a portion of the difference is driven by the ideological/partisan overlap between parties and state governments. The rest is built on the state-level desire to affect the nomination process by holding an earlier primary date or devising a delegate allocation plan to benefit a certain candidate or type of candidate or to attract a full field of candidates to campaign in the state. Some states are willing to make those changes, but that willingness is not always sufficient. It also requires the ability to change as well. Regardless of willingness, in terms of shifting primary dates around, states that combine their presidential primaries with primaries for state and local offices have traditionally been less able to move than states that have separate presidential primaries and primaries for state and local offices.[6] Those states with separate presidential primaries have already incurred the startup costs associated with creating a separate—and more mobile—presidential primary. All states, then, are not equal when it comes to making rules changes or reacting to national party rules changes. That patchwork affects the interactions between the national parties and the states in the context of delegate selection.

THE RATIONALE BEHIND 2016 DELEGATE SELECTION RULES CHANGES

2008 Problems

All of this is the environment in which these decisions on delegate selection and allocation are made. The 2016 cycle is no different. The basis for the 2016 delegate selection rules created by both national parties finds its roots in the 2008 and 2012 election cycles. The former was the last competitive nomination race for the Democratic Party while the latter was the same for the Republican Party. What was unique about both cycles was that some states were more willing to break the national party rules in order to maximize their positions in the process than had been the case throughout much of the post-reform era. It was not so much the fact that states were challenging the privileged positions of Iowa and New Hampshire on the presidential primary calendar in 2008, but rather *which* states were threats.

Delaware, for example, had tethered its primary to New Hampshire's for the 1996 cycle, but New Hampshire Republicans were able to persuade most of the viable Republican candidates to sign a pledge that they would not campaign in Delaware.[7] That type of response is more effective when the state is a small state like Delaware. What was different in 2008 (and again in 2012), though, was that larger states—bigger delegate prizes like Florida and Michigan—were the states threatening the national party rules as well as early carve-out states, Iowa, New Hampshire, Nevada, and South Carolina.

Both national parties, however, dealt with the threat—the breaking of national party delegate selection rules within the 2008 cycle—differently. In May 2007, the Florida state legislature passed legislation that was subsequently signed into law by Governor Charlie Crist moving the Florida presidential primary from the second Tuesday in March to the last Tuesday in January.[8] The Florida state government made the move under the auspices of shifting the presidential primary in the Sunshine State to a more advantageous spot on the primary calendar and also while knowing that the penalty from both the DNC and RNC would be a 50 percent reduction in the size of the Florida delegation to the national conventions.[9] Legislators and the governor in Florida wagered that the penalties to deter an early and non-compliant primary date were not severe enough and/or, more importantly, they would not be enforced at the convention.

The 50 percent penalty meted out by the DNC and RNC was where the similarities ended. The Democratic National Committee added for the 2008 cycle a rule akin to the pledge that New Hampshire Republicans pushed the 1996 Republican presidential candidates to sign regarding Delaware. Under the 2008 Democratic provision (Rule 20.C.1.b), any candidate who campaigned in a state with a non-compliant primary would not be eligible for any pledged delegates from that state.[10] Additionally, the Democratic Rules and Bylaws Committee (RBC) had the ability to increase the severity of that penalty as well (Rule 20.C.6). When Florida Democrats failed to make any changes by August 2007, the Democratic RBC stripped the Florida Democratic delegation of *all* of its delegates, rendering any subsequent contest meaningless to the candidates and the overall delegate count in the 2008 race.[11] The Michigan Democratic delegation met the same fate after the state government there shifted the presidential primary in the Great Lakes state up to January 15 from the last Tuesday in February.[12]

At the time, in the fall of 2007, this signaled to other states that the DNC was serious about cracking down on states attempting to leapfrog the four earliest states. However, that signal to states for future cycles was weakened over the course of the 2008 primary process, culminating in the Democratic

RBC restoring 50 percent of the Florida and Michigan convention delegations just before the final round of primaries in early June.[13] Then the previous move to strip both states of their full delegations was threatened
completely when the delegates from Florida and Michigan were seated in
full at the 2008 Democratic National Convention in Denver. Members of
the Rules and Bylaws Committee have contended in the time since that the
100 percent penalty was effective when it needed to be: during the primary
phase when delegates were being counted.[14]

On the Republican side, the approach was slightly different. The RNC, as
was the case with the DNC, had the same 50 percent penalty to use against
states that both scheduled a presidential primary and began allocating delegates before the first Tuesday in February.[15] However, the Republicans were
stuck with the delegate selection rules and penalties that were drafted and
passed by the 2004 Republican National Convention. There was no provision in those rules that allowed the RNC to increase the penalty on any
states that violated the rules. That meant the question for the Republican
Party was one of enforcement at the convention in lieu of the see-saw, take-
and-give process witnessed on the Democratic side. And again, unlike the
Democrats, the Republican National Committee opted to follow through
on the 50 percent penalty at the convention. Not only did Florida and
Michigan receive delegation reduction penalties, but so too did the carve-
out primary states forced to move to earlier dates to stay first, New Hampshire and South Carolina.

2010 National Party Reaction

As the primary season transitioned to the general election in 2008, the
national parties' sights turned toward the next cycle. Most of that was
driven by the natural sequence of events. The Democratic Party at their
national convention in Denver had to lay the groundwork for the commission that would reexamine the rules and recommend any changes to the
Rules and Bylaws Committee for 2012. Similarly, as had historically been
the rules-mandated custom for the Republican National Committee, the
decisions concerning any changes to the rules in 2012 had to be made at
the 2008 convention in Minneapolis. The DNC, then, had institutionalized
a process of allowing some additional time to consider any rules changes,
while the RNC had kept those decisions confined to the convention. That
pattern was broken in the 2008 cycle as the Republican National Convention adopted rules tasking a Temporary Delegate Selection Committee with
reexamining the delegate selection rules and recommending changes to the
(Permanent) Republican National Committee Rules Committee.[16] The
move brought the RNC more in line with the DNC procedure, but also
served as a signal that both parties saw some need in standardizing the

rules-making process: creating a united front in combating some of the rogue activity plaguing both national parties on the state level.

Yet this standardization across parties extended beyond just the sequencing and the process behind drafting changes to delegate selection rules. Both national parties had in the wake of 2008, and have regardless of cycle, a common interest in managing the various interests—national parties, state parties, state governments, candidates, and voters—involved in the process. Effective management breaks down when there is a lack of cohesion across the national parties. It is a collective action problem. For the national party process to work takes buy-in from the states. However, those states for myriad reasons have incentives to break the rules in order to maximize their position—and that of their voters—in the nomination process. If the penalties for violation are not high enough, states shirk. If the state government is controlled by one party, the actors in that legislature are not bound by the delegate selection rules created by the opposite party. If the penalties are different across parties, it can differently motivate states based on partisan alignment within the state government in addition to state election law.

All of these were factors in the decision making in Florida in 2007. The aftermath of that decision and how it affected the 2008 process in both parties weighed heavily at the national party level as the rules for 2012 were being considered in 2009 and 2010. One of the side effects of the Florida and Michigan decisions was that scheduling of those contests in January pushed the early states up even earlier and the beginning of the process up against the beginning of the year. That was a point of contention for all of the players involved with the exception of Florida and Michigan. The national party rules set the first Tuesday in February as the earliest date any state other than the four carve-out states could hold a delegate selection event in 2008. Through informal discussions across parties, there was some consensus, if not coordination, behind the idea of moving the starting point back to the first Tuesday in March in order to provide some additional calendar cushion for the carve-out states. Both the Republican Temporary Delegate Selection Committee and the Democratic Change Commission recommended changes and the national parties set rules consistent with that guideline and allowed the four carve-out states to go as early as February.[17]

While there was some intracycle informal coordination across parties in terms of the basic outline of a presidential primary calendar, that was where the rules similarities ended. The Democratic Party faced a different set of motivations than the Republican Party. First, the DNC was content with the penalties placed on rules violators from the 2008 cycle. Second, there were no indications in the summer of 2010 that President Obama would face any opposition for the Democratic nomination. Parties in the White

House typically face fewer incentives to tweak the rules for determining their nominees in that setting.[18] Out-parties, however, have a greater incentive to tinker with their delegate selection rules as they are collectively attempting to change party fortunes in the next election. This was the position the RNC was in relative to the 2012 election—out of the White House and trying to figure out the best way to nominate a candidate who could beat an incumbent president.

Given those circumstances, the RNC made one additional change to its rules in an effort to increase the deliberation around its eventual nominee. The Temporary Delegate Selection Committee recommended placing states into three tiers: the carve-out states; March states barred from using winner-take-all allocation rules; and April to June states that could employ allocation rules of their choosing. The addition relative to the previous national party guidelines was the March proportionality window. The third tier—states in the April to June period on the calendar—operated much the same way that the post-Iowa/New Hampshire period had worked in prior cycles: State parties were free to allocate delegates in any method they saw fit. In other words, there were restrictions on when states scheduled their delegate selection events but not on how those delegate slots were allocated to candidates. Early winner-take-all events could have the effect of speeding up the decision-making process through the primaries and caucuses. The new Republican rule for the 2012 cycle required that states with contests before April 1 had to have an element of proportionality to their delegate allocation plans.[19] In some small way, this brought March, under the 2012 Republican rules, in line with the Democratic National Committee rules mandating a true proportional allocation of delegates regardless of the timing of the contest. The goal was to slow the process down.[20]

2011 State Response and 2008 Redux in 2012

The changes made to the Republican delegate selection rules cross-pressured states in a number of interesting ways as states were making decisions on delegate selection and allocation throughout 2011. The intent of the changes was to get states to move back, whether it was states that were scheduled too early in 2012 relative to their 2008 positions or states that were insistent upon maintaining a winner-take-all allocation of delegates. And that worked for the national parties in most cases.

In a few cases, however, 2012 was a repeat of 2008. Coming into calendar year 2011 there were nineteen states with laws scheduling their presidential primaries in February, a period non-compliant with the revised national party delegate selection rules.[21] Those nineteen states represented nineteen rules-breaking possibilities. Most states moved back, but several—

Florida, Michigan, and Arizona among them—opted to maintain February or earlier primary dates.[22]

The problem for the RNC was that while the rules had changed in terms of the timing of delegate selection events and the method of allocation, the penalties associated with violations had not increased at all. State-level decision makers, then, were faced with a similar wager to the one they had made ahead of 2008. It was all based on a simple question: Is it more important to hold an early and potentially influential contest than it is to avoid a 50 percent reduction to the national convention delegation? Again, most states complied, but others did not. And the actions of that handful of rogue states had a similar effect in 2012 to the one they had had in 2008. It pushed Iowa, New Hampshire, and South Carolina well into January and forced Nevada Republicans to hold caucuses at a position on the calendar outside of the top four slots.

The result was that even before primary season officially kicked off with the 2012 Iowa caucuses, one thing was clear: The flexibility that the Democratic Rules and Bylaws Committee was granted to increase penalties beyond the baseline 50 percent penalty on states in violation of the rules gave them an advantage in dealing with rogue activity as compared to the RNC. With just a 50 percent penalty to dole out, the RNC and, in turn, the states faced the same dilemma as in 2008. From the RNC perspective, the problem was that the penalty was not sufficient enough to force state-level compliance.

That was just one front in the 2012 rules battle between the national parties and the states. The Republican Party had also added the new proportionality requirement for states with contests before April 1. The move was made to elongate the nominations phase of the process, but it did not have that effect. The reasons were twofold. First of all, the interpretation of the new requirement itself was different in states across the country. Texas Republicans, expecting a March 6 primary, rushed to create a plan that called for a true proportional delegate allocation.[23] On the other end of the spectrum, Florida Republicans opted to flout the new RNC rule and maintain a winner-take-all allocation plan in addition to the non-compliant January 31 primary.[24] In between both were plans like the one in Ohio where statewide, at-large delegates were proportionally allocated and congressional district delegates were allocated in a winner-take-all fashion based on the results within the congressional district.[25] Both Texas and Ohio were compliant with the RNC rules for states with contests before April 1, but with very different allocation plans. Florida, on the other hand, was not compliant.

Secondly, the changes to state-level Republican delegate allocation plans from 2008 to 2012 were minor. This was also based on the interpretation of the rules changes both within and outside of the RNC and the state parties. The thinking was that states would make moves similar to that of Texas—to a true proportional allocation—or move an early and non-compliant winner-take-all primary back to a later and compliant date, as was the case with Wisconsin. Outside of the RNC—in the press—the assumption was that all states with pre-April 1 contests would move from a true winner-take-all allocation to a true proportional allocation, maximizing the impact. The reality was that few states had the type of true winner-take-all method assumed, and additionally states were already in or had moved to calendar positions that were consistent with the allocation methods utilized in 2008.[26] That minimized the effect of the new proportionality rule.

As the primary phase of the Republican nomination race dragged on into the spring of 2012, exacerbating the divisions within the Republican Party among the candidates and voters supporting them, the change to proportionality rules was assumed to be the culprit. However, the actual allocation changes were more subtle than assumed and the lengthening of the process was more a function of the state-level reactions to the new timing requirement.[27] Again, most states moved to compliant positions on the calendar—March or later—but states like Florida, Michigan, and Arizona pushed the start point of primary season to the beginning of January and created a void of contests in the middle three weeks of February. That had a bigger influence on stretching the Republican process out in 2012 than the addition of the proportionality requirement.

ON TO 2016

The National Parties

As the 2012 nomination process moved toward the national conventions, the national parties' sights turned toward 2016 and laying the groundwork for the rules that would govern the primary process. Both the 2008 and 2012 cycles demonstrated the tenuous control the national parties sometimes have over their processes. Each cycle highlighted the fact that primary season is the only time—in real time—the parties have to try out new rules and often find out too late, in the form of unintended consequences, that there were loopholes or other problems. That trial-and-error approach from the national parties fits well within the sequential and iterative process of making rules but also of implementing them.

Facing a competitive nomination race for the first time since 2008 in 2016, the Democratic National Committee had an additional consideration in deliberating over the process of setting their rules at the 2012 convention in Charlotte. Again, the DNC and its Rules and Bylaws Committee had been content with maintaining in 2012 most of the delegate selection rules from 2008. The start point for states other than the carve-out states was moved back from the first Tuesday in February to the first Tuesday in March. The party had also carried over its delegate incentive structure and added a new clustering enticement.[28] For the most part, however, the DNC was content with its rules from 2008 and with how the minor changes had worked in an uncompetitive environment in 2012. On the Democratic side, then, there was little motivation to make any changes to the rules. In fact, the biggest change at the convention was that the DNC did not empower a commission to revisit the rules and recommend any changes. Instead, that duty—to finalize the rules for 2016—went directly to the Rules and Bylaws Committee.

For the Republican National Committee, things were different heading into their convention in Tampa. Primary season had not necessarily gone as planned, and there was still lingering division in the party over the primary process and the rules that had governed it. To deal with problem states in 2016, the Republican National Convention passed a revised set of delegate selection rules that would levy a 50 percent penalty against states that violated the proportionality requirement added to the 2012 rules and carried over to 2016.[29] Additionally, states that broke the timing rules—holding a primary or caucuses before the first Tuesday in March—would be reduced to twelve delegates overall, an increasingly significant reduction the bigger a state is. This not only solved the penalty-severity problem but accounted for the lack of an answer to the double-violation issue that Arizona and Florida raised in 2012. To clean up the issue of non-binding contests, the convention also adopted a contentious rule that would bind delegate allocation to particular candidates based on the results of the initial statewide vote. This closed off the path that many caucus states had utilized in the past to circumvent the timing rules. Caucus states under this rule would have to allocate delegates based on the statewide vote in the precinct caucuses rather than the vote of delegates selected to attend the state convention at the state convention. Finally, the national convention adopted a rule that would allow the Republican Rules Committee to convene in a way similar to the Democratic Rules and Bylaws Committee to meet outside of the convention to consider any further rules changes for the 2016 cycle.

Both parties' rules committees had the discretion to recommend changes to the rules with a deadline of the end of summer 2014. Between the conventions and summer 2014, the Democratic Rules and Bylaws Committee essentially made no changes to the 2016 Democratic delegate selection rules. As was the case for 2012, the party carried over the bulk of the rules to 2016 with only technical changes that did not really affect the rules or penalties as they apply to states. Importantly, the Rules and Bylaws Committee retained the ability to increase the severity of a penalty against a rogue state on a case-by-case basis.[30]

The Republicans, on the other hand, spent time at each of the three annual meetings of 2013–2014 considering additional changes to the rules adopted at the 2012 convention. The changes here were technical like the Democratic changes but carried additional importance for the enforcement of the rules on would-be violators. Some of the changes were based on the language of the rules adopted at the national convention, but others strengthened the super penalty on timing violations, tightened the proportionality window to the two weeks between March 1 and 15, and created a temporary committee charged with developing rules to guide the 2016 Republican primary debates.[31]

The problem with the so-called super penalty crafted to deal with timing violations was that reducing a delegation to just twelve delegates theoretically works well on large states, but the penalty was less severe or nonexistent for states with smaller delegations.[32] The RNC tweaked the rule to add a caveat for those smaller states that could have received a penalty less than the 50 percent penalty they would have faced for a similar violation in 2012. In 2016, states with delegations of thirty or more delegates would receive the reduction to twelve delegates, while those with twenty-nine or fewer delegates would have their delegations downsized to nine total delegates.

The rules regarding the proportionality requirement were also augmented in a couple of ways. As mentioned, the proportionality window was shrunk from all of March to just March 1–15. The intent of the change was to reverse the effect of the rule in 2012—to compress the primary process instead of drawing it out. That would have to occur indirectly, though, based on states with winner-take-all rules being enticed to move to a late March position on the calendar. The direct effects of the proportionality requirement were negligible with respect to lengthening the process. Again, that was more a function of the timing rules. The second change to the proportionality rule was to remove the 50 percent penalty for violations. Instead, the RNC gained the power to automatically "proportionalize" a state's delegation at the convention if such a state failed to adopt a combination of early state and proportional allocation rules.

The States' Reactions So Far and Heading into 2015

In the wake of the delegate selection rules changes for 2016, the early indications are good for the national parties being able to avoid the problems of the past couple of cycles. The increased Republican penalty for timing violations triggered 2013 and 2014 changes to primary laws in Republican-controlled Florida and Arizona, respectively. Both states moved back into March, compliant with the national parties' guidelines.[33] In the other rogue state from 2008 and 2012, Michigan, the state Republican Party has also endorsed a March 15 primary date.[34] That change will have to go through the state legislature first, however.

Past problems aside, other states are also revisiting old ideas like regional primaries. There is a concerted effort on the part of Georgia Secretary of State Brian Kemp to coordinate an "SEC primary" among a handful of southern states on the first Tuesday in March.[35] Throughout 2014 Secretary Kemp has reached out to his counterparts in Alabama, Arkansas, Louisiana, and Mississippi. That March 1 date already has Florida, Oklahoma, Texas, and Virginia primaries scheduled on it as well.[36] Other states may move into that position also, but heading into the 2015 state legislative sessions, March 1, 2016, appears as if it is a date that will take on a decidedly southern flavor. On the one hand, a set of conservative contests early and on the heels of the four carve-out state could impact the course of the nomination race, helping a more conservative candidate. However, on the other hand, those contests would all fall within the proportionality window. Depending upon how proportional those contests are, it could mute the delegate count impact of a string of contest wins. If history is a guide, the states in these regional primaries do not always coalesce behind one candidate. That was the case in the 1988 Southern Super Tuesday on the Democratic side when southern states split their votes among Michael Dukakis, Jesse Jackson, and Al Gore. A repeat of that in the Republican contests in 2016 could also dampen the effect of the SEC primary effort.

One other factor that works in the favor of a more orderly assembly of the 2016 calendar and the state-level rules for delegate allocation is the partisan alignment between where the bulk of national party changes took place and the control of state legislatures and state governments following the 2014 elections. The RNC could get an assist from states under Republican control. That is certainly true in the case of the rogue states cited above, but also in terms of potentially tamping down on any other states that might consider breaking the rules.

This is a sequential process, though. The national parties both finalized 2016 delegate selection rules in 2014. The process now shifts to the state level for 2015, and it is an open question as to whether states will or can see past the strengthened penalties for the 2016 cycle. Some may once again see that the costs of moving to a non-compliant date—a reduced delegation—are outweighed by the benefits of such a move—affecting the course or outcome of the nomination races. That said, the new dynamic of the last couple of cycles is that the national parties are working together, even if informally, against a common problem. The result has been a standardization of the delegate rules on dealing with those problems. The intent is to significantly decrease the state-level willingness to break the rules. While the 2016 delegate selection rules represent the most united front the national parties have rolled out to date in the post-reform era, it is still up to the involved actors in the states—state parties and state governments—to decide their own rules in 2015. And that is the other marker of the post-reform era: rules changes more often than not yield unintended consequences from the state level. That is what 2015 will reveal.

NOTES

1. Shafer, Byron E. Shafer, *Bifurcated Politics: Evolution and Reform in the National Party Convention* (Cambridge, MA: Harvard University Press, 1988).

2. This differs from the traditional model the Republicans have employed in the past. Setting the rules at the convention provides states with ample time—three years—to react to any changes the national party may have put in place at the preceding convention.

3. John H. Sununu, "2012 Presidential Primaries Recap & Review: Roundtable Discussion," comments made at 2013 National Association of Secretaries of State Winter Conference, Washington, DC, January 24–27, 2013.

4. There may be disagreements within factions of a national party about what constitutes "orderly" and "fair" and which candidates or types of candidates that advantages. However, the national parties are motivated to avoid a process that ends too quickly without sufficient voter deliberation or goes on long enough that it can or will be injurious to the eventual or presumptive nominee. Achieving that balance can be difficult.

5. Scott R. Meinke, Jeffrey K. Staton, and Steven T. Wuhs, "State Delegate Selection Rules for Presidential Nominations, 1972–2000," *Journal of Politics* 68 (2006): 180–93.

6. Joshua T. Putnam, "The Frontloading of Presidential Primaries and Caucuses from the States' Perspective" (PhD diss., University of Georgia, 2010).

7. Joshua T. Putnam, "On Ignoring Laws to Schedule Primaries and Caucuses," *Frontloading HQ*, October 7, 2011, accessed December 17, 2014, http://frontloading .blogspot.com/2011/10/on-ignoring-laws-to-schedule-primaries.html.

8. "Governor Signs Early Primary Bill into Law," *Fox News* (*AP*), May 21, 2007, accessed December 17, 2014, http://www.foxnews.com/story/2007/05/21/florida -governor-signs-bill-to-move-up-presidential-primary-to-january/.

9. "The Rules of the Republican Party as Adopted by the 2004 Republican National Convention," Republican National Convention, August 30, 2004, accessed December 1, 2014, http://campus.murraystate.edu/faculty/mark.wattier/The %20Rules%20Of%20The%20Republican%20Party%20As%20adopted%20by%20 the%202004%20Republican%20National%20Convention%20August%2030.doc; "Delegate Selection Rules for the 2008 Democratic National Convention," Democratic National Committee, August 19, 2006, accessed December 1, 2014, http://s3 .amazonaws.com/apache.3cdn.net/3e5b3bfa1c1718d07f_6rm6bhyc4.pdf.

10. This was a rule that was added based on an agreement among the major likely candidates and their surrogates on the Democratic National Committee Rules

and Bylaws Committee when the rules were being finalized in 2006 (Fowler and Roosevelt 2012).

11. "DNC Rules and Bylaws Committee Memo on Florida and Michigan (May 2008)," DNC Rules and Bylaws Committee, May 2008, accessed December 1, 2014. https://www.scribd.com/doc/164027958/DNC-Rules-and-Bylaws-Committee-Memo-on-Florida-and-Michigan-May-2008. Florida Democrats found making any changes to the primary date difficult. Republicans controlled both chambers of the state legislature and the governor's mansion. The Democratic Party in Florida also never really considered shifting to caucuses on a later date because it was too expensive for the party and due to the potential for a far smaller turnout (from personal communication with Carole Fowler and James Roosevelt, Jr. in May 2012).

12. Joshua T. Putnam, "It Is Official in Michigan and Nebraska Dems Embrace an Early Caucus," *Frontloading HQ*, September 6, 2007, accessed December 1, 2014, http://frontloading.blogspot.com/2007/09/it-is-official-in-michigan-and-nebraska .html; "Democrats Punish Michigan for Early Primary," *NBC News (AP)*, December 1, 2007, accessed December 1, 2014, http://www.nbcnews.com/id/22054151/ns/ politics-decision_08/t/democrats-punish-michigan-early-primary/.

13. Katherine Q. Seelye and Jeff Zeleny, "Democrats Approve Deal on Michigan and Florida," *New York Times*, June 1, 2008, accessed December 1, 2014. http://www.nytimes.com/2008/06/01/us/politics/01rules.html.

14. Carole Fowler and James Roosevelt, Jr. personal communication with author, May 2012.

15. Non-binding caucus states were excluded from this rule. The delegate selection process began in states like Iowa and Nevada in January 2008, but the final selection and ultimate allocation of the delegates did not take place in those states until later state conventions. More importantly, the allocation was not bound to the results of the first-round precinct caucuses.

16. "The Rules of the Republican Party as Adopted by the 2008 Republican National Convention," Republican National Convention, September 1, 2008, accessed December 1, 2014, https://www.scribd.com/doc/137196443/2008-RULES -Adopted.

17. *Ibid.*; "Delegate Selection Rules for the 2012 Democratic National Convention," Democratic National Committee, August 20, 2010, accessed December 1, 2014. https://www.scribd.com/doc/143258280/DNC-2012-Delegate-Selection-Rules. The rules regarding the scheduling of the carve-out states was slightly different across the parties. The Democrats were clearer in laying out a specific schedule for Iowa, New Hampshire, Nevada and South Carolina. Iowa was allowed to hold its precinct caucuses as early as the first Monday in February with the other three falling in line thereafter with approximately a week in between each. Comparatively, the Republican rules lacked clarity, merely restricting those four contests to the month of February with no regard for a specific order.

18. Philip A. Klinkner, *The Losing Parties: Out-Party National Committees, 1956– 1993* (New Haven, CT: Yale University Press, 1994).

19. "New Timing Rules for 2012 Republican Nominating Schedule," Republican National Committee, February 11, 2011, accessed December 1, 2014. https://www .scribd.com/doc/49655712/Presidential-Nominating-Schedule-Memo-021111. At a

bare minimum this meant that a state's share of statewide delegates—each has ten plus bonuses for a loyal partisan voting history—had to be proportionate to the percentage a candidate received in the statewide vote. There were numerous other ways to arrive at the RNC Legal Counsel Office's definition of "proportional."

20. Beth Reinhard, "RNC Wants a Longer Primary Season," *National Journal*, March 4, 2011, accessed December 1, 2014, http://www.nationaljournal.com/poli tics/rnc-wants-a-longer-primary-season-20110304.

21. Joshua T. Putnam, "The 2012 Frontloading Problem: What's Our Incentive?" *Frontloading HQ*, May 27, 2010, accessed December 1, 2014, http://frontloading .blogspot.com/2010/05/2012-frontloading-problem-whats-our.html.

22. Joshua T. Putnam, "The 2012 Presidential Primary Calendar," *Frontloading HQ*, March 1, 2012, accessed December 1, 2014, http://frontloading.blogspot.com/ p/2012-presidential-primary-calendar.html. Maine, Minnesota and Washington Republicans all held caucuses ahead of the first Tuesday in March date designated by the national party rules as the earliest point non-carve-out states could hold a primary or caucuses. Those caucuses were joined by a non-binding primary in Missouri in February (or early March).

23. Joshua T. Putnam, "2012 Republican Delegate Allocation: Texas," *Frontloading HQ*, May 29, 2012, accessed December 1, 2014, http://frontloading.blogspot .com/2012/05/2012-republican-delegate-allocation_29.html. The Texas primary was scheduled for the first Tuesday in March by law, but due to a court battle over redistricting, the primary was shifted back to late May (Putnam 2011b). Delegate allocation could not take place without new maps in place because Texas had added two districts after the 2010 census, and district boundaries were necessary for the delegate allocation process.

24. Joshua T. Putnam, "2012 Republican Delegate Allocation: Florida," *Frontloading HQ*, January 29, 2012, accessed December 1, 2014, http://frontloading.blog spot.com/2012/01/2012-republican-delegate-allocation_29.html. This was another shortcoming of the RNC delegate selection rules. Florida and Arizona not only held primaries before the first Tuesday in March but also maintained a winner-take-all method of delegate allocation. The double violation was an issue that the Republican Rules Committee had failed to anticipate. The lone option available to the party was a 50 percent delegation reduction. It could be applied to one of the two violations but could not be levied twice. That meant that both states got away with one violation in 2012.

25. Joshua T. Putnam, "2012 Republican Delegate Allocation: Ohio," *Frontloading HQ*, October 26, 2011, accessed December 1, 2014, http://frontloading.blog spot.com/2011/10/delegate-allocation-rules-hinged-on.html.

26. Joshua T. Putnam, "Republican Delegate Allocation Rules: 2012 vs. 2008," *Frontloading HQ*, December 24, 2011, accessed December 1, 2014, http://frontload ing.blogspot.com/2011/12/republican-delegate-allocation-rules.html.

27. Joshua T. Putnam and John Sides, "Republican Rules Are Not to Blame for Primary War," *Bloomberg View*, March 22, 2012, http://www.bloombergview.com/ articles/2012-03-22/republican-rules-are-not-to-blame-for-primary-war.

28. Similar to the tiered system the Republicans developed for allocation methods, the Democratic National Committee adopted a system of incentives to entice

states to move to later dates on the calendar. States with primaries or caucuses in the second tier—during April—received a 10 percent bonus added on to their delegation and states in the third tier—May and June—were granted a 20 percent bonus (Democratic National Committee 2010b). Additionally, states that held contests after the third Tuesday in March *and* with "at least two neighboring states" received a bonus of 15 percent on their delegations. The latter was a new addition to the Democratic rules for 2012.

29. "The Rules of the Republican Party as Adopted by the 2012 Republican National Convention," Republican National Convention, accessed December 1, 2014, https://www.scribd.com/doc/122649980/2012-Rules-of-the-Republican-Party.

30. "Delegate Selection Rules for the 2016 Democratic National Convention," Democratic National Committee, August 23, 2014, accessed December 1, 2014, https://www.scribd.com/doc/237924369/2016-Democratic-Delegate-Selection-Rules.

31. "The Rules of the Republican Party as Adopted by the 2012 Republican National Convention," Republican National Convention, as last amended August 8, 2014, accessed December 1, 2014. https://s3.amazonaws.com/prod-static-ngop -pbl/docs/Rules_of_the_Republican + Party_FINAL_S14090314.pdf. Two significant rules tweaks dealt with the language of a couple of rules that opened up significant loopholes that states could exploit to their advantage against the national party. The first concerned the proportionality requirement. A one word change in the 2012 rule at the convention—*shall* to *may*—suggested a proportionality rather than mandating it on all contests in the proportionality window. Until that word was changed, there was no proportionality requirement for 2016 (from Josh Putnam, "Thoughts on Where the 2016 Presidential Primary Rules Stand, Party One," *Frontloading HQ*, January 29, 2013, accessed December 1, 2014, http://frontloading .blogspot.com/2013/01/thoughts-on-where-2016-presidential.html). That change was made at the 2014 Winter meeting of the Republican National Committee. The second technical tweak dealt with a discrepancy between the timing rule and the penalty associated with it. The rule deemed states in violation of the timing provisions if the state held a contest prior to the first Tuesday in March. The penalty, however, only penalized states with contests scheduled before the last Tuesday in February. That opened up a week in which states could schedule contests penalty free. That, too, was altered. Both points were synced to March 1.

32. Joshua T. Putnam, "A Closer Look at the RNC Super Penalty for 2016," *Front-loading HQ*, April 16, 2013, accessed December 1, 2015, http://frontloading.blog spot.com/2013/04/a-closer-look-at-rnc-super-penalty-for.html.

33. Joshua T. Putnam, "2016 Florida Primary: Out of January, But Confined to March?" *Frontloading HQ*, May 4, 2013, accessed December 13, 2014, http://front loading.blogspot.com/2013/05/2016-florida-presidential-primary-out.html; Joshua T. Putnam, "So, It Turns Out Arizona Has Actually Moved Its Presidential Primary Back on the Calendar," *Frontloading HQ*, August 25, 2014, accessed December 1, 2014, http://frontloading.blogspot.com/2014/08/so-it-turns-out-arizona-has-act ually.html.

34. Joshua T. Putnam, "Michigan Republicans Green Light March 15, But . . . " *Frontloading HQ*, September 22, 2014, accessed December 13, 2014, http://front loading.blogspot.com/2014/09/michigan-republicans-green-light.html.

35. Joshua T. Putnam, "An SEC Primary in 2016? Not so fast . . . (Part I)," *Front-loading HQ*, February 20, 2014, accessed December 13, 2014, http://front loading.blogspot.com/2014/02/an-sec-primary-in-2016-not-so-fast-part.html.

36. Joshua T. Putnam, "The 2016 Presidential Primary Calendar," *Frontloading HQ*, December 12, 2014, accessed December 13, 2014, http://frontloading.blog spot.com/p/2016-presidential-primary-calendar.html.

12

The Path to the Presidency

The Past and Future Look of the Electoral College

Sean Trende

It is a bit of an oddity that most analyses of American elections focus on the popular vote, either implicitly or explicitly. Consider political science models, almost all of which explicitly purport to show a candidate's likely share of the two-party vote.[1] Only a few models examine the Electoral College.[2]

Or consider demographic analysis, which tends to focus indirectly on the popular vote. The projections for Hispanic population growth, for example, are typically national, as are debates over what share of the Hispanic population the Republican Party would need to win in order to emerge victorious in future elections.

This is an oddity, of course, because we don't conduct our elections via the popular vote. Instead we have the Electoral College, a venerable American institution that awards states votes based on the number of representatives that they send to Congress, plus two votes for the state's senators. To be sure, the distinction between popular and electoral vote is typically one without a difference, but as those who recall the 2000 elections know all too well, when the distinction is meaningful, it matters a lot.

If our focus is to be on the Electoral College instead, our approach must be different. This isn't to say the popular vote isn't relevant: It very much is, as we'll see below. But consider again our example of demographic change. Hispanics are a powerful, growing bloc in terms of the popular vote. But in the Electoral College? They exceed their share of the overall population in only nine states, only three of which could be considered swing states (Colorado, Florida, and Nevada). While Hispanics account for 17 percent of the United States population, they only account for just over 8 percent of the population of the median state. Only one other swing state (North Carolina) has a higher-than-median share of the Hispanic population.[3]

The African American population raises similar issues. Blacks make up about 14 percent of the population but only exceed that share in sixteen states; the median state's population is only 8 percent African American. There are a fair number of swing states with above-median African American population shares, but only a handful (Florida, North Carolina, Virginia, and arguably Michigan) with above-average African American populations.[4] That leaves non-Hispanic whites disproportionately represented, with thirty-seven states sporting above-average non-Hispanic white populations.[5]

The upshot of this is that, while Republicans could have theoretically won the popular vote in 2012 by increasing their share of the Hispanic vote to 48 percent, they would have had to increase it to over 70 percent (assuming a uniform swing in vote share across states) to pull in enough Electoral College votes to win.[6] Obviously, our approach with respect to the Electoral College must be slightly different than with the popular vote.

When we think about the Electoral College, our focus must instead be primarily upon geographic coalitions, rather than demographic ones. We must think in terms of states. That's not to say that demographics are irrelevant to this sort of consideration; rather, it is only to say that they are subordinate to a larger consideration.

The purpose of this chapter is to explore Electoral College coalitions over time and discuss what changes we might see going forward. Might we expect a realignment in the next few years? Are Republicans separated from electoral bliss by a "Big Blue Wall"? By focusing primarily at the state level, we can see that the answers to these questions appear to be "maybe, but probably not" and "no."

These two questions are not randomly plucked from the ether: They are ancillaries to the key questions for evaluating the Electoral College. First, what will be the ordering of states (from most Democratic to least Democratic)? Second, how will the national environment drive the popular vote to interact with this rank ordering of states?

Think, if you will, of a 51–rung ladder descending into a tidal pool. At the bottom of the ladder is the most Democratic state in the country (in the 2012 elections, this was technically the District of Columbia, but among states it was Hawaii). At the top of the ladder is the most Republican state in the country (unsurprisingly, Utah). The water represents the Democratic tide, driven by national forces such as the economy, presidential popularity, and so forth. As the tide rises, increasingly red states cast their ballots for the Democratic candidates. As it falls, blue states begin to turn crimson. Obviously, both the "ladder" and the "water" are complex and are driven by multiple factors. But it really is the interaction between these two factors that creates an electoral victory, at base.

We'll focus primarily on the makeup of the ladder. What will be the ordering of the states in 2016?

The classic way to approach would be with realignment theory. Realignment theory proposes that certain elections remake the American political landscape, bringing sharp, durable changes to the electorate.[7] Under this theory, there are a more-or-less agreed-upon (at least among those who accept realignment theory) set of elections that qualify as "critical": 1800, 1828, 1860, 1896, and 1932.[8] The 1968 and 1992 elections are often held up as other potential realignments. Under realignment theory, these "critical" elections are often accompanied by new maps, spikes in turnout, new issues, and the rise of third-party candidacies. I'll briefly describe each coalition, along with the problems with considering each one "realigning."

The 1800 election is marked as a "critical election" because the Democratic-Republicans rose to power in the place of the Federalists. Now, this is certainly an extremely important election, if only because it saw the first peaceful transition of power from one party to the other. It wasn't without its speedbumps—a last-minute slew of appointments led to a little case called *Marbury v. Madison*—but it nevertheless set a precedent that proved, for lack of a better word, critical for future American elections.

But can we really think of the period from 1800 to 1824 as a "period"? After winning unanimously in 1792 behind George Washington, the Federalists received 51 percent of the electoral vote in 1796, 47 percent in 1800, 8 percent in 1804, 27 percent in 1808, a rally to 41 percent in 1812, and just 15 percent in 1816 before giving up the ghost and failing to field a candidate at all in 1820 and 1824. Our first party system isn't so much a party system as it was a gradual suffocation of a party system in its infancy.

As is often the case, the precise emergence of the subsequent party system is difficult to pin down, with 1824, 1828, 1832, and 1836 all making decent claims to being the "critical" election. But most historians and political scientists engaged in these sorts of inquiry settle on 1828, when Andrew Jackson emerges victorious over his intraparty rival, John Quincy Adams. The modern Democratic Party emerges during this time period and wins most of the presidential elections through 1856.

What makes this system so interesting, though, is how completely non-systemic it was. The Jacksonians didn't have a regular foil: They faced Henry Clay's National Republicans in 1832, Whigs in the five elections from 1836 to 1852, and Republicans in 1856. There were clearly overlaps between these parties, but there were also important differences.

More importantly, there is little electoral stability during this time. In 1832, Jackson lost (moving north to south) Vermont, Massachusetts, Rhode Island, Connecticut, Delaware, Maryland, Kentucky, and South Carolina.[9] There's some regionalism on display here, especially when you consider that Kentucky was Clay's home state.

But compare this result with Martin Van Buren's win in 1836 against a slate of regional Whig candidates. Van Buren lost two New England states (Vermont and Massachusetts), some mid-Atlantic states (New Jersey, Delaware, and Maryland), and then a swath of states across what was then the middle of the country: Georgia, Indiana, Kentucky, Ohio, South Carolina, and Tennessee. Van Buren's loss in 1840 saw him carry what can only be called a mish-mash of states: Alabama, Arkansas, Illinois, Missouri, New Hampshire, South Carolina, and Virginia. Compare this with 1856, which really does see a well-defined North-South split emerge.

But eyeballing maps presents the same danger as looking at clouds: We're programmed to detect patterns, even when none really exists. So let's be more rigorous. We can take the popular vote in each state in a given election and compare those to the popular votes in states in subsequent elections.[10] If there really is a system at work, we should see a high degree of correlation, with a previous election explaining, say, 75 percent of the variance in subsequent elections. If, however, electoral coalitions are shifting, the variance explained should be much lower, as state vote shares from one year will be of limited utility in explaining subsequent elections.[11]

So what are the correlations between the various elections in the second party system?

As you can see in Table 12.1, at least from an electoral perspective, the second party system doesn't hold together that well. There are a few elections where coalitions resemble each other: 1828 and 1832, 1840 and 1844, 1844 and 1848. But overall, the correlations are low: You can explain, on average, about 30 percent of the variance in the state vote shares by using any other year for reference. This will not do.

We'll examine the next two coalitions together. The subsequent coalition emerges with the election of Abraham Lincoln, and concludes with Grover Cleveland's second victory in 1892. Then the next coalition begins in 1896 and culminates in the election of Herbert Hoover in 1928.

From an electoral perspective, we can identify several problems at the outset. Republicans do win hefty victories in 1864, 1868, and 1872. But

Table 12.1. Comparison of Popular Vote Results by State, 1828–1856 (R-squares)

Year	1852	1848	1844	1840	1836	1832	1828
1856	0.1452	0.1774	0.07238	0.01307	0.0429	0.3488	0.583
1852		0.4586	0.5064	0.3768	0.3381	0.256	0.2665
1848			0.6227	0.4991	0.3748	0.1238	0.1237
1844				0.7377	0.5147	0.2907	0.2598
1840					0.5198	0.1762	0.09415
1836						0.01981	0.04712
1832							0.8093
Average:	**0.314233**						
Median:	**0.2786**						

they lose the presidency in 1892 and 1884, lose the popular vote (but win the presidency) in 1888, and lose the popular vote and likely the Electoral College as well in 1876. James Garfield wins both in 1880, but only wins the popular vote by 9,000 votes.

If we look at the correlations between elections here, we see the following in Table 12.2:

Table 12.2. Comparison of Popular Vote Results by State, 1860–1892 (R-squares)

Year	1888	1884	1880	1876	1872	1868	1864	1860
1892	0.6452	0.5391	0.4716	0.417	0.09557	0.381	0.4192	0.5607
1888		0.9035	0.742	0.4874	0.09921	0.3206	0.5232	0.5613
1884			0.7955	0.6235	0.1786	0.2997	0.4301	0.5321
1880				0.797	0.3523	0.4678	0.4024	0.6102
1876					0.5716	0.3917	0.3226	0.5096
1872						0.2244	0.1215	0.3097
1868							0.3469	0.3339
1864								0.7489
Average:	**0.459349**							
Median:	**0.44895**							

This is weak tea. There are some election pairs that meet our 75 percent threshold. All but one of these pairs, however, are composed of sequential elections. There is little evidence for *durable* electoral coalitions here. The average correlation between election pairs is slim, and if we exclude sequential elections, it falls to a paltry 40 percent.

What about the so-called system of 1896? David Mayhew devotes much of his seminal work on the topic of realignment to this, and I have little to add.[12] I will simply add that, from an electoral perspective, there really does appear to be a durable correlation, as shown in Table 12.3.

Table 12.3. Comparison of Popular Vote Results by State, 1896–1928 (R-squares)

Year	1924	1920	1916	1912	1908	1904	1900	1896
1928	0.5744	0.547	0.5649	0.4127	0.5948	0.6272	0.5682	0.2101
1924		0.9303	0.7175	0.7406	0.8071	0.875	0.7394	0.2863
1920			0.81	0.7135	0.8658	0.9007	0.8047	0.3773
1916				0.5834	0.8683	0.78	0.8837	0.5722
1912					0.7017	0.8303	0.6664	0.2521
1908						0.8928	0.905	0.4912
1904							0.783	0.2993
1900								0.6824
average:	0.663							
median:	0.708							

Almost every election here explains at least half of the variance in any other election. This isn't altogether surprising, given that the South votes as a bloc for most of this time period (note that the correlations between 1928, which saw the weak performance in the South by Democrat Al Smith, and the other elections are relatively weak). But this does appear to be something of a system.

But is it a system *of 1896*? Taking a page from Mayhew, let's suppose that we took 1876 as our critical election, and extend that alignment through William Howard Taft's election in 1908 (see Table 12.4). The 1876 elections meet many of our criteria for a critical election: a spike in participation, the rise of third parties (the Liberal Republicans of 1872 are arguably the most successful third party in American history), and new issues dominating the landscape.

Table 12.4. Comparison of Popular Vote Results by State, 1876–1908 (R-squares)

Year	1904	1900	1896	1892	1888	1884	1880	1876
1908	0.8928	0.905	0.4912	0.4164	0.785	0.6323	0.6054	0.2825
1904		0.783	0.2993	0.58	0.8472	0.7151	0.7	0.4208
1900			0.6824	0.3121	0.724	0.5915	0.5828	0.2753
1896				0.02629	0.419	0.3471	0.4119	0.2167
1892					0.6452	0.5391	0.4716	0.417
1888						0.9035	0.742	0.4874
1884							0.7955	0.6235
1880								0.797
Average:	0.56575							
Median:	0.58715							

This works about as well as the 1896–1928 periodization. The correlations here are stronger than for the second or third party systems, and as we'll see, are stronger than the New Deal party system as well. But what we should focus on here is the 1888 election. Note how strongly it correlates with later elections: It more or less meets our earlier 75 percent standard for what we'd expect to see in a stable coalition with respect to 1900, 1904, and 1908. In fact, the electoral maps from 1880 to 1888 correlate, on average, more strongly with the maps from 1900 to 1908 than do the 1892 and 1896 maps. Perhaps 1892 and 1896 are actually deviating elections, and we really have a system of 1880! Regardless, even though we might see 1896 as bringing about durable change, it is hard to claim that it brought about a *sharp* change.

Finally, the mighty New Deal coalition:

Table 12.5.   Comparison of Popular Vote Results by State, 1932–1964 (R-squares)

Year	1960	1956	1952	1948	1944	1940	1936	1932
1964	0.00285	0.3528	0.1765	0.01406	0.3856	0.4093	0.4517	0.4468
1960		0.2803	0.5718	0.05937	0.365	0.3328	0.2061	0.1436
1956			0.6587	0.1969	0.6137	0.5951	0.5905	0.561
1952				0.09099	0.5847	0.5896	0.3828	0.3151
1948					0.2264	0.2166	0.2199	0.234
1944						0.9702	0.8004	0.7064
1940							0.8115	0.7216
1936								0.8848
average	0.421374							
median	0.3842							

It is actually the weakest of the bunch, save for the second party system. In fact, if we eliminate the pairs where an FDR win is compared to another FDR win, the average variance explained falls to just 34.2 percent.

If realignment theory were true, we'd actually be about due for a realignment, and we might expect some massive shifts in 2016 (or certainly by 2020). But as we've seen, the story just doesn't hold together well. We can see this better if we take each election from 1832 to 2008, calculate the average correlation between that election and the subsequent five elections, and then subtract that amount from the average correlation with the preceding five elections.

If realignment theory is true, we should expect to see something akin to an EKG readout. That, is, because a critical election should have a lot in common with subsequent elections, and little in common with previous elections, the resulting figure should be strongly positive. The fifth election after a critical election should be around zero, since it should have as much in common with subsequent elections as previous elections (it is the midpoint of the realignment). The ninth election should be negative, as it has little in common with subsequent elections, and quite a lot in common with previous elections. There should then be a sharp spike at the critical election.

Instead of a neat EKG pattern, we see this in Figure 12.1:

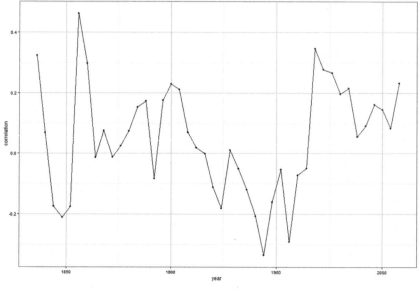

Figure 12.1

There are peaks, but they don't match up with our aforementioned critical elections at all: The peaks occur in 1856, 1888, 1900, 1928, 1952, and 1968. The 1932 election—often held out as the seminal realigning election—offers more in common with the preceding five elections than with the subsequent five elections. Moreover, the peaks are highly irregular, with some (e.g., 1952) actually having negative correlations. If this is an EKG readout of realignment theory, the patient is headed for a heart attack.

Our electoral history is filled with randomness and unpredictable swings. We'd be unwise to rely on it for making future predictions. Instead, I think we have to look at recent elections on their own terms. We start with two basic observations, which are somewhat in tension: Our elections are increasingly polarized and increasingly rigid.

We see this plainly in Figure 12.2, which takes the standard deviation for state vote shares in each election. To smooth things a bit, the data are presented as a three-election rolling average (that is, the data for 2012 are actually 2004 to 2012).

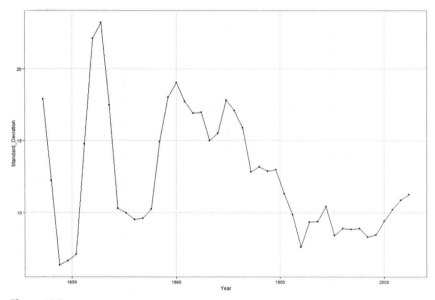

Figure 12.2

As you can see, our Electoral College really is becoming more polarized, a trend beginning in 1992. To be sure, we aren't approaching the heights reached in the wake of Reconstruction's end, but we're still more polarized than we've been since the mid-1900s.

Or consider the percentage of states in each election that were within five points of the national average. Once again, as shown in Figure 12.3, we're on a steady downward trend, but we also really are approaching historic territory by this measure:

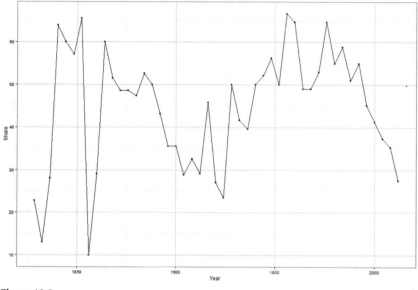

Figure 12.3

On the other hand, we've seen sharp reversals in the trend before, including the sharp turnaround from 1924 to 1928, which continued through 1952. Might we expect another sharp reversal in 2016? The problem is that not only are we becoming more polarized, we're becoming more rigid. In other words, the order of the rungs on our ladder has been awfully stable in recent elections. The following chart, Table 12.6, shows the top and bottom rungs on our ladder since 1988:

Table 12.6. Most and Least Republican States Since 1988

Rank	2012	2008	2004	2000	1996	1992	1988
1	UT	WY	UT	UT	UT	UT	UT
2	WY	OK	WY	WY	ID	NE	ID
3	OK	UT	ID	ID	NE	ID	NH
4	ID	ID	NE	AK	AK	ND	AK
5	WV	AK	OK	NE	KS	AK	SC
...							
47	RI	NY	NY	HI	HI	AR	MA
48	NY	RI	VT	NY	NY	VT	HI
49	VT	VT	RI	MA	MA	RI	IA
50	HI	HI	MA	RI	RI	MA	RI
51	DC	DC	DC	DC	DC	DC	DC

To put this in perspective, since 2000, only seven states have been in the top five most Republican states, and only six have appeared in the bottom five. If we push back to 1988, eleven states have appeared in the top five, while just eight have appeared in the bottom five.

As a further illustration of this phenomenon, let's return to our correlations. To simplify, we'll take each election since 1832, and take the average correlation among the states over the preceding five elections (if five are available). The data are presented in Table 12.7.

Table 12.7.   Strongest and Weakest Correlations across Five Election Periods

First Year	Last Year	Avg. Correlation	First Year	Last Year	Avg. Correlation
1984	2000	0.724	1828	1836	0.03347
1992	2008	0.73234	1840	1856	0.09019
1900	1916	0.73752	1952	1968	0.16199
1924	1940	0.74752	1948	1964	0.18636
1928	1944	0.77056	1844	1860	0.20451
1816	1832	0.8093	1956	1972	0.21615
1988	2004	0.8122	1932	1948	0.23742
1908	1924	0.8141	1828	1840	0.26338
1996	2012	0.81516	1852	1868	0.26565
1904	1920	0.81894	1960	1976	0.26837

As you can see, four of the ten most stable electoral maps in the past 180 years have been drawn in the past few cycles; none of the recent cycles qualify as unstable.

Now again, this doesn't tell us anything about who wins or loses. The strength of these correlations simply confirms that the ladder is consistent; it doesn't tell us anything about the depth of the pool. But we still should view any claims that that the Electoral College is about to shift radically with skepticism.

To be clear, we've seen sharp reversals in individual states' partisan orientations in recent years. Arkansas moved ten points to the left, relative to the country as a whole, from 1988 to 1992, and ten points to the right from 2004 to 2008. Wyoming lurched nine points rightward in 2000 (this is probably a testament to how strongly Ross Perot ran in Wyoming, and which party he drew disproportionately from there). Iowa, Nebraska, and North Dakota moved nine points toward Republicans in 1992 as the farm crisis receded, and New Jersey swung seven points toward the New Democrats in 1996.

So, we might see some individual state shifts in 2016. Sources with ties to Hillary Clinton have suggested that she could put Arizona, Arkansas, Georgia, Indiana, and Missouri into play if she is the Democratic nominee.

If Clinton is winning by nine or ten points in 2016, most of these states really will be in play. But can she can substantially re-arrange the order of the rungs on the ladder? Probably not. Clinton hasn't been an Arkansan since Boyz II Men's "End of the Road" topped the charts, and the Razorback State, along with Missouri, has swung strongly against Democrats since then. Demographic change is coming to Georgia and Arizona, but it has been slow, as increased non-white populations have found themselves stubbornly offset by an increasing Republican lean of non-Hispanic whites. Republicans have won the last four presidential elections in Arizona by seven, ten, eight, and nine points; they've likewise won the past two governor's races by twelve points. That doesn't seem ripe for change. There might be some shifts here, but those shifts will likely be slight.

What about Republicans? The increasing shift of white working-class voters toward Republicans offers interesting opportunities for the party of Lincoln. Mitt Romney won whites in Ohio by a larger margin than George W. Bush did, notwithstanding the change in the national environment.[13] If you adjust for the national environment, whites shifted toward Republicans from 2004 to 2012 in states like Wisconsin and Iowa as well.[14] If the Democrats are unable to replicate President Obama's showing and turnout among African Americans in 2016, the Upper Midwest—which is largely unaffected by demographic change—could move toward Republicans. But once again, any such shift will be small and likely secondary to shifts in national forces.

What about the second half of the equation: The water level? Obviously, other contributors to this volume, such as Alan Abramowitz, have ably discussed Republican prospects for the popular vote. This chapter does not venture into that discussion.

There is, however, one frequently proffered hurdle to Republicans taking the White House that should be dealt with here: The so-called "Big Blue Wall." This theory, which grows out of a Ron Brownstein article from shortly after the 2008 elections,[15] goes something like this: Since 1992, Democrats have won 18 states plus the District of Columbia in every election, for a total of 242 electoral votes. Republicans, by contrast, have only won 14 states worth 105 electoral votes.

Different writers use different variations of this approach—some look at states where Democrats have gone five-of-six to get Democrats up to 257 electoral votes as a baseline, while one observer throws Virginia into the mix to get the Party of Jackson up to 270 votes, which would end the election before it even starts.[16] But the shared view is that Democrats begin with a significant head start, electorally speaking.

But all of these analyses suffer from the same problems. We might start by asking: Why limit ourselves to the past six elections? It's true that Republicans have only won, say, Iowa once since 1988. But if we want to look at the past twelve elections, rather than the past six, the Republicans have won there half of the time. This isn't to say twelve is a magic number, either. Rather, the point is simply that your answer to the question "how big is this 'blue wall'?" will change depending on the number of elections in our sample. Since there isn't any non-arbitrary way to determine the proper number of elections to examine, it might not be a question worth asking.

Remember, it wasn't that long ago that peer-reviewed articles appeared in political science journals analyzing the Republican "lock" on the Electoral College (my junior year elections seminar from spring of 1994 also studied the Democrats' supposed lock on the House).[17] There was a reasonable case to be made for this: from 1952 to 1988, Republicans won Electoral College landslides in six elections, won one narrowly, lost two narrowly, and suffered only one major defeat.

But researchers who wondered why Republicans had a lock on the Electoral College were barking up the wrong tree. The answer was that Republicans won their Electoral College landslides because they were *supposed* to win Electoral College landslides. There was nothing magical about any of these elections.

In 1952, Dwight Eisenhower was a war hero running against a party with an unpopular incumbent president who was effectively forced not to seek reelection in large part due to his conduct of an unpopular war. In 1956, Eisenhower was overseeing peace and prosperity. These races were supposed to be landslides, and they were. In 1972, Nixon was running on getting the nation out of Vietnam, with massive economic growth at his back. Unsurprisingly, he won a landslide. In 1980, Ronald Reagan was running against an unpopular Democratic incumbent in a recession year. In 1984, he had economic growth at his back. In 1988, voters again saw a strong economy and opted to give Reagan a third term by voting for his vice president, George H.W. Bush.[18]

But the one year where Democrats were governing in a strong economy (1964), they were able to put together a landslide victory. This should have served as a warning sign for Republicans, because it suggested that their advantage in the Electoral College could prove fleeting. Indeed, the first time a Republican president was up for reelection in a recession year, he lost badly, and Republicans have had relatively weak showings since. It behooves us, though to ask ourselves, "In which of the years where Republicans lost should they have breached the 'blue wall' states?"

Should Republicans have won Democratic-leaning states like Wisconsin or Pennsylvania in 1992? Probably not, given the tepid growth, slow recovery from the recession, and electorate that was primed for change from twelve years of Republican control of the presidency. What about 1996? Economic models suggest that Republicans performed about as well as we would have expected given the growing economy and the relative popularity of the incumbent administration. This was not a year to push into blue territory.

We can probably rule out 2008 as well on this basis: John McCain was not going to win historically Democratic states when the economy was contracting on Election Day and a president of his own party controlled the White House. McCain performed about as well as he probably should have given the economy and presidential job approval (maybe a bit better, in fact), so there's nothing unusual about this showing.

That leaves 2000, 2004, and 2012 as years where Republicans could have broken down the blue wall. In fact, many of these states were quite close in those years. Al Gore carried Wisconsin by two-tenths of a point, Minnesota by two points, and Pennsylvania by four points. John Kerry—without Ralph Nader siphoning away votes—won those states by four-tenths of a point, three points, and two points, respectively. In 2012, Barack Obama won comfortably in these states, but they were still only a couple of points more Democratic than the country as a whole.

Of these, the only year we can really say was a pro-Republican environment was 2004, and that year was only modestly so. Had the Iraq War been going a little bit better (or avoided altogether), or had the economy been growing a bit more briskly, these states would have flipped. In other words, the "big blue wall" is merely a construct of how the coin flips have landed the past six cycles, not an intrinsic feature of our politics. Give Republicans a better environment in which to run, and the wall will be breached, just like Democrats broke the Republican wall when the coin tosses started to land their way.

To return to our analogy, we probably should expect the ladder in 2016 to look an awful lot like the ladder did in 2012. But this tells us nothing about national forces or the level of the pool. In a good enough environment, Republicans can absolutely paint the map red. But likewise, Democrats can paint it blue. American elections remain unpredictable, except in the shortest of terms, which is precisely what makes them interesting to analyze.

NOTES

1. For an overview of forecasting in the 2012 election, see James Campbell, "Forecasting the 2012 American National Elections," *PS: Political Science & Politics* 45 (2012): 610–13, doi: 10.1017/S1049096512000856.

2. Oddly, state-level forecasts have tended to perform poorly in predicting elections. See, e.g., Michael J. Berry and Kenneth N. Bickers, "Forecasting the 2012 Presidential Election with State-Level Economic Indicators," http://polisci.colorado

.edu/sites/default/files/Berry_Bickers_2012_Forecast.pdf (suggesting Barack Obama would win only 218 Electoral College votes).

3. "State and County Quickfacts," U.S. Census Bureau, accessed December 8, 2014, http://quickfacts.census.gov/qfd/index.html; see also "List of U.S. States by Hispanic and Latino Population," http://en.wikipedia.org/wiki/List_of_U.S._states_by_Hispanic_and_Latino_population.

4. "State and County Quickfacts," U.S. Census Bureau, accessed December 8, 2014, http://quickfacts.census.gov/qfd/index.html; see also "List of U.S. States by African-American Population," http://en.wikipedia.org/wiki/List_of_U.S._states_by_African-American_population.

5. "State and County Quickfacts," U.S. Census Bureau, accessed December 8, 2014, http://quickfacts.census.gov/qfd/index.html; see also "Non-Hispanic Whites," http://en.wikipedia.org/wiki/Non-Hispanic_whites.

6. Byron York, "Winning Hispanic Vote Would Not Be Enough for GOP," *Washington Examiner*, May 2, 2013, accessed December 8, 2014, http://www.washington examiner.com/byron-york-winning-hispanic-vote-would-not-be-enough-for-gop/article/2528730.

7. V.O. Key, Jr., "A Theory of Critical Elections," *The Journal of Politics* 1 (1955): 11.

8. E.g., Walter Dean Burnham, *Critical Elections and the Mainsprings of American Politics* (New York: W.W. Norton, 1971), passim.

9. Unless otherwise indicated, all elections data are taken from Dave Leip's Atlas of U.S. Presidential Elections, http://www.uselectionatlas.org/.

10. To keep comparisons "apples to apples," I only take into account states that voted in both elections. So, for example, when comparing 1960 to 1956, Hawaii and Alaska are eliminated.

11. Note that we don't have to take account of national vote totals, as a regression analysis will push any national vote shift into the constant.

12. See David R. Mayhew, *Electoral Realignments: A Critique of an American Genre* (New Haven, CT: Yale University Press, 2002).

13. Compare http://www.cnn.com/election/2012/results/state/OH/president #exit-polls, with http://www.cnn.com/ELECTION/2004/pages/results/states/OH/P/00/epolls.0.html. Some might dispute the accuracy of the exit poll findings, but the Current Population Survey, when adjusted for non-response bias, shows similar results.

14. Compare http://www.cnn.com/election/2012/results/state/WI/president#exit-polls and http://www.cnn.com/election/2012/results/state/IA/president#exit-polls, with http://www.cnn.com/ELECTION/2004/pages/results/states/WI/P/00/epolls.0.html and http://www.cnn.com/ELECTION/2004/pages/results/states/IA/P/00/epolls.0.html.

15. The actual article appears to be unavailable, but as of this printing, a follow-up can be found at Ronald Brownstein, "Playing Their Hand: Will Hard Times Allow Mitt Romney to Breach the Democrats' Formidable 'Blue Wall' in November?" May 10, 2012, http://www.nationaljournal.com/columns/political-connections/breaching-the-blue-wall-20120510.

16. Chris Ladd, "The Missing Story of the 2014 Election," November 10, 2014, http://blog.chron.com/goplifer/2014/11/the-missing-story-of-the-2014-election/#28114101 = 0.

17. For example, David J. Smyth, "Why Do the Republicans Win the White House More Often Than the Democrats?" *Presidential Studies Quarterly* 22 (Summer, 1992): 481.

18. Alan I. Abramowitz and Jeffrey A. Segal, "Beyond Willie Horton and the Pledge of Allegiance: National Issues in the 1988 Election," *Legislative Studies Quarterly* 15 (1990).

13

Through a Glass Darkly

The Outlook for the 2016 Presidential Election

Alan I. Abramowitz

Although most Americans are probably still recovering from the incredibly long, expensive, and negative 2014 midterm election campaign, it is clear that the 2016 presidential campaign is already well under way. Potential presidential candidates have been descending on Iowa and New Hampshire for many months. On the Democratic side, former First Lady, United States Senator, and Secretary of State Hillary Clinton appears to be in a dominant position based on the early polls. On the Republican side, in contrast, there is no clear frontrunner and it might be easier to list the current and former GOP office-holders who are definitely not running than to list those who are thinking about running. Prominent Republicans rumored to be considering a 2016 presidential candidacy include Kentucky Senator Rand Paul, Florida Senator Marco Rubio, former Florida Governor Jeb Bush, Wisconsin Governor Scott Walker, New Jersey Governor Chris Christie, and Texas Senator Ted Cruz.

The identities of the Democratic and Republican presidential candidates will probably not be known until March or April 2016 at the earliest. But whether Hillary Clinton does or does not end up as the Democratic nominee, and regardless of who wins the Republican nomination, there are many things that we already know about the first presidential election of the post-Obama era. What we know is based on longstanding trends in American politics and well-established features of the presidential selection process. Some of the most important things that we already know about the 2016 presidential election involve the characteristics of the American electorate in the second decade of the twenty-first century.

THE TWO AMERICAN ELECTORATES

One thing we already know is that the 2016 electorate will be much larger than the 2014 electorate. Despite record campaign spending and intense voter mobilization efforts by candidates, parties, and outside groups, turnout in the 2014 midterm elections was extraordinarily low. According to data compiled by Michael McDonald's United States Elections Project, only 36 percent of eligible voters cast ballots in 2014. It was the lowest turnout in a midterm election since 1942. And the decline in turnout from 58 percent in 2012 to 36 percent in 2014 was the largest drop in turnout between a presidential and midterm election since 1940–1942.[1] Approximately eighty-three million Americans cast ballots in the 2014 midterm election compared with over 130 million in the 2012 presidential election.[2] In other words, forty-seven million voters dropped out of the electorate between 2012 and 2014.

Midterm elections have always been characterized by much lower turnout than presidential elections. However, the difference in turnout between these two types of elections has been especially large in recent years, and this growing gap between the presidential and midterm electorates has had important political consequences. Although lower turnout in midterms affects every group in the electorate, it especially affects the types of voters that Democrats now rely on very heavily—younger voters, racial and ethnic minorities including Latinos, and unmarried women. Midterm elections almost always result in losses for the president's party, but the results of recent midterm elections have been especially bad for Democrats due to their party's growing dependence on groups of voters with especially high dropout rates in midterm elections.

Because 2016 is a presidential election year, voter turnout will be much higher than it was in 2014. It is therefore safe to predict that the 2016 electorate will look much more like the 2012 electorate than like the 2014 electorate. The 2016 electorate will be considerably younger, less white, and almost certainly more Democratic than the 2014 electorate. In fact, based on the expected replacement of predominantly white older voters departing the electorate by much more racially diverse younger voters entering the electorate, the 2016 electorate is very likely to have a smaller proportion of non-Hispanic whites and a larger proportion of Latinos and other nonwhites than the 2012 electorate. Even without Barack Obama at the top of the Democratic ticket, demographic trends almost guarantee that the nonwhite share of the electorate will continue to grow over the next several election cycles at about the same rate that it has been growing since the early 1990s. A reasonable guess would be that nonwhites will make up about 30 percent of the 2016 electorate with Latinos comprising around 11 percent of the electorate.

None of this means that Republicans cannot take back the White House in 2016. When it comes to presidential politics, demography is not destiny—the outcome of the next presidential election will depend on a variety of factors besides the racial and ethnic composition of the electorate, including the state of the American economy and voters' evaluations of President Obama's job performance in 2016. Moreover, Democratic gains due to the party's growing support from African Americans, Latinos, and other nonwhites have been offset to a considerable extent by a substantial erosion of Democratic support among white working-class voters since the early 1990s. In 2014, for example, Republican House candidates defeated Democratic House candidates by a whopping 30 percentage points among white voters without a college degree, according to the national exit poll. The ability of the 2016 Democratic presidential candidate to reduce the Republican margin among white working-class voters, who were once a vital component of the Democratic electoral coalition, may be just as important as turnout among nonwhites in determining the outcome of the election.

A CLOSELY DIVIDED AND PARTISAN ELECTORATE

What we can predict with a high degree of confidence even at this early stage is that individual voting patterns in 2016 will closely resemble those in 2012, the electoral map in 2016 will closely resemble the electoral map in 2012, and party loyalty and straight ticket voting will be the rule in 2016 just as in 2012. With the country closely divided between supporters of the two parties, this means that the outcome in 2012 is likely to be very close unless one party or the other chooses a candidate so extreme as to alienate large numbers of moderate partisans and independents. Right now, the risk of this happening appears to be greater on the Republican side than on the Democratic side because of the wide open nature of the GOP contest and the tendency of Republican primaries to magnify the influence of the Tea Party wing of the party.

In the first two decades of the twenty-first century, the United States has entered a new era of electoral competition. This new era of competition has three main characteristics that distinguish it from the patterns of electoral competition that were evident for half a century following the end of World

War II. First, there is a close balance of support for the two major political parties at the national level, which has resulted in intense competition for control of Congress and the White House. Second, despite the close balance of support between the parties at the national level, there is widespread one-party dominance at the state and local level. Third, there is a very high degree of consistency in the outcomes of elections over time and across different types of elections. These three characteristics are closely related. All of them reflect the central underlying reality of American electoral politics in the current era: an electorate that is strongly partisan and deeply divided along racial, ideological, and cultural lines.

While swings in party control of the White House occurred frequently between the 1950s and 1990s, many of the elections during those years were decided by very large popular vote margins. In contrast, the popular vote margins in recent presidential elections have been fairly small. Of course there have been closely contested presidential elections throughout American history, but there have also been many landslide elections in which one candidate defeated his opponent by a margin of ten percentage points or more in the popular vote. In fact, during most of the twentieth century, landslide elections were the rule and not the exception. Of the seventeen presidential elections between 1920 and 1984, ten were won by a double-digit margin. But there hasn't been a landslide election since Ronald Reagan's drubbing of Walter Mondale in 1984.

The 2012 results continued the recent pattern of presidential elections that are decided by a narrow margin at the national level but by a landslide or near-landslide margin in many states. This pattern of many deep red and blue states, including several of the nation's most populous states, represents a dramatic change from the pattern of electoral competition seen in close presidential elections during the 1960s and 1970s. In 1960 and 1976, when John F. Kennedy and Jimmy Carter won close, hard-fought battles for the White House, twenty states were decided by a margin by less than five percentage points. Moreover, in those elections every one of the nation's most populous states was closely contested, including California, Illinois, New York, and Texas. In 1976, states decided by less than five points accounted for 299 electoral votes while states decided by fifteen points or more accounted for only sixty-six electoral votes. In 2012, in contrast, states decided by less than five points accounted for only seventy-five electoral votes while states decided by fifteen points or more accounted for 289 electoral votes.

We can be confident that the 2016 electoral map will closely resemble the 2012 electoral map. The large majority of states that voted for Obama in 2012, including almost all of the states carried by Obama by ten points or more, are very likely to end up in the Democratic column while the large majority of states that voted for Romney in 2012, including almost all of the states carried by Romney by ten points or more, are very likely to end up in the Republican column. The outcome of the election will once again be decided by a relatively small number of swing states, almost all of which were swing states in both 2008 and 2012. While there could be some additions or subtractions from the group of swing states, it would be very surprising if Colorado, Florida, Iowa, New Hampshire, North Carolina, Ohio, Pennsylvania, Virginia, and Wisconsin are not major battlegrounds in 2016.

The remarkable consistency in the results of recent presidential elections as well as the large number of deep blue and deep red states can both be explained by the fact that the American electorate today is sharply divided along party lines. The results of elections closely reflected the underlying strength of the parties and the fact that while the nation as a whole is closely divided between supporters of the two parties, the large majority of states now clearly favor one party or the other.

The partisan divide was clearly evident in the results of the 2012 election at the individual level as well as at the state level. Thus, according to the national exit poll, 93 percent of Republican identifiers voted for Mitt Romney while 92 percent of Democratic identifiers voted for Barack Obama. This was the highest level of party loyalty in any presidential election since the beginning of exit polls in 1972, and it continued a pattern of strong partisan voting by Democratic and Republican identifiers in recent presidential elections. Data from the 2012 American National Election Study confirm this pattern: 91 percent of party identifiers, including leaning independents, voted for their own party's presidential candidate while only 7 percent defected to the opposing party's candidate. This was the highest level of party loyalty in any presidential election since the ANES began asking the party identification question in 1952.

Independents made up 29 percent of the electorate according to the national exit poll, and they divided their votes relatively evenly—50 percent for Romney to 45 percent for Obama. But that 29 percent figure undoubtedly exaggerates the significance of the independent voting bloc because the exit poll does not ask independents whether they usually lean toward one party or the other. Based on data from the ANES and other surveys, however, we know that the large majority of self-identified independents lean toward a party and that these leaning independents vote very similarly to regular partisans. In fact, in recent elections, leaning independents have been more loyal to their party than weak party identifiers. In the 2012 ANES, 72 percent of independent voters leaned toward one of the two major parties and only 9 percent of these leaning independents defected to the opposing party's presidential candidate compared with 14 percent of weak party identifiers.

DIVERGING PARTY COALITIONS

The high levels of party loyalty and straight ticket voting in 2012 extended a trend that has been evident in American elections for some time. Recent elections have seen consistently higher levels of party loyalty and straight ticket voting than elections from the 1970s and 1980s. Both increased party loyalty and increased partisan consistency in voting reflect the fact that over the past several decades, the party divide has become increasingly associated with other, deeper divisions in American society: a racial divide between a declining white majority and a rapidly growing nonwhite minority, an ideological divide over the proper role and size of government, and a cultural divide over values, morality, and lifestyles.

Over the past several decades, growing racial, ideological, and cultural divisions within American society have resulted in a growing divide between the electoral coalitions supporting the two major political parties. This can be seen in Table 13.1, which compares the racial and ideological composition of the Democratic and Republican electoral coalitions in 1972 and 2012 based on data from the American National Election Studies. The results in this table show very clearly that in terms of race and ideology, the Democratic and Republican electoral coalitions are much more distinctive today than they were in 1972—and the contrast would undoubtedly be even greater if we could go back further in time. Unfortunately, we cannot because the ideology question was not added to the ANES survey instrument until 1972.

In 1972, while conservative whites made up the single largest Republican voting bloc, they were less than half of all Republican voters, and they barely outnumbered moderate whites. In 1972, moderate-to-liberal whites actually outnumbered conservative whites among Republican voters. In contrast, in 2012, conservative whites made up more than two-thirds of Republican voters, greatly outnumbering moderate and liberal whites combined. In terms of its electoral base, the Republican Party is much more

Table 13.1.   Diverging Electoral Coalitions, 1972–2012

	Democratic Voters		Republican Voters	
Race and Ideology	*1972*	*2012*	*1972*	*2012*
Nonwhites	17%	42%	3%	12%
White Liberals	22%	32%	10%	2%
White Moderates	43%	21%	42%	18%
White Conservatives	18%	6%	45%	68%

Note: Respondents who opted out of ideology question coded as moderates.
Sources: American National Election Studies surveys

conservative today than it was in 1972. And while nonwhites comprise a slightly larger proportion of GOP voters today than they did in 1972, they remain a very small minority of Republican voters despite the dramatic increase in the minority share of the overall electorate during these four decades.

African Americans made up only 1 percent of Republican voters in 2012 compared with 23 percent of Democratic voters. Moreover, although nonwhite Republicans are somewhat more moderate than white Republicans, they are much more conservative than nonwhite Democrats. According to the data from the 2012 ANES survey, 66 percent of nonwhite Republican voters described themselves as conservative compared with only 15 percent of nonwhite Democratic voters. Nonwhite Republicans were only slightly less conservative than white Republicans, 77 percent of whom chose the conservative label. The presence of a relatively small group of rather conservative nonwhite Republicans has very little impact on the overall conservatism of the modern GOP base.

The Democratic electoral coalition has also undergone a makeover since 1972. In the case of the Democrats, however, the result has been to increase the influence of nonwhites and white liberals at the expense of moderate-to-conservative whites. In 1972, moderate-to-conservative whites made up about three-fifths of Democratic voters. In contrast, in 2012, moderate-to-conservative whites made up only about one-fourth of Democratic voters. Today's Democratic electoral coalition is dominated by nonwhites and white liberals. These two groups together made up only about two-fifths of Democratic voters in 1972. In 2012, they made up about three-fourths of Democratic voters. As a result of these changes, the center of gravity of the Democratic Party in the electorate has shifted considerably to the left of where it was in the 1970s. The electoral coalition that put Barack Obama in the White House was very different from the one that put Jimmy Carter in the White House or even the one that put Bill Clinton in the White House.

WILL IT BE TIME FOR A CHANGE?

It is easy to predict that voting patterns in the 2016 presidential election will closely resemble those seen in 2012, that the electorate will be sharply divided along party lines and that the outcome will be decided by a fairly small number of swing states, most of which were also swing states in 2008 and 2012. However, it is much harder to predict something else about the 2016 presidential election: who will win. We know that President Obama will be completing his second term in 2016, which means that the Democratic nominee will be trying to do something that is always difficult: hold the White House for her party for a third consecutive term. That has only happened once since 1952, when George H.W. Bush succeeded Ronald Reagan in 1988, although Al Gore likely would have repeated the feat in 2000 if not for a host of problems with the vote-counting in the state of Florida. Three second-term elections resulted in narrow defeats for the president's party (1960, 1968, and 1976) and three resulted in decisive defeats (1952, 1992, and 2008). On average, however, these elections have been close: the candidate of the president's party has won an average of 49.1 percent of the major-party vote in second- or later-term elections since World War II.

Two other variables that appear to influence the outcomes of third-term presidential elections like 2016 are the condition of the U.S. economy and the public's evaluation of the current incumbent's performance. In the three third-term elections since World War II in which the president's party won the popular vote—1948, 1988, and 2000—the incumbent president's approval rating was an average of seventeen points higher than his disapproval rating at the time of the election, and real GDP grew by an average of 4.2 percent during the year of the election. In contrast, in the six third-term elections in which the president's party lost the popular vote—1952, 1960, 1968, 1976, 1992, and 2008—the incumbent president's approval rating was an average of three points lower than his disapproval rating and real GDP grew by an average of 3.4 percent during the year of the election.

In the six third-term elections without a running incumbent, the contrast between the electoral environments for successful and unsuccessful incumbent party candidates is even sharper. In the two open-seat elections in which the president's party won the popular vote—1988 and 2000—the incumbent president's approval rating was an average of fifteen points higher than his disapproval rating, and real GDP grew by an average of 4.1 percent. In the four open-seat elections in which the president's party lost the popular vote—1952, 1960, 1968, and 2008—the incumbent president's approval rating was an average of eight points lower than his disapproval rating, and real GDP grew by an average of only 2.9 percent during the year of the election.

CAN THE ELECTORAL COLLEGE
SAVE THE DEMOCRATS?

Of course, the outcome of the 2016 presidential election will be decided by the electoral vote, not the popular vote, and the electoral vote is based on the election results in the states. Table 13.2 displays the results of the 2012 election in the states along with the number of electoral votes cast by each state. Safe states were won by a margin of at least fifteen points, solid

Table 13.2.   Electoral Vote Results for 2012

Safe D	Solid D	Lean D	Toss-up	Lean R	Solid R	Safe R
CA (55)	NM (5)	CO (9)	FL (29)	AZ (11)	AK (3)	AL (9)
CT (7)	OR (7)	IA (6)	NC (15)	GA (16)	IN (11)	AR (6)
DE (3)	WA (12)	MI (16)	OH (18)	MO (10)	MS (6)	ID (4)
DC (3)		MN (10)	VA (13)		MT (3)	KS (6)
HI (4)		NV (6)			SC (9)	KY (8)
IL (20)		NH (4)				LA (8)
ME (4)		PA (20)				NE (5)
MD (10)		WI (10)				ND (3)
MA (11)						OK (7)
NJ (14)						SD (3)
NY (29)						TN (11)
RI (4)						TX (38)
VT (3)						UT (6)
						WV (5)
						WY (3)
167	24	81	75	37	32	122

states were won by a margin of ten to fifteen points, leaning states were won by a margin of five to ten points, and toss-up states were won by a margin of less than five points.

The results of presidential elections at the state level have been remarkably stable since 2000, with forty states and the District of Columbia supporting the same party in all four elections. Based on these results, the Democratic candidate in 2016 is very likely to carry the District of Columbia and fifteen states with a total of 191 electoral votes that Barack Obama won by at least ten points in 2012. Fourteen of those states along with the District of Columbia have voted for the Democratic candidate in every presidential election since 2000, and New Mexico, which supported George W. Bush in 2004, has shown a clear Democratic trend since that year as a result of its growing Latino electorate. Likewise, the Republican candidate in 2016 is very likely to carry twenty states with a total of 154 electoral votes that Mitt Romney won by at least ten points in 2012. Nineteen of these states have voted for the Republican candidate in every presidential election since 2000, and Obama's narrow victory in Indiana in 2008 looks like a one-time aberration given Mitt Romney's double-digit margin in 2012, and the Hoosier State's record of voting for every other Republican presidential candidate since World War II except Barry Goldwater in 1964.

The results in Table 13.2 suggest that the Democratic candidate in 2016 will start off with a somewhat larger bloc of electoral votes that she can count on compared with the Republican candidate. In addition, there are eight states with a total of eighty-one electoral votes that Obama carried by a margin of between five and ten points in 2012, compared with only three states with a total of 37 electoral votes that Mitt Romney carried by a margin of between five and ten points. If the Democratic nominee just carries the District of Columbia and all of the states that Obama won by at least five points in 2016, that would give her a total of 272 electoral votes, which would be two more than the 270 needed to win the election.

The question raised by these results is whether, notwithstanding what happened in the 2000 presidential election, Democrats now enjoy an advantage in the Electoral College so that even if the Democratic candidate loses the popular vote by a relatively narrow margin, she would have a good chance of winning the electoral vote. However, an analysis of the relationship between the popular vote and the electoral vote in recent presidential elections indicates that any Democratic advantage in the Electoral College is extremely small and could easily be overcome if the Republican candidate wins the popular vote by more than a tiny margin.

Figure 13.1 displays a scatterplot of the relationship between the Democratic two-party popular vote margin and the Democratic percentage of the electoral vote for the six presidential elections since 1992 along with the estimated regression line for predicting the Democratic share of the electoral vote from the Democratic popular vote margin. There are three things to observe about the relationship shown in this figure. First, there is a very close fit between the two-party popular vote and the electoral vote—the Democratic popular vote margin explains over 96 percent of the variance in the Democratic share of the electoral vote during this time period. Second, the slope of the regression line is very steep—every 1 percent increase in the Democratic popular vote margin produces an increase of almost 4.5 percent in the Democratic share of the electoral vote. This means that even a fairly narrow popular vote margin for either party's candidate can be expected to produce a decisive electoral vote margin. Finally, and perhaps most importantly, there is very little partisan bias in the translation of popular vote margin into electoral vote margin. That is, neither party has a significant advantage due to the Electoral College.

Based on the results displayed in Figure 13.1, in order to win the 270 electoral votes needed to become president, a Democratic candidate would need to win 49.8 percent of the popular vote while a Republican candidate would need to win 50.2 percent of the popular vote. A tie in the popular vote would be expected to result in a very narrow electoral vote win for the Democratic candidate by 277 electoral votes to 261 electoral votes. However, given the margin of error in these estimates, even this very small Democratic advantage may not be real.

Looking back at the results in Table 13.2, it is apparent that it would not be very difficult for a Republican presidential candidate to carry enough states to win at least 270 electoral votes in 2016. Merely adding the three

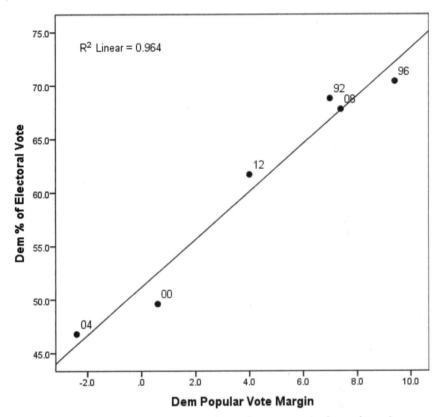

Figure 13.1 Democratic Share of Electoral Vote by Democratic Share of Popular Vote in Presidential Elections, 1992–2012

toss-up states won by Obama in 2012—Florida, Ohio, and Virginia—to the states won by Mitt Romney would result in a total of 266 electoral votes. So the Republican nominee in 2016 would only have to add a single state won by Obama by between five and ten points to reach the magic number of 270. Right now, Iowa and Colorado look like inviting targets given Republican victories in 2014 Senate contests in those states, and a relatively small swing in the national popular vote could put almost any of these states in the GOP column in 2016.

These results indicate that the current Electoral College system for choosing the president represents a very close approximation to a national popular vote system. Of course misfires can occur if the popular vote is extremely close, as it was in 2000. However, the 2000 misfire should probably be attributed more to vote-counting problems in the state of Florida than to the operation of the Electoral College. What this means for 2016 is that the candidate who wins the national popular vote will almost certainly become the next president.

THE SIGNIFICANCE OF THE 2016 PRESIDENTIAL ELECTION

Democratic candidates have won four of the last six presidential elections and have won the popular vote in five of the last six. The 2016 election should provide a critical test of the theory that the Democratic Party now enjoys a significant advantage in presidential elections as a result of demographic trends, generational replacement, and the growing liberalism of the American public on a variety of cultural issues. The Democratic nominee in 2016 will not have the first-term incumbency advantage that helped Barack Obama win a second term in the White House in 2012 despite slow economic growth and mediocre approval ratings. This is an important electoral factor: The only first party-term incumbent to lose a bid for reelection in the past century was Jimmy Carter in 1980. Without that advantage, history indicates that the Democratic candidate will need President Obama's approval rating to at least be in positive territory and the U.S. economy to be growing briskly during 2016 in order to extend the Democratic hold on the White House beyond eight years. In addition, the nomination of a Tea Party candidate by the GOP would almost certainly aid the Democratic cause in 2016.

Given the track record of successor candidates in presidential elections, a Republican victory in the 2016 presidential election would not be surprising despite long-term demographic and cultural trends that seem to favor the Democratic Party. Should this happen, however, Democrats will be able to take some consolation from the fact that having a Republican in the White House is the most likely scenario that could eventually restore Democratic control of Congress. There is clear evidence of a presidential penalty in American politics: The party that controls the presidency almost inevitably sees its power erode in Congress, especially in the House of Representatives. Since 1992, Democrats have won a majority of seats in both chambers in three of five elections under Republican presidents but in none of the seven elections under Democratic presidents. Democrats have won an average of 233 House seats and 52 Senate seats in elections under Republican presidents compared with only 203 House seats and forty-nine Senate seats in elections under Republican presidents.

It is not entirely clear why the party controlling the presidency generally sees its power diminish in Congress, although the prevalence of negative voting in midterm elections is certainly part of the explanation. But whatever the cause of this phenomenon, the implication is that as long as the overall balance of support between the two parties in the electorate remains very close, periods of one-party control of government are likely to be brief. Regardless of which party captures the White House in 2016, divided government is likely to prevail most of the time for the foreseeable future. Given the deep ideological divide that exists between Democrats and Republicans, that means that we can probably expect to see a continuation of the politics of confrontation and gridlock in Washington for the foreseeable future as well.

NOTES

1. Jennifer Burnett, "Voter Turnout: 1940–2014," The Council of State Governments, November 19, 2014, accessed December 11, 2014, http://knowledgecenter .csg.org/kc/content/voter-turnout-1940-2014.

2. "2014 November General Election Turnout Rates," last updated December 16, 2014, accessed December 16, 2014, http://www.electproject.org/2014g.

Index

Note: Page numbers in *italics* indicate figures (tables, charts, etc.).

About the Contributors

Alan I. Abramowitz is the Alben W. Barkley Professor of Political Science at Emory University and a nationally renowned expert on American elections and voting behavior. He is a senior columnist for *Sabato's Crystal Ball*, and his latest book is *The Polarized Public: Why American Government Is So Dysfunctional*.

Mark Blumenthal is the senior polling editor of *Huffington Post* and the founding editor of Pollster.com. Prior to that, Blumenthal worked in the political polling business for more than twenty years, conducting and analyzing political polls and focus groups for Democratic candidates and market research surveys for major corporations.

Jamelle Bouie is a staff writer for *Slate* magazine, where he covers politics, policy, and race. He previously worked at *The Daily Beast* and *The American Prospect* and also wrote for *The Nation*.

Rhodes Cook was a political reporter for *Congressional Quarterly* for more than two decades. Currently, he publishes a bimonthly political newsletter, *The Rhodes Cook Letter*, serves as a senior columnist for *Sabato's Crystal Ball*, writes political posts for the *Wall Street Journal*'s "Capital Journal," and works with *ABC News* on election nights to help project the outcome of congressional races. Since 1996, he has also authored *America Votes*, a biennial collection of election results.

Robert Costa is a national political reporter for the *Washington Post* and a frequent commentator on television and radio. He previously was *National Review*'s Washington editor, a CNBC political analyst, and a fellow at the *Wall Street Journal*.

Ariel Edwards-Levy is a reporter for the *Huffington Post*, where she covers politics and public opinion. Previously, she worked as an associate polling editor during the 2012 and 2014 elections. She also co-writes the *HuffPost* Pollster newsletter.

James Hohmann is a reporter for *Politico*, where he covers campaigns and elections. He previously wrote for the *Washington Post, Los Angeles Times, Dallas Morning News,* and *San Jose Mercury News.*

Kyle Kondik is the Washington director of the University of Virginia Center for Politics and managing editor of *Sabato's Crystal Ball,* the center's nonpartisan newsletter on American campaigns and elections. His analysis of presidential, congressional, and gubernatorial politics has been cited by the BBC, *New York Times, Wall Street Journal, BuzzFeed,* and many other publications, and he is a frequent contributor to *Politico Magazine.*

Jill Lawrence is a national columnist for Creators Syndicate and a contributing editor to *U.S. News & World Report.* She has covered every presidential campaign since 1988 for news organizations that include *USA Today, National Journal, The Daily Beast, Politics Daily,* and the Associated Press. An award-winning political writer, Lawrence is the coauthor of the Brookings Institution report "Phoning It In and Failing to Show: The Story of the 2014 House Primaries."

Joshua T. Putnam is a visiting assistant professor of political science at Appalachian State University specializing in campaigns and elections. He is also the author of FrontloadingHQ, a widely cited blog that tracks the presidential primary process.

Larry J. Sabato is the Robert Kent Gooch Professor of Politics at the University of Virginia and director of its Center for Politics. He is the author or editor of more than twenty books on American politics and elections, including, most recently, the *New York Times*–bestselling *The Kennedy Half Century.*

Geoffrey Skelley is media relations coordinator for the University of Virginia Center for Politics and associate editor of *Sabato's Crystal Ball,* the center's nonpartisan newsletter on American campaigns and elections. As a political analyst, Skelley has been quoted or cited in numerous print and online publications, such as the *New York Times, Politico,* and *Huffington Post,* among others.

Michael E. Toner is a former chairman of the Federal Election Commission and is co-chair of the Election Law and Government Ethics Practice Group at Wiley Rein LLP in Washington, DC. Mr. Toner previously served as general counsel of the 2000 Bush-Cheney presidential campaign, general counsel of the Bush-Cheney Transition Team, and chief counsel of the Republican National Committee.

Karen E. Trainer is a senior reporting specialist at Wiley Rein LLP and previously served as a senior campaign finance analyst at the Federal Election Commission.

Sean Trende is the senior elections analyst for *RealClearPolitics*. He is the author of *The Lost Majority: Why the Future of Government is Up for Grabs and Who Will Take It,* and he is a coauthor of the *Almanac of American Politics 2014.*